CW01082409

FERGUSON
TE20

In Detail

FERGUSON
TE20

In Detail

BY MICHAEL THORNE

Herridge & Sons

Published in 2006 by
Herridge & Sons Ltd
Lower Forda, Shebbear,
Beaworthy, Devon EX21 5SY

Reprinted 2010

Designed by Ray Leaning, MUSE Fine Art & Design Ltd
Special photography by Andrew Morland

ISBN 978-0-9549981-3-4
Printed in China

Picture Acknowledgements
The author and the publisher are grateful to the following for supplying photographs for exclusive use in this book: AGCO, Keith Base, Tim Bolton, Peter Boyd-Brent, John Burge, Robert Crawford, Peter Drinkwater, John French, Stuart Gibbard, Merethe Hansen, Lawrence Jamieson, Nigel Liney, Andrew Morland, Hans Goran Person, Duncan Russell, Jim Russell, Jamie Sheldon, Ron Stanbrook, Alan Starley, Peter Warr, David White, H Willet and Fred Wilson.

Contents

Foreword by Jamie Sheldon

Five years ago Peter Warr and I started a small collection in honour of my grandfather, Harry Ferguson. These were mainly pieces which had been in the family ever since his death in 1960. Sadly I was only four at the time and can barely remember him, yet luckily I did have many happy memories of my grandmother, who was an extraordinarily kind and generous person. As they say, "Behind every successful man lies a very special woman". Maureen Ferguson was certainly that.

It was because we started our own small family collection that I came to meet Mike Thorne, who kindly invited me to Coldridge to open the Ferguson Shed. He has built up the most amazing collection at Coldridge, and he not only opened my eyes to the extent of Harry Ferguson's influence, but also inspired me to take a much greater interest in my grandfather's life.

There are several books dedicated to his life and achievements but Mike Thorne's stands out as being remarkably informative and well researched. The life of Harry Ferguson continues to be a fascination for many people and I would like to thank Mike for all his hard work, his enthusiasm, and his ability to bring this story into other people's lives.

Jamie Sheldon
July 2006

Introduction and Acknowledgements

Little Grey Fergies

A fair number of books have been written about Harry Ferguson the man, his tractors, and his pioneering work on four-wheel drive systems. It was a great privilege and challenge to be asked to put together this book, but prudently the publisher suggested it should focus mainly on the TE20 range of tractors, the "little grey Fergies", together with the large range of implements, accessories, options and equipment produced by unconnected manufacturers, so this is what I have endeavoured to do. This book celebrates both the anniversaries of the grey Fergie: sixty years since its introduction, fifty years since its demise.

As well as my own involvement in the use, collecting and restoration of these classic examples of farm mechanization, I have drawn heavily on the experience and writings of others. I make no apology for this: one gains insight, knowledge and understanding of the historical and evolutionary context of such a major development as the Ferguson System by many routes.

Over the years, I have been privileged to meet and talk extensively to many of those men who were involved in the development, testing, marketing, and servicing aspects of the TE20, as well as several who worked closely with Harry Ferguson himself. In my opinion they were all touched by the magic of "HF". Since his death in October 1960 there has been a growing interest in all things Ferguson among people of widely

"A tractor without an implement is like a pen without ink."

(Harry Ferguson)

differing ages and backgrounds. These people are known collectively as Ferguson enthusiasts, and I count myself among that fraternity. Almost without exception these people share freely and openly their knowledge and experience of the Ferguson system. This has produced a snowball effect – let's keep it rolling!

I make no claim that this book is in any way definitive, but I have endeavoured to find "new" material to complement the story as it is already known. I hope the book may help to foster a widening appreciation of what this man and his small team of engineers developed and gave to the world.

I must acknowledge all the written works I have used as sources of reference, and thank AGCO for permission to use the Ferguson trademark as well as Ferguson sales statistics and technical material.

I offer my warmest thanks to those who have given their time and happily shared their knowledge and experience to make this work a much more rounded volume than it would have been without their valuable input. I have encountered them all through my exploration of all things Ferguson, and to introduce the reader to them I will tell the story of my journey through this fascinating land.

My interest in Fergusons developed when I was a young teenager. I made annual visits to the Smithfield show, where I was the bane of the sales people on their stands, grabbing copious quantities of sale brochures and any small gifts like badges and key fobs. The brochures were my reading matter, for I was not interested in sport or novels. I did however have a strong interest in most things electrical and mechanical, and the brochures substantially increased my understanding of machinery.

Another bonus was the fact that my family had a two-acre garden, so there was a Rotoscythe lawn mower, a Howard Rotovator Bantam and other power garden tools. In fact I had to earn my pocket money by doing grass cutting, cleaning out chicken runs and preparing seed beds with the Rotovator. Around this time I also worked on a nearby dairy farm on Saturday mornings, free of charge, just for the joy of being on a farm and of course for having the opportunity to drive the Fordson Major E/27N. What a crude tractor it was: a TVO model with hand start! By the age of fifteen I was convinced I wanted to go into farming, so my father arranged a trip to a 1000-acre mixed farm on the Berkshire/Oxfordshire border near Wallingford, owned by one of his customers who had a couple of businesses in the London area. This farm was not run on strict business lines - it was more of a nice estate for the owner and his family to live on. We had lunch in the impressive dining room, with the food served by their butler, and afterward we were taken for a full tour of the 1000 acres, taking in two Aberdeen Angus beef herds, a Guernsey dairy herd, an impressive grain drying and handling facility, and needless to say a tractor shed, this one housing at least nine tractors, all of which today might be seen on rally fields. There were two Fordson Standards, two Allis Chalmers B American models, two Caterpillar R2s, a Farmall 15-30, an International McCormick Deering F20, a Minneapolis Moline GT and a new arrival, a new-type Fordson Major Diesel.

Back at the Home farm the owner's son, who was about two years younger than me, asked if I would like to see his new tractor, a Ferguson TE.D20. First he drove it around the farmyard with me sitting on the mudguard, and then he asked me if I would like to have a drive. This was my first experience of a TE20, and what a beautiful piece of engineering it felt when compared to the Fordson E27N. I was hooked, at 15 years of age! On leaving school at 16 I went to work on this farm for a year prior to attending Oaklands, the agricultural college in Hertfordshire, where there was also a Ferguson in the fleet, this time a TE.F20 with "banana" loader. After a year at Oaklands I returned to the farm near Wallingford as a farm worker, doing mostly tractor driving and relief milking. Luckily for me most of my driving was done on the TE.D20, often hauling a 3-ton Ferguson trailer and using the Ferguson post-hole digger, which were the only Ferguson implements we had. After a year had elapsed I left there on my BSA Bantam motorcycle to take a farm worker's job on a dairy farm in south Hertfordshire, where a couple of Fordson Major Diesels were used.

Leaving there after two years, I worked for

the Milk Marketing Board as an inseminator of cattle. At one of their main centres they used a TE.D20 to move bulls from the bull housing to the fields where they were tethered. This "towing procedure" involved passing a loop of rope around the bull's horns, down over his face and through the ring in his nose, the free end being tied to the tractors 11-hole draw bar. Most bulls seemed quite happy with this form of guidance and went along with it quite easily. I can remember one bull, an elderly Hereford called Porch Jumbo, deciding to stop one day as I was taking him into the field – the Ferguson just stalled.

The next move, after three years with the MMB, was into a joint farm partnership with an MMB colleague. This resulted in buying a farm in North Devon, where we inherited a Fordson Major Diesel and a TE.F20 minus its fuel injection pump. I soon sourced and fitted a secondhand part and had it working. We also had a two-furrow Ferguson plough, a rear-mounted Ferguson mower and the mounted Ferguson fertilizer spreader. However, the partnership did not last long, and after three years I withdrew and got myself a job in a steel fabrication shop in Exeter. This was like a condensed apprenticeship but after nine months I became disillusioned with the management and decided to start out on my own.

It was now the autumn of 1968, and I took on any work that farmers in the area wanted done: ploughing, mending washing machines, respraying cars and tractors, relief milking, electrical installation, and steel fabrication. At this line we produced gates, cow cubicles, over 2500 farm trailers and, of course, some steel-framed buildings, which are our core business today. I rebuilt and repainted some Fergusons for customers, but otherwise the grey tractors took a back seat.

Building up the business was a period of hard work and long hours, but my interest in Fergusons re-surfaced about 22 years ago when an estimator for a scaffolding company told me of a TE.D20 standing forlorn in a field near Tiverton; the owner, a solicitor, was asking £100 cash for it. I agreed to buy it, and that tractor, No.1 in the Coldridge Collection, is now restored and fitted with tyre tracks. From that day many tractor purchases followed, of differing makes and models, but close in the wake of No.1 was No.4 a TE.A20 in very nice original condition. After about four years, more than 60 tractors had been acquired, including a pair of early Ferguson Browns. It was around this time that I joined the Ferguson Club and met George Field, who was a living encyclopaedia of all things Ferguson. A few years later we had our first open day at Coldridge – just to enable tractor enthusiasts to share the collection. This has become an annual event.

It was at this point I encountered Ernie Luxton, an ex-Massey Ferguson indentured mechanic – in fact a mechanic par excellence. He had been made redundant by the changing structure of the MF dealership here in North Devon, so he came to work for me on tractor restoration and has done the mechanical restoration of almost all the tractors in the Coldridge Collection. It is Peter Clarke who has done the painting on most of those in the collection. Through open days and club involvement I began to meet many people who during their working lives had been involved with Harry Ferguson Ltd. It is people like Sandy von Behr, Keith Base, John Burge and the late Michael Winter who all kindly shared their experiences with me and thereby enhanced my understanding of the Ferguson System. It was on one of the early Coldridge open days that Keith Base introduced me to his long-standing friend the late John Armstrong, who had spent time in India with Ferguson.

As the Fergusons began to dominate the collection most of the other makes of tractors were sold off. About ten years ago only a handful of other makes remained in the collection and that holds true to this day.

At a ploughing event at Stoneleigh I took along the two Ferguson Browns and an FE35 diesel, together with a 1936 two-furrow plough. The late John Chambers was there and it was not long before he was being asked to pose for photographs on my Ferguson-Brown with plough. After a while I suggested he might like to do some ploughing; he thought yes he would like to do a couple of rounds, and was ploughing for two hours, smiling like the cat who got the cream. I have a much cherished photo of him ploughing, but nine months later he sadly died.

It was at the Ferguson Club AGM in 1996 held in Northern Ireland that I got to know the late Dick Dowdeswell and his wife Beryl. Dick had been a field test driver and head demonstrator for Harry Ferguson Ltd, and later in a similar role worked for Massey-Ferguson. The stories he told would fill a book, but he reminded me of the LTX project and enthused at length about the amazing performance of those prototypes. It is the fond regard for these tractors that triggered in me the idea of building a replica of one of them. Then I thought it was no use building a mock-up - one would want it to work! The cost was calculated: at least £200,000 and thus quite out of the question. The alternative would be to build a ⅟₁₈th fine scale model; that way other enthusiasts could also indulge!

The following year at Moreton-in-the-Marsh the Ferguson Club had arranged that their main speaker would be Ray Fardeon – Harry Ferguson's head gardener at Abbotswood. He gave us a wide-ranging talk about his life and involvement with Harry Ferguson. In the afternoon he gave us a tour of the gardens in pouring rain. It was through him that the Tractor Research prototype for the BMC Mini tractor came to the Coldridge Collection in 2005.

By this time I had made contact with the late Erik Fredriksen, who had a lifetime of work with MF in product design and development. He had recently retired but eagerly responded to my request for help in researching the LTX story. (It should be remembered that none of the tractors had survived and information was very scanty). On my first visit to the Midlands Erik had laid out a programme of visits to different people who had been involved in the LTX project and on this and a subsequent visit I was able to gain an enormous amount of information on these tractors and their performance. This afforded me the privilege of meeting Nigel Liney, who by chance had been "unofficial" photographer for the project; we have him to thank for some of the photos used in Chapter 13. I also heard at first hand the experiences of Jack Biddy and Colin Stevenson who, like Nigel, were Field Test drivers. I met farmer Derrick Hiatt of Upton who had an LTX on his farm for almost 22 years until MF took it away and cut it up.

It was through Erik that I met Jim Russell, a retired Warwickshire farmer, and his wife Jane, conservationists of national standing, Jim is a cine film maker and Ferguson enthusiast of a high order, not to mention his amazing collection of Ferguson and MF models, with the odd Cuneo painting thrown in.

Another new friend was Andrew Morland, the respected tractor photographer, who contacted me to ask if he could photograph some of the tractors in the collection for a book he was involved in. We struck up an easy rapport on this first assignment and it was not long before he was back again for more photographs. A good friendship has been fostered by this collaboration and I was delighted when told that Andrew would undertake for the colour photography for this book.

Through the Ferguson Club I met and became a good friend of their one-time chairman Ian Halstead and his wife Ann. Ian, a long standing Ferguson collector, has some lovely original tractors and implements and has over the years sourced obscure items for me. It was Ian who introduced me to Stuart Gibbard and his wife Sue. These people too have become good friends. I have bought a good number of Ferguson sales brochures from Stuart, and have most of his excellent tractor books in my library, including his *The Ferguson Story*. John and Grace Popplewell have always shared their extensive knowledge of Ferguson things with me, and over the years have sold me a number of the rare items now in the collection.

The next notable part in this story was the hosting of the Ferguson Club AGM at Coldridge in 2000. This coincided with the completion of a second tractor building, known as the Ferguson Shed, to house the collection. I thought it appropriate to ask Jamie Sheldon, Harry Ferguson's grandson and president of the Ferguson Club, if he would agree to open the new building. He said yes and we have a plaque to celebrate that. Jamie bought along Peter Warr, who had worked for Harry Ferguson as estate manager at Abbotswood, had worked for Tony Sheldon, who had married Harry's daughter Betty, and now works part time for Jamie. Peter gave us all a most interesting and entertaining account of his work with Harry Ferguson and the Sheldon family. This of course led me to establishing a friendship with Jamie, who kindly wrote the introduction to this book, and a friendship with Peter Warr, who gave freely of his time as curator of The Ferguson Family Museum in the Isle of Wight. My thanks to Jamie for the use of some of the family's photographs.

At the 2000 AGM I also met Andrew Boorman, whose career was based in the agricultural engineering trade with Olivers. In his retirement Andrew has put together an impressive document, *Ferguson Publications Index 1922-1964*, which lists no less than 10,000 different items. Access to this has to be gratefully acknowledged.

In 2004 the publishers of this book, Herridge and Sons, approached me with the idea of producing a book devoted to the TE20. After some deliberation I committed myself to the task, which I have enjoyed enormously, so now may I turn my attention to those people who have contributed in their different ways to making this possible.

Fellow collector and joint author with John Farnsworth of the book *The Hunday Experience*, John Moffitt was full of enthusiastic support for my book about the TE20, and I have to thank him for finding me some obscure American Ferguson items. Alan Starley a retired Ferguson development engineer, responded most positively to my asking him to read each chapter as it was produced. This he did in a most professional way by returning alongside my script what he termed "grist". Grist was a subtle mixture of corrections, anecdotes, questions and a spicing of Alan's extensive engineering experience. I hope the flavour bubbles through! Thank you, Alan.

Another provider of enthusiastic assistance was John French, who helped me out enormously in the area of Reekie conversions and supplied photographs from his own collection; John is also one of those people who has helped me source obscure tractors and implements. Peter Drinkwater, farming vegetables in the Cotswolds with his brothers, is himself a major Ferguson collector and gave me help with photographs and finding certain implements.

Thanks must go to Mark Flynn for translating at my request chunks of text and captions from *Tracteurs Ferguson*. This gave me some insight into Ferguson tractor production in France during the period covered by this book.

When it came to Ferguson in India Peter Boyd Brent came to the rescue. He spent several years in India but now lives nearby in Devon and helped out with photographs and the story of his time in India with Ferguson. Lawrence Jamieson, long-time membership secretary of the Ferguson Club, with his wife Jane, was most helpful in bringing to my attention photographs he had of oddball Ferguson attachments and modifications floating around in Scotland and Northern Ireland. Chris Massingham of Friends of Ferguson Heritage kindly spent hours on the phone sorting out production figures for me. In the area of industrial Fergusons, Graham Holland from Norfolk, who shares my passion for the "industrial", was able to fill in most of the missing gaps. Fellow Ferguson enthusiast Fred Wilson shared his experiences as a Ferguson Distributor with me, and one or two of the photographs he loaned me are reproduced here.

From abroad, my long-standing friend from Denmark Merethe Hansen provided the backbone to that section of the book, together with some very nice photographs. Sandy von Behr for his help in in the areas of India and Japan. Bill Brox from Norway was able to communicate over the telephone his knowledge and experience of Ferguson in his part of the world.

Hans Göran Person in Sweden helped enormously with photographs and written information. Angus Macleod-Henderson, who farmed extensively in Africa with Ferguson, and has visited the Coldridge Collection at least twice, was able to fill me in for that part of the book. From Holland, Piet Mooij, who has his own extensive Massey-Harris and Ferguson collection, was able to give me some background to Ferguson in Holland.

My good friend and fellow MF collector in Germany Norman Tietze researched the information for me that provided the section on Ferguson in Germany. He has also been able to find me a rare MF in Austria. For a fair bit of the detail on the Meadows-engined Ferguson I must thank its previous owner, engineer David White, who by the way brought the tractor back to life. Tony Turner of Turner Engineering, one-time manufacturer of the Turner Ranger Four, helped me by sharing his experiences with these vehicles, as did Peter Warr.

My neighbour and friend Harold Beer, with his wife Eileen, has one of the most impressive collections of Ferguson working implements, together with some suitable TE20s to power them; has always been most willing to share not only his extensive knowledge but also his almost equally extensive collection of Ferguson brochures and technical publications, some of which are reproduced here.

And finally I thank Duncan Russell for kindly (but unwisely, he must now think) agreeing to take on the task of proof reading. That was a very big favour.

Michael Thorne
Coldridge
May 2006

Chapter One

Harry Ferguson The Man

Only one inventor in 10,000 succeeds!

Harry Ferguson was born on 4 November 1884 at Lake House, a farm of about 100 acres (40 hectares) in the village of Growell, Co. Down, Northern Ireland. He was the fourth child of a flock of eleven, eight boys and three girls, produced by the union of James and Mary Ferguson: an example of the good fecundity of those times! By the standards of the day, his parents were reasonably comfortable financially, as a result of hard work in the rather harsh environment of that part of Northern Ireland. Ferguson's father James could trace his ancestry back to the protestant Scots, who had migrated to that part of Ireland during the reign of James I in the early seventeenth century. These people had the tough spirit so necessary for their survival. James Ferguson was a God-fearing member of the Plymouth Brethren who by all accounts ruled the household with stern discipline. The fourth child was christened Henry George, but was always known as Harry. Today, Lake House stands neat and tidy, painted grey like a Ferguson tractor, owned by Mr and Mrs Allan Pootsway. To the right of the front door is set one of those blue plaques that are used throughout the land to designate houses where famous people have lived. No one could doubt or argue the justification for that plaque.

This book is dedicated to him and his achievements. If he had been born the seventh son, one could speculate on that old legend that the seventh child is often a genius, yet he achieved that status at number four in the series! The date of his birth was a few months before Daimler's and Benz's invention of the first motor cycle and the first car, so he was born in an age as yet unaffected by the internal combustion engine. According to Colin Fraser in his book *Harry Ferguson Inventor and Pioneer* (1972), the young Harry manifested his early mechanical talents by opening the various private drawers which his siblings shared in a communal chest of drawers – each child had its own drawer with its own key. Harry worked out that he was able to unlock all the drawers by the simple expedient of unlocking and taking out his own drawer, and then working his way down the locks. This ingenuity seemed to set the stage for a person who was going to go far in his lifetime and claim great achievements.

At fourteen he left school to work on his father's farm, but being of small stature he hated the drudgery of the work, as much as he hated the religious indoctrination of his father. He and some of his siblings countered this by smuggling books into the house and reading in their bedrooms at night, the only "official" reading being the Bible. By 1902 Harry Ferguson had become totally disenchanted with the farm and joined his brother Joe, who had a car business in Shankill Road, Belfast. Joe was four years older than Harry and the first-born child. It was this thorough questioning of his family's religious beliefs that led Harry Ferguson to become an agnostic in his teens, and to adhere to this concept throughout his life. It is also safe to assume that the questioning nature with which he was blessed fostered the development of his many engineering innovations over a lifetime. He was aware of his individuality and proud of it; he was true to his own convictions and beliefs, for he had thought them through for himself. They were not just taken from others, but had passed through the filtering process of his reasoning.

The apprenticeship Joe offered Harry at the Shankill garage was an ideal opportunity for Ferguson to hone his natural engineering talent. He found great delight in driving cars and motorcycles, exploring their mechanics, meeting customers and in due course found a particular skill in tuning car engines. The business prospered, because the two brothers were not only good with cars and customers but were also sticklers for good practice in the workshop, no doubt an effect of their father's discipline at home. As time went on, the garage came to be considered the best in Belfast. From 1903 to 1905 Harry Ferguson took engineering classes at Belfast Technical College, where he met John Lloyd Williams, who became a life-long friend.

Concurrently in this period, Harry Ferguson met one of their more wealthy customers Thomas McGregor Greer, who owned a large estate at Tullylagen and several motor cars. Harry Ferguson was often sent by Joe to the estate to repair Greer's cars on site. At first, Harry slept overnight in the bothy, but as Greer's regard for him blossomed, he was eventually welcomed into the house – a friendship slowly developed, which was to be of lasting importance. By this time, Harry had begun to take part in competitive car and motorcycle events in the locality, with some fair measure of success. The reason given for these activities was to promote interest in Joe's garage business, but perhaps it was also a way of converting profits into fun.

In 1908, Harry Ferguson and his friend John Williams decided to visit aircraft meetings at Blackpool and Reims in France. These visits fuelled their interest in flying and flying machines, to the extent that they made dimensional sketches of some of the aeroplanes they saw. Eventually Ferguson decided to build his own monoplane in the loft above his brother's workshop. By December of 1909, the plane was ready for its test flight, and was taken to Lord Downshire's estate near Hillsborough, Co. Armagh, where it was recorded that it flew for 130 yards (119m), so Harry Ferguson became the first man in Britain to build and fly his own aircraft. In April 1910 he took his plane to Massereene Park in Co. Antrim where after

H F in pensive mood beside the aircraft he built.

Plaque in Donegal Square, Belfast. There is a similar one at HF's birthplace, Lake House, near Dromore in Co Down.

several runs he achieved a flight of just over one mile (1.6km). Later that year he went on to achieve a flight of three miles' length (4.8km), and in doing so won an aviation prize. It is worth bearing in mind that since these events aircraft designers have considered the fundamental design of his aircraft to be quite sound, and while they are of the opinion that Harry Ferguson was not a natural pilot, he made up for it in daring, courage and persistence. However in October 1910 Ferguson crashed his plane, injuring himself quite badly. Although he flew again in 1911-12, he now increasingly turned to motor racing.

Ferguson's interest in flying and racing obviously took up some of the time that he should have spent working for his brother Joe. This led to friction between the brothers, and in 1911 Harry left to set up his own motor works, known as May Street Motors. He took on his old friend from college days, John Williams, as well as Willie Sands, who had been an engineering apprentice in the linen industry. In May 1912 Harry Ferguson Ltd became incorporated. The company continued to trade in motor car repairs and tuning at the May Street premises, and became agents for such cars as Vauxhall and Darracq. (It is interesting to note that this company title was retained until the sell-out to Massey-Harris in August 1953. Following that merger, Harry Ferguson Research Ltd was set up primarily to explore motor car development, with a strong bias towards higher standards of safety, especially four-wheel drive and anti-lock braking systems. The current company Harry Ferguson Holdings was incorporated on 9 July 1981, with its head office in the Isle of Wight.)

In 1913 Harry married Maureen Watson, the daughter of a grocery shop owner living at Dromore. Their only child, a daughter called Betty, was born a few years later. Whether or not it was the stimulation of falling in love and getting married to Maureen, this was the time of Ferguson's life when he seriously started his career as an inventor. In the year of his marriage he took out two patents for the refinement of carburettors. Also in 1913, he became politically active with the Ulster Volunteer Force (UVF), and was even involved in importing guns and ammunition into Northern Ireland from Hamburg. In 1914 his friend John Williams joined the Royal Flying Corps on the outbreak of war with Germany.

As a result of the outbreak of World War I, the British Government felt it prudent to import American tractors, as part of a programme to increase food production throughout the UK, but farmers used to horses had to be educated to use the tractors efficiently. To this end, thirty-year old Harry Ferguson, who had taken on an agency for the American Overtime tractor, was asked by the Irish Department of Agriculture to supervise the training of farmers in the use and maintenance of these imported tractors and

A Ferguson "Belfast" plough fitted to an Eros tractor conversion of a Ford model T car, around 1917.

ploughs. This gave Harry and his friend Willie Sands the opportunity to perfect their ploughing techniques, and to travel extensively around Ireland, undertaking demonstrations and providing training. Ferguson and Sands became familiar with the shortcomings of these early tractors, especially their tendency to tip over backwards when the implement met an obstruction, often injuring or even killing the driver. Harry Ferguson's inventive, questioning mind set itself to resolving this problem.

By the end of 1917, Sands had made a plough that fitted the Ford Eros tractor, which was a conversion based on the Ford Model T car. Undoubtedly his designs and work were the products of Harry Ferguson's inventive mind, but it is reasonable to say that the two men worked very closely together. At the close of that year, the plough was given a public demonstration at Coleraine in Northern Ireland. This first mounted plough is frequently known as the Belfast Plough.

The same year saw the new Fordson Model F tractor being tested by the British Board of Agriculture to ascertain its suitability for British conditions. It passed with flying colours, and Henry Ford agreed to start production of it at his plant at Cork in Southern Ireland. However, before production got under way, 6000 Fordson Model Fs were imported into the UK from America to help speed up food production. Also in 1917, Harry Ferguson Ltd took on an apprentice draughtsman, Hugh Reid, who later ended up running Ferguson's garage business in Belfast.

In 1918, Ferguson and Sands proceeded to the next and obvious phase of plough development, and designed and tested a plough to be mounted on the Fordson Model F, which was becoming a popular and reliable tractor. They actually took a plough out to Detroit to demonstrate to Henry Ford and his right-hand man Charles Sorensen, whom Ferguson had sought out in London, but the two parties failed to reach an agreement at this time. In 1920, Sands decided to leave Harry Ferguson Ltd to work on his own, so Archie Greer, a one-time pattern maker who had joined Ferguson in 1917, progressed to become Harry Ferguson's right-hand man. In 1921 Ferguson and Greer were sufficiently satisfied with the plough to arrange a visit to the Cork plant, where they met Patrick Hennessey, later chairman of Ford in Britain, who was at that time involved in Fordson tractor production.

By 1922 the problem of maintaining a constant working depth of the plough had been partially overcome, and the Ferguson Duplex plough was produced and marketed by Harry Ferguson Ltd from the May Street Premises in Belfast. Ferguson and John Williams then visited the USA, wanting to find a manufacturer to produce 50,000 Ferguson ploughs a year. They thought they had reached agreement with a large blacksmith business with a plant at Bucyrus in Ohio, owned by one John Shank, but he eventually shied away from the idea, so Harry Ferguson approached Roderick Lean, a harrow manufacturer in Mansfield, Ohio. This arrangement lasted until 1924, when Lean's firm went into receivership. Ferguson then had to look for an alternative producer, which he found in the Sherman Brothers, Fordson tractor distributors of Evansville in New York State. Their partnership was known as Ferguson Sherman Inc.

In 1924 Willie Sands, who was a brilliant designer and a creative mind in his own right, decided to come back to work for Harry Ferguson. The plough designs were taken further, and the idea was born of adapting the system of automatic draft control also to other implements. A patent application for draft control was lodged in February 1926, and by June 1926 the master patent number 253566 was

The Ferguson plough Mark I Duplex of 1922, fitted to a Fordson F. The gentleman in the bowler hat has his right hand on the lever that is used to put the plough in and out of work.

Ferguson and his friend Poppe at Brooklands in 1929.

Harry Ferguson's first three-point linkage system, using one lower link and two top links.

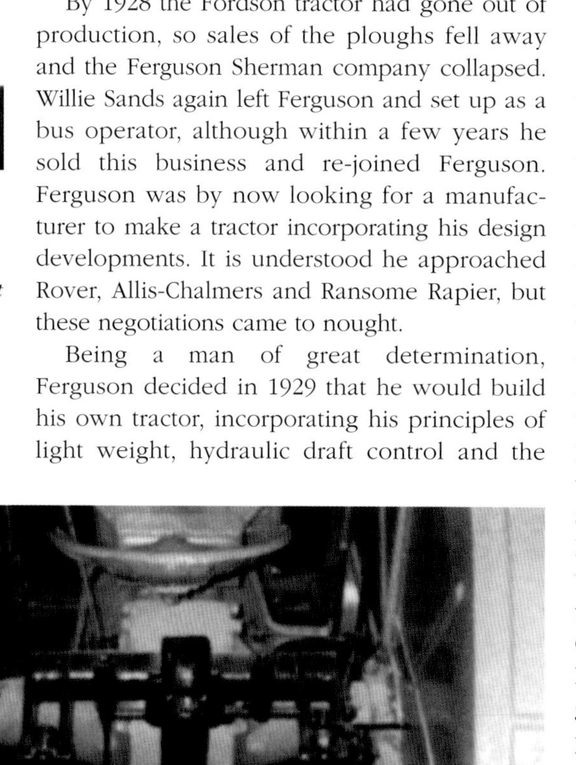

granted for "Apparatus for Coupling Agricultural Implements to Tractors and Auto- matically Regulating the Depth of Work", carried out by either electrical, mechanical or hydraulic means. The patent was also filed in the USA.

By 1928 the Fordson tractor had gone out of production, so sales of the ploughs fell away and the Ferguson Sherman company collapsed. Willie Sands again left Ferguson and set up as a bus operator, although within a few years he sold this business and re-joined Ferguson. Ferguson was by now looking for a manufacturer to make a tractor incorporating his design developments. It is understood he approached Rover, Allis-Chalmers and Ransome Rapier, but these negotiations came to nought.

Being a man of great determination, Ferguson decided in 1929 that he would build his own tractor, incorporating his principles of light weight, hydraulic draft control and the three-point linkage. Around this time, in 1930, Ferguson was keenly demonstrating his own Fordson F, which had been fitted with an embryonic three-point linkage system with lower link sensing covered by patent 253566. One demonstration was held in a field near Ascot, Berkshire, before a selected group of people including the Prince of Wales, who apparently was very impressed and took the trouble to inform the motor car manufacturer William Morris. Morris sent a technical assistant to Ascot to evaluate Ferguson's invention. Likewise he was most impressed, and thought the tractor could be put into mass production by Morris Motors.

The discussions between Ferguson and the Morris team went well until they came to the matter of a name for the tractor. This was where things became heated. Ferguson wanted his name on the tractor but he also wanted the tractor put into mass production, so the name issue was put on hold and a draft agreement was thrashed out. However, just when it was about to be signed by both sides, Morris Motors withdrew from the deal "on the grounds of the economic situation prevailing at the present time", although the author's guess is that the Morris people were scared off by Ferguson's pernickety and stubborn personality. One wonders how Ferguson reacted to this sudden change of heart by Morris Motors. No doubt it spurred him on to produce his own prototype, the Black Tractor (now in the Science Museum, London, but still owned by the Sheldon family), which was completed by 1933. One can only speculate what might have been, if the Morris-Ferguson tractor had gone into production.

In 1931 the skills and ideas for the proposed tractor came together. Trevor Knox and John Chambers came on board with Sands and Ferguson, and design and development work got under way. The pioneering nature of this project, about to be undertaken by such a small team of dedicated, talented and determined people, cannot be overestimated. First and foremost, the tractor incorporated several patents from the past. These included the three-point linkage with what became the standard Category I attachment points, as well as the top link sensing which controlled the hydraulic pump on the suction side, and the stepped wheel rims and centres which provided an adjustable track. Like all later Ferguson designs,

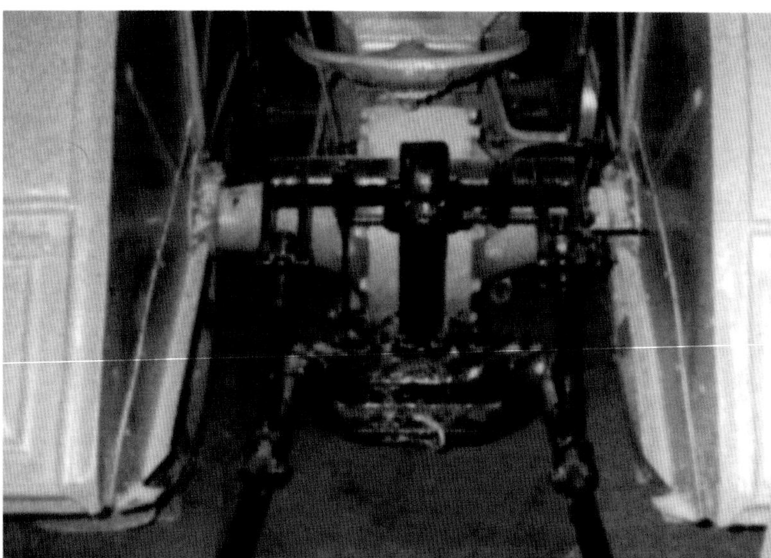

The first true three-point linkage as we know it, fitted to a Fordson F tractor. Draft sensing is through the lower links in this case.

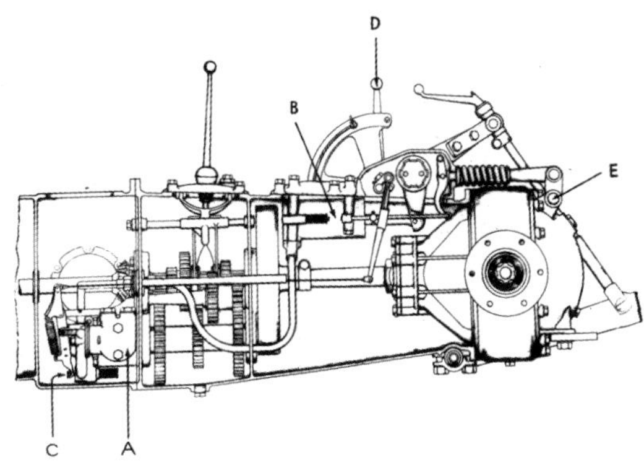

A sectional drawing of the Ferguson Type A transmission hydraulic system. A is the hydraulic pump driven by the input shaft. B is the lift cylinder. C is the inlet port to the pump, which is controlled by the draft control lever D, conveniently placed next to the driver. E is the pivot point for the rocker that connects the top link to the compression spring and control linkage.

Rear view of the Ferguson Type A connected to a two-furrow plough.

Offside view of the Ferguson Type A, an early example fitted with a dry air filter. The fenced enclosure was to enable HF to demonstrate the ease of handling possible with mounted implements.

the Black Tractor was built on the unit principle and had no frame as such, the engine, gearbox and rear axle being integrated into one load-bearing unit. This idea had been pioneered back in 1916 by the Hungarian engineer Eugene Farkas, who was employed by Ford of Dearborn, and it was therefore copied by Ferguson from the original Fordson. The Black Tractor's 20hp engine was made by Hercules of America and was of cast-iron construction, but the remainder of the transmission housing was of cast aluminium, as were the radiator top and bottom tanks, which in turn supported the forged steel front axle. The rear axle was made of pressed and fabricated mild steel. Total weight was in the region of only 16.5cwt (839kg) or about half the weight of the Fordson Model F at 1.5 tons (1500kg). The cogs for the gearbox and steering box were supplied by the foremost gear cutter in England at the time, David Brown of Huddersfield. The author has heard it suggested that the differential unit came

This 1936 Austin 10 van was used by Harry Ferguson Ltd as a service vehicle. It has probably arrived to attend to the needs of the Type A tractor alongside.

The first English demonstration of the Ferguson system, held in Herefordshire in May 1936. Harry Ferguson is placing a chunky fence post under the front wheel of the Type A. He was doing this to demonstrate to spectators that the depth of ploughing would not be affected: the draft control system would take care of that.

from a Morris-Commercial lorry axle, but that has not been verified. Evidence to support this is the fact that an interna-toothed ring gear reduction unit was used between the output shaft of the gearbox and the pinion drive shaft of the differential unit.

Various trials had to be carried out on the experimental tractor before a satisfactory performance was achieved and it could be made into a marketable product. By 1935 this had more or less been achieved, and Ferguson changed the title of his trading company, Harry Ferguson Ltd of Belfast, to Harry Ferguson Motors Ltd, and set up a second new company as Harry Ferguson Ltd, which included his old friend and backer McGregor Greer, and John Williams, his fellow college student. It was planned to bring in John Turner as a financial adviser; Turner, a Huddersfield accountant, at that time worked for David Brown, and while he remained independent of the company, he was to become a life-long friend and adviser to Ferguson. David Brown undertook to manufacture Ferguson's tractor, which was to be known as the Type A, or more commonly the Ferguson-Brown, and was to be fitted with a Coventry Climax engine. The public was first shown this tractor in May 1936 at a demonstration near Hereford.

In 1937 Ferguson-Brown Ltd was formed, with F E Brown as Chairman, David Brown and Henry G Ferguson as joint managing directors. They were joined on the board by Ernest de Silly Hamilton Brown, Thomas McGregor Greer and Arthur Sykes. This did not last long, as in 1938 David Brown Tractors Ltd was formed, and Ferguson, McGregor Greer and Hamilton Brown were removed from the board. In 1939 production of the Ferguson-Brown Type A ceased, with about 1300 units sold in total. Approximately 350 are thought to have survived, not bad going for a light and rather frail piece of agricultural machinery. This was a depressing time for Ferguson and his small team, but nevertheless there was one positive development: the rear centre placed power take-off (PTO), derived from a constantly running layshaft in the gearbox, was success-

Harry Ferguson in the driving seat, demonstrating how th eimplement can be lowered in corner of a restricted space. A farmer who attended an early demonstration once told me that he went home and said to his family "I have seen a system of tractor ploughing that is a revolution for farmers".

Front cover of a 1938 brochure, over-printed with the new name David Brown Tractors Ltd.

fully patented on 31 July 1939.

In October 1938 Ferguson and John Williams travelled to the USA to meet Henry Ford and make the famous "handshake" agreement. Ferguson's erstwhile US business partner Eber Sherman had kept Henry Ford informed of the development of the Ferguson tractor, and the intrigued motor tycoon, who was himself exper-

John Chambers driving Ferguson Type A no. 88 with a two-furrow plough at the Deer Park, Stoneleigh, about nine months before he died. He told me he had helped assemble this tractor in 1936. Today it is part of the Coldridge Collection.

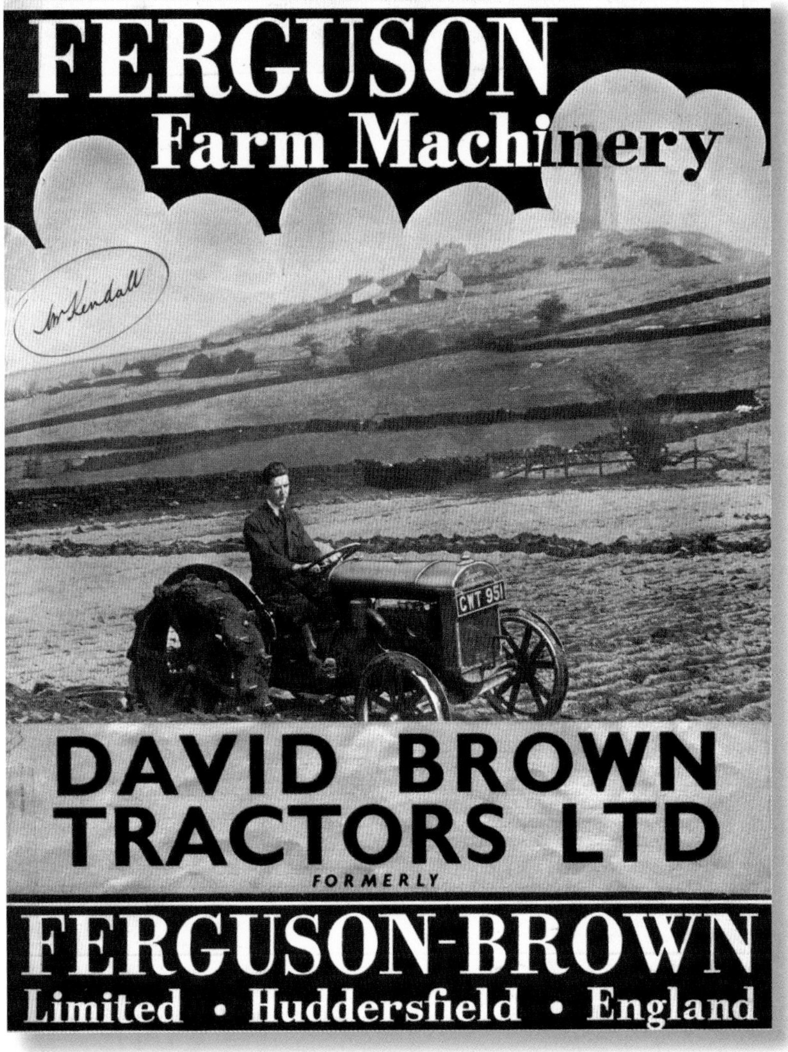

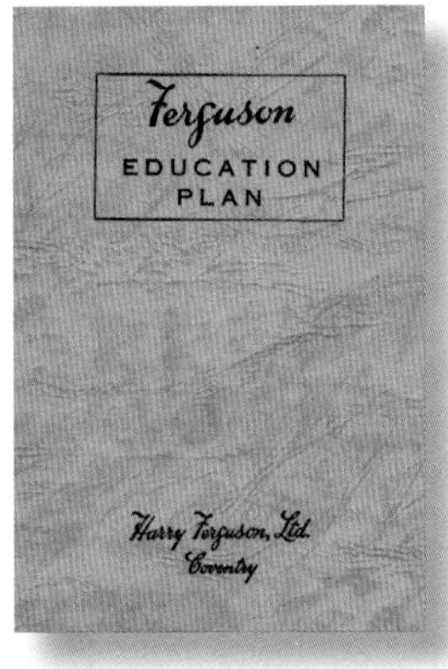

The front cover of a Ferguson training booklet for salesmen. It covers all aspects of selling not only the tractor but also a fair range of the implements, as well as setting up and running a successful demonstration.

imenting with tractor designs at this time, asked for Ferguson to come to Detroit and demonstrate his machine. Their meeting and its portentous outcome are discussed in detail in Chapter 2.

Things now happened very quickly. Ferguson travelled to the USA again in January 1939. By April of that year, the first Ford-Ferguson prototype was ready for testing and by June production of the tractor was under way, together with a wide range of implements. The Ferguson System took off. A very satisfied Ferguson returned to Northern Ireland in September 1939. In October he set up a demonstration at Greenmount Agricultural College to show off the Ford-Ferguson and implements, and this was followed by another demonstration in Bedfordshire in 1940. By 1942, the American government was contributing a huge amount of equipment and men to the war effort, creating a shortage of materials for home market production which led to a drop in production of Ford-Fergusons. However, a fair proportion of the tractors manufactured were sent to Britain, to help increase food production here.

At the end of World War Two, in 1945, Ferguson turned his attention to getting his tractor produced in the UK. His first effort was a plan for production in Northern Ireland, but that concept fell on stony ground. After a second and equally fruitless discussion with William Morris, now Lord Nuffield, an agreement was eventually reached with the Standard Motor Company, under the chairmanship of Sir John Black, for production to start at the then redundant aero engine shadow factory at Banner Lane, on the outskirts of Coventry. By late 1949 when production of the TE20 model was well established, the design and development teams had received feed-back from their sales people that farmers with larger acreages were looking for a tractor that incorporated all the positive features of the TE20 but had more horsepower. This led to work starting on the LTX model, described in Chapter 13.

In July 1947 Ford Motor Company in the USA announced production of a new tractor, the 8N, which relied on Ferguson's patents. Ferguson was incensed by this violation of his patents by Henry Ford's grandson, Henry Ford II. At the time he happened to be in a Zürich clinic for what he himself described as chronic toxaemia, in a way not surprising bearing in mind the stresses and pressures he had been subject to. In November 1948 he went to America with his friend and financial adviser John Turner, to whom David Brown had introduced him back in 1935, to confront Henry Ford II over the

The first agricultural show at which TE20s were present was at Bakewell, Derbyshire, in June 1947. The local Ferguson dealer's service van is also on hand.

IN THE

District Court of the United States

FOR THE SOUTHERN DISTRICT OF NEW YORK.

Civil Action No. ....

HARRY FERGUSON and HARRY FERGUSON, INC.,
Plaintiffs,

v.

FORD MOTOR COMPANY, DEARBORN MOTORS CORPORATION, HENRY FORD II, ERNEST R. BREECH, ERNEST C. KANZLER, FRANK R. PIERCE, THOMAS A. FARRELL, JOHN R. DAVIS, ALBERT J. BROWNING, GRANT COOK, OHIO TRACTOR & IMPLEMENT CO., and SHERMAN TRACTOR & EQUIPMENT CO., INCORPORATED,
Defendants.

COMPLAINT.

Dated, New York, January 8, 1948.

CAHILL, GORDON, ZACHRY & REINDEL,
Attorneys for Plaintiffs,
63 Wall Street,
New York 5, N. Y.

CARLSON, PITZNER, HUBBARD & WOLFE,
1 North LaSalle Street,
Chicago 2, Illinois,
Of Counsel.

The front cover of the complaint by Harry Ferguson against the Ford Motor Company. It runs to 45 pages.

violation of patents and the handshake agreement. At first Ferguson and Turner tried to negotiate a deal, but Ford was intransigent, and as a result Ferguson decided to build his own production plant in Detroit, Michigan.

This was a great gamble but it paid off. The plant, set in 72 acres (29 hectares), was of the highest quality, it was built in 116 working days, and Ferguson drove the first tractor off the production line in October 1948. With production running at about 100 units per day in America, and with a similar figure coming out of Banner Lane, Ferguson tractor sales were really hitting Ford. No doubt filled with buoyant confidence, Ferguson filed a lawsuit against the Ford Motor Company charging them with "violating the agreement of trust and confidence made in 1939", with infringing his patent rights by "deliberately copying Ferguson System tractor and farm implements, unlawfully seizing and using Ferguson inventions, engineering and developments, designs and ideas", and with endeavouring to destroy his American market so as to establish their own monopoly, an offence under United States Anti-Trust Laws.

He alleged that besides conspiring to destroy his source of implement supply and his distribution organization, the defendants had also tried to obstruct his efforts to raise capital and arrange for an alternative source of manufacture. This sent a shockwave through the Ford organisation. Harry Ferguson instructed the firm of attorneys Cahill, Gordon, Zachry and Reindel of Wall Street, New York, to claim a total sum of

HF at his home, Abbotswood, in 1948, with a demonstration model of the Ferguson system. The front, rear and steering wheels are from the Meccano range.

HF next to his beloved Bentley.

$251,100,000 (nearly £90,000,000, after the 1949 devaluation), together with reasonable attorneys' fees, costs and disbursements of this action. During the court hearing, Ferguson himself answered over 60,000 questions, his evidence running to over 10,500 pages of record. He stood up to the strain of this well, even enjoyed the trial, as he always maintained that the small man must never submit to the business magnate. One witness (Philip Page, an ex-Ford employee who was by now a vice-president of Ferguson's American company), under the strain of cross-examination and conflicting loyalty, left a suicide note saying "my head feels tighter than a drum", and then proceeded to jump to his death from the fourteenth floor of his New York hotel. In contrast, Ferguson by all accounts seems to have enjoyed the case. A newspaper reporter asked him about his amazing stamina, "Have you no feeling of strain – are you not worried about the outcome?" Ferguson laughed in his face, "Worried! Certainly not – I've never been happier in all my life", he chuckled. "The case" had become his hobby!

Henry Ford II on the other hand found it a great strain, perhaps because he knew in his heart that he had been deceitful and conspiratorial, and during the case he made several offers to settle out of court, but Ferguson would stubbornly refuse, saying that he would cease the fight only on a legal ruling. In April 1952 the judge ordered the Ford Motor Company to stop production of the 8N by the end of that year. Ford finally agreed to pay Ferguson $9,250,000, or at the time £3,303,570. This was considered to be the largest amount paid out so far in the USA to a plaintiff in a patent claim. Ferguson was at his Abbotswood home in the Cotswolds mowing the lawn when he was given the news, and is said to have shown little emotion over this great and long protracted victory, except "it is a victory for the small inventor."

By this court decision Ferguson suddenly became significantly more wealthy, and at the age of sixty-eight must have considered what next? He had a great interest in combine harvesters, and although he had been working on a demountable design of his own, he respected the achievement of the long-standing Canadian firm Massey-Harris. Their president James Duncan, who had started as an office boy with the firm at the age of seventeen, happened to be in England at the time, and Ferguson arranged a meeting to suggest a pooling of their resources. The two men got on well, and before long Duncan had instructed his directors and lawyers to get to England as quickly as possible, to enter into the negotiation of terms and financial settlement. All these discussions proceeded fairly smoothly, but there was haggling over one million Dollars (then around £357,000), for Ferguson's company. To break the deadlock,

Ferguson suggested they toss for it. This startled the Massey-Harris people but Ferguson assured them that he always lost a toss. So a half crown was tossed and Ferguson lost. They then tossed for the coin itself and Ferguson won! Thus he lost £357,000 but gained 12.5p... The Massey-Harris team later presented Ferguson with a silver cigar box with the half-crown on the lid and the inscription "The million dollar coin", followed by "To our friend and partner Harry Ferguson, a gallant sportsman".

This merger of the two companies to form Massey-Harris-Ferguson took place in August 1953, but all was not well. Ferguson had not told any of his staff about the merger, so resentments soon came to the fore, and it was not long before quite a bit of internal political fighting erupted between the Massey-Harris people – known as the "reds" from the colour of their tractors – and the Ferguson people – inevitably called the "greys". This discord was not just between staff of the two companies, but between James Duncan and Harry Ferguson

HF with newspaper cuttings of his action against Ford Motor Company.

A publicity shot from the time of the merger with Massey-Harris. Denis Purchase (on the Ferguson), who was involved with the training school, is seen with M McCutcheon, engineering director of Massey-Harris.

This makes interesting reading and is surprisingly up to date, apart from rule 14 which states "Smoking is permitted in the offices during working hours".

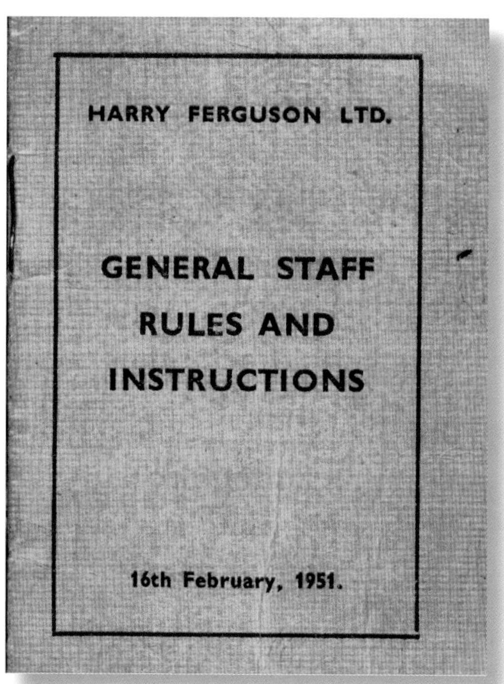
HARRY FERGUSON LTD.

GENERAL STAFF RULES AND INSTRUCTIONS

16th February, 1951.

himself, over fundamental questions of how design, production and marketing should be approached. For example, Ferguson was very keen to get the LTX or TE60 tractor (see chapter 13) into production, but Duncan thought the capital cost was too great, and suggested using a Perkins engine to power it, or even building a bigger tractor using some existing FE35 parts. This in fact is what eventually happened with the MF65, which used a Perkins P4TA engine and the FE35 gearbox and transmission with the addition of epicyclic reduction hubs and dry disc brakes on the rear axle, together with 11x32 rear tyres. This tractor went into production in 1958.

By this time Ferguson was not involved in what was going on within Massey-Harris-Ferguson, but was actively involved with Harry Ferguson Research, which concentrated on motor car development. It should be remembered that in 1954 Ferguson was seventy years old and had suffered on and off for half of his life from bouts of depression, along with back pain that possibly stemmed from his aeroplane crash back in 1910. He also had a general tendency towards hypochondria, so it is not surprising that these factors combined with the stress of a five-year court case and protracted negotiations in selling his business to Massey-Harris left him tired, run down, and in a mentally distressed state.

However, when he rallied round and became himself, he took up the challenge of hawking his four-wheel drive prototype car to the major UK car manufacturers, including Jaguar, Rootes, and BMC, but all these endeavours came to nought. No doubt his lack of diplomacy in the latter part of his life in dealing with the captains of the motor industry did not help, and this was exacerbated by his sometimes bigoted attitude. A lot of people in their mature years become nostalgic and interested in the past; Ferguson was no exception to this generalization, for he and his wife often returned for long holidays to Dunmurry Bay and Dundrum near Belfast.

On one occasion while in Belfast, he was re-introduced to his old colleague Willie Sands – who had testified against Ferguson in the Ford suit – but when they were reconciled, Ferguson decided to give Sands an annuity. Despite the profound refreshment he found in familiar parts of Northern Ireland, he and his wife were to spend one more holiday abroad, this time in Jamaica early in 1957. One night Ferguson was attacked as he slept by a hooded figure with a gun, and after a struggle was shot through the leg as the intruder was shouted out of the room. Obviously, Ferguson capitalised on this event when he returned to England, pointing with his walking stick at his left leg where the bullet had gone in just below the knee cap and come out at the back of the calf muscle, making the point to the assembled journalists "you can see I was not running away! And the intruder did not get a single cent."

Peter Warr, Ferguson's estate foreman and general factotum, indicated to me that this incident was probably a crucial point in Ferguson's decline. He became even more regimented in the structure of his day, but there were days when his old youthful sparkle and enthusiasm surfaced. At one point he and Bob Annat sketched out plans for a small tractor of 20bhp that could pull a two-furrow plough. He wrote to Massey-Harris-Ferguson offering a design and development service. Also at this time he took up a claim against Charles Sorensen, the former Ford executive, over statements in his book *My Forty Years with Ford* (1956) in which he slandered Ferguson. The book was withdrawn from British bookshops as a result of this action.

In May 1960, the last year of Ferguson's life, Peter Warr took him to Silverstone, and the stimulation of meeting the people among the racing cars in the pits fired Ferguson up with the idea of producing a four-wheel drive racing car to Formula One specification. The outcome of this was the decision to launch Project 99. But on 25 October 1960 just after 8.30am Maureen, his wife of forty-seven years, found him drowned in his bath. Later, at the inquest, it was established that a drug overdose of about twice the lethal requirement had been found in his body. According to Ferguson's wishes as a through-and-through agnostic, he was cremated without the usual religious ceremony. His ashes were spread over Abbotswood from an aeroplane. An observation made by George Bernard Shaw could well relate to Harry Ferguson, "Since the reasonable man adapts himself to his circumstances, all progress must be made by the unreasonable man."

To round off this opening chapter, may I quote a few verbal snapshots of this highly inventive and individual man.

Meeting a young draughtsman in the gents, he asked him, "Are you not going to wash your hands before you go back to work?"

"No sir – I am going to lunch now."

"Well that's alright then", said Ferguson.

Ray Farden, Ferguson's head gardener, when asked how he found his employer, said, "He was my friend and I was his friend."

The telegraphic address of Harry Ferguson Research Ltd was PROGRESS, COVENTRY.

"Farm machinery should be foolproof".

"Beauty in engineering is that which performs perfectly the function for which it was designed and has no superfluous parts." This saying was printed on notices hung on the walls of his engineering departments.

"Nothing must be left to chance" and "Attention to detail" were further maxims.

"He is a remarkable fellow...bit of a one track mind though, but remarkable." Winston Churchill on Harry Ferguson.

Another shot of HF with his Mk VI Bentley - not the car which Michael Winter and Betty Ferguson both crashed in France.

Chapter Two

The Ford-Ferguson

Despite a promising start, both Harry Ferguson and David Brown soon became disenchanted with their working relationship, and it is worth investigating the causes of this friction. Harry Ferguson was adamant that his tractor design was just right, yet on the other hand David Brown was not selling the numbers that Ferguson expected, bearing in mind that in 1936 Brown had set up a most up-to-date production and assembly line for tractors and implements. The plant had such exceptional standards of quality control that even the nuts and bolts were made on site and the nuts were cyanide hardened, the sort of attention to detail that Harry Ferguson demanded. BSF threads were used, and the head sizes chosen so that by and large the famous double-ended Ferguson spanner could be used for all field adjustments. All the engines were dynamometer tested for power output, and the implements as well as the tractors were treated with rust-proofing material, prior to painting to "show finish standard".

On the one hand Harry Ferguson insisted pedantically on all these and other high standards of production, and on the other hand David Brown found that the tractors he was producing for Ferguson were not selling as well as anticipated. Ferguson owned the marketing company, and had built into the agreement with Brown that he would only pay for each tractor when he had a sale lined up. Ferguson suggested to Brown that he should cut the price of the tractors and step up production. It was not surprising that Brown refused, suggesting to Ferguson that the tractor needed design changes to promote sales. Harry Ferguson stubbornly refused to consider this. As Brown recalled, "The battles we had to change even a split pin!"

In close secrecy, David Brown now pushed ahead with the development of a tractor of his own design. By the summer of 1937 the Ferguson sales company was in serious financial trouble. It had spent large sums of money advertising the Ferguson Model A and its small range of implements, but the tractors were not selling fast enough. By June 1937, accountants had developed a plan to merge the two firms of Harry Ferguson Sales Ltd and David Brown Tractors Ltd under the new title of Ferguson-Brown Tractors Ltd, with Harry Ferguson having only a minority share holding.

At the time of these events in England, Henry Ford in America was experimenting with prototype lightweight tractors, with the intention of eventually producing a good working tractor for the small farmers of the world. Although Ford invested quite an amount of money and engineering expertise to further this objective, progress was spasmodic. Harry Ferguson had worked with Eber Sherman on plough designs back in 1928. Sherman had been present at a demonstration of the Ferguson type A, and was most impressed by its performance, as well as by the revolutionary concept of its three-point linkage and draft control system. It was Eber

A nice publicity shot showing how easy it is for a young boy to lift a Ferguson two-furrow plough.

Sherman who told Henry Ford about Ferguson's design, suggesting that it would be of interest in developing Ford's small tractor concept. Ford was intrigued and asked for Ferguson to come to out Detroit to demonstrate his tractor, which was exactly what Ferguson and Sherman wanted to happen.

In the autumn of 1938 Harry Ferguson prepared to ship two Ferguson-Brown tractors, numbers 661 and 662, and the small range of Ferguson implements, from Huddersfield to Belfast en route to Dearborn, USA. Ferguson told David Brown that he was going to America, but was vague and evasive when Brown asked whether he might see Ford. Ferguson's demonstration to Ford in October 1938 was set in Mrs Ford's nursery garden at the Fords' Fairlane Estate. Just a small group assembled. On the American side, Henry Ford, his chauffeur Wilson, Ed Malvitz who was the assistant to development engineer Karl Schultz on Ford's tractor programme, and George and Eber Sherman, as well as an employee of the Sherman Brothers who had driven the truck carrying the tractors and implements. The British contingent was Harry Ferguson with daughter Betty, and his right-hand man John Williams.

It was arranged that Malvitz would drive the tractor and plough so that Ferguson could give Henry Ford a running commentary on what was happening. After a few rounds of ploughing, Malvitz changed the plough to a cultivator, carrying out the demonstration in a tiny roped-off enclosure, as was characteristic of Ferguson demonstrations. Evidently Ford was very impressed, but he asked for an Allis-Chalmers model B and a Fordson from the farm machinery pool to be brought in for comparative assessment. These two tractors performed very poorly in comparison with the Ferguson; the loose surface on the gradient conspired against them. "Well", said Henry Ford, "you're ploughing in my wife's garden. Let's see how the tractor does in some heavier ground. We'll take it into the Deerfield."

This was the largest field on the Ford Estate, 250 acres (101 hectares) of heavier land. The Ferguson pulled the two-furrow plough with ease. Ford was most impressed and thoughtful. He instructed his chauffeur Wilson to fetch a couple of chairs and a table from the nearby lodge, and these were set up adjacent to the ploughing patch. Harry Ferguson had brought along one of his demonstration clockwork models with Meccano wheels, which were used to illustrate the benefits of the Ferguson System, and Ford and Ferguson sat down facing each other, over the table with the model. It is quite amazing how much these two men had in common. They were both farmers' sons, they shared a passion to relieve the drudgery of farm work, they were both idealists and pacifists, they were equally eccentric and strong-willed, some said they even looked alike. Perhaps most importantly, each recognised in the other man a kindred spirit.

No doubt this establishment of common ground and their mutual empathy quickly led them to discussions of how they could work together. Henry Ford apparently offered to buy Ferguson's patents for a large sum of money. The following exchanges are based on the version that appeared in Colin Fraser's biography of Ferguson, and are apparently based on Ferguson's own recollection of their meeting:

Ferguson told Ford directly, "You have not got enough money because they are not for sale to you or anyone else."

"Well I am determined to go into business, and you need me and I need you, so what do you suggest?" asked Ford.

"A gentleman's agreement", Harry Ferguson replied, and went on to explain, "You're proposing to stake your reputation and your resources on this idea, even if a billion Dollars is involved, and so no agreement could protect you fully. I've spent my whole career thinking out this great economic idea, and I put everything I and my family have into it, and I reckon my designs and inventions are worth more than

Nearside view of a Ford-Ferguson 9N - not an early example because the slats in the radiator grill are aligned vertically. Earlier examples had the slats more or less horizontal.

a billion Dollars, so I don't see how I can make an agreement. I'll trust you if you'll trust me and I'll put all my services at your disposal for future design, education and distribution. It will have to be world education, because there is a new world economy involved. For your part, you will put all your resources, energy, fame and reputation behind the equipment and manufacture it in volume at low cost, and I'll sell it."

"That's a good idea", said Ford. "I'll go along with you on those terms."

They then went on to work out five further points:

(i) Ferguson would be fully responsible for all design and engineering work and would have full authority in that area.

(ii) Ford would manufacture the tractor and assume all risks involved in manufacture.

(iii) Ferguson would distribute the tractor which Ford would deliver to him f.o.b. (free on board) for sale wherever and however he pleased.

(iv) Either party could terminate the agreement at any time without obligation to the other, for any reason whatever even if it was only "because he did not like the colour of his hair".

(v) The Ford plant at Dagenham in England would ultimately build the Ferguson System Tractor on similar terms to those established at Dearborn.

In today's world this type of gentleman's agreement seems bizarre but it is obvious that both men got on well together and intuitively trusted each other. They must have done, with so much at stake. So the pair of them stood up and shook hands across the table, thus sealing a traditional gentleman's agreement of trust and commitment. A deal was done which has become known over the years as the "handshake agreement". Following this agreement, the Ferguson-Brown was demonstrated to Ford's son Edsel, and then to Ford's top management people. They were all impressed with the tractor, but a good many were sceptical about the handshake agreement, although this did not deter Ferguson and Ford. Harry Ferguson was obviously delighted that he had pulled off such an amazing deal, and he and Williams returned to England.

Ferguson realised that he would have to terminate his agreement with David Brown on the best possible terms. Asked by Brown on his return whether he had seen Ford, Ferguson replied, "You can't get near the man." Critics of Harry Ferguson have often cited this as an example of a devious nature but, to be realistic, in the world of big business these things sometimes have to be done for survival. Ferguson

Rear view of the Ford 9N showing the linkage draw bar.

knew that David Brown was working on designs for his own tractor; in fact Brown showed Ferguson the drawings. Ferguson considered this a violation of the agreement that they had both been a party to. This blew up into a row, but of course David Brown was in reality pleased, because a break would free him to produce and market his own tractor, the VAK 1. He offered to buy out Harry Ferguson's stake in Ferguson-Brown Tractors Ltd, as well as the remaining stock, and to take on the service commitment to the tractors. Up to January 1939, approximately 1200 Type A tractors had been sold, together with a limited range of implements. David Brown sold off the remaining stock, and it is generally believed that a total of about 1350 were produced.

As an aside, David Brown's VAK 1 was launched in July 1939. This was a larger tractor with a 35bhp engine, and it was fitted with a three-point linkage but not of course the Ferguson-patented draft control system. It had styled bodywork with a touch of the American design aesthetic of that period, and it was painted Hunting Pink, no doubt due to David Brown's strong connection with the Yorkshire-based Badsworth Hunt. It is reported that when Harry Ferguson saw the new tractor, he was not impressed, but then he was very biased.

In January 1939 Ferguson, with wife Maureen and daughter Betty, set off to America on the Cunard liner *Aquitania*, accompanied by his team of John Chambers and Willie Sands and their families, and also Harold Willy, who had been involved with the sales at Ferguson-Brown. They arrived in New York on 14 January, and then went on to Dearborn, where they stayed in country accommodation adjacent to the Dearborn Inn, the world's first airport hotel, owned of course by Henry Ford.

In the time that had elapsed between the handshake agreement and Ferguson's party arriving at Dearborn, Ford engineers had stripped down the Ferguson Type A to evaluate its workings, and to do some basic laboratory tests on its physical performance, especially in the area of front end stability. In November and December of 1938, Ford had also built three prototypes incorporating the Ferguson System patents. These were tested at Ford's Richard Hill plantation near Ways in Georgia, as the freezing conditions of a Michigan winter precluded field testing near Detroit.

On their arrival at Dearborn in January 1939, the Ferguson team was working with Ford engineers at the old airport building, and then moved to the River Rouge car plant experimental building. They had brought the full set of working drawings, together with some more recent patent drawings, one of which was patent number 510352, filed on 30 November 1937, relating to the PTO (Power Take-Off) drive and hydraulic pump. This feature was achieved by having a constantly running layshaft in the gearbox so that, providing the main clutch was engaged, the PTO and hydraulic pump would run, though drive to both could be disengaged by a sliding-coupling type of clutch. The PTO output shaft was positioned on the centreline of the tractor within the three-point linkage, as per patent 421983 filed on 3 July 1938. The other significant improvement the Ferguson team brought to the Ford experimental shop was the adjustable row-crop front axle, which allowed track width to be varied from 48in (1219mm) to 76in (1930mm), without altering the front wheel alignment. It is generally thought that Greer and Sands were responsible for this design, but the patent was filed in Ferguson's name.

In his handshake deal with Ferguson, Henry Ford had promised to put all the resources of his organisation behind the team that were

A sectioned view of the gearbox in the Ford Ferguson 9N, showing well the straight-cut sliding gears, the taper roller bearing on the mainshaft and the constant-running layshaft. Note the interlock on the starter switch linkage with the gear lever, and the mechanical press button to energize the starter, which can only be done when the gear lever is in neutral.

putting together this prototype tractor. The Ford side was headed up by Charles "Cast-Iron Charlie" Sorensen, Ford's production genius and chief executive, aided by a young engineer, Harold Brock, who at the time was working on automotive drivetrains under chief automotive engineer Larry Sheldrick. At the age of twenty-five, Brock was asked by Sheldrick to head up the tractor design project with the title of project manager while continuing his involvement in transmissions.

Thus on the Ford side were Henry Ford himself, Sorensen and Harold Brock, plus the mass-production methods and experience for which Ford was world renowned. They already had in mass production many components that could be worked into the tractor design, thereby saving production costs and reducing the number of extra parts needed to be held in stock by dealerships.

On the other side of the equation was Ferguson with his team of Willie Sands, John Chambers and John Williams, their Ferguson-Brown Type A with plough and cultivator, together with its working drawings, and at least two additional patents that could be worked into the new design. A small team of stubborn Irishmen, who together had worked out a functional application of hydraulic draft control built into a lightweight tractor of 16.5cwt (839kg) – but the design was far from perfect. Its main drawback was that the hydraulics did not function unless the driven wheels were turning. The offset PTO shaft did not meet the engineering SAE standard of the day. The tractor was costly to produce, and in general rather weak structurally, with a limited range of implements available.

After much argument and negotiation between the two camps, and sheer hard work by both, the 9N eventually emerged – 9 stood for 1939 and N was the Ford designation for tractors. Harold Brock writes in his book *The Fords in my Past* that he found it very difficult dealing with four bosses: Sheldrick (chief engineer), Charles Sorensen (chief executive officer), Henry Ford and finally Harry Ferguson, who with his team had overall control of engineering and held most of the patents incorporated into the design.

By March 1939 a successful working prototype was being tested. Ford felt it appropriate to mark this achievement and ordered that on 1 April the prototype should be taken to be tried out in Mrs Ford's garden at Fairlane, the scene of the demonstration the previous autumn. This time there would be an invited audience of the Ford and Ferguson families, together with the Sherman brothers and a few others who had shown interest in marketing this tractor once it went into production.

Harry Ferguson with Charles Sorensen of Ford.

The engineers working on the prototype designs found that the hydraulic linkage had a tendency to bobbing when ploughing. It was considered that because pneumatic tyres were used rather than steel wheels, the rubber tended to deflect slightly due to variations in draft loadings. The problem was solved by Willie Sands, who had the idea of putting a slight taper on the shaft of the control valve, which proved to have a damping effect.

Another development to come out of the liaison was the spring-loaded linchpin we all take for granted today. Prior to this being conceived, the Ferguson-Brown tractors had used a linchpin with a simple ring that flopped down by gravity. The field testers found that these had a tendency to flip out of place when working through vegetation. It is claimed by Harold Brock that Ford engineers overcame this by designing a linchpin with two small off-set

A very early demonstration of the 9N tractor, probably in England. Archie Greer is on the left of the bonnet, Harry Ferguson on the right.

This early handbook has 72 pages text, photographs and line drawings. It highlights how Ferguson expected operators to care for their tractors and implements.

holes on its top end, and a loop of spring steel whose ends engaged in these holes. This gave a strong positive bias for the ring to remain tight against the pin when closed, or vertical when open, and therefore much less likely to be flipped out.

Let us now turn to the specification that was finally reached. The petrol engine was a four-cylinder sidevalve unit of 119.7 cu in (1962cc) with a compression ratio of 6:1. It was in effect "half" of the Ford Mercury V8 engine in production at the time. It was fitted with a governor to give a speed range of 800rpm to 2200rpm, and produced 17.5bhp. The pressure lubrication system was fed by pump from a wet sump, and included a replaceable cartridge type of oil filter. The carburettor was a Marvel-Schebler, supplied with air through an oilbath filter. The electrics were 6-volt as was common practice at the time, with an eighteen-plate battery of 85Ah capacity. This was charged by a dynamo with its charging rate controlled by a cut-out and a vibrating current regulator on early models, later changed to a third-brush design. The starter switch could only be operated if the gear lever was in neutral.

Cooling was by water circulated by a belt-driven pump, with a fan drawing cooling air through the radiator, and temperature control by thermostat. The system was not pressurised on early models. Ferguson was not in favour of the sidevalve engine, arguing, rightly, with Ford engineers that an overhead-valve design was more efficient, but Ford had a suitable sidevalve engine in production so that is what was used. Transmission was via a 9in (229mm) single dry plate clutch, designed so that clutch plate pressure was increased by centrifugal force as engine revs increased. The clutch transmitted power to the input shaft of the three-speed and reverse gearbox, which featured straight-cut gears, sliding into mesh for selection. All shafts were mounted on taper roller bearings, except the reverse idler. The gearbox featured the constant-running layshaft, which in turn drove the hydraulic pump and PTO shaft via a separately controlled sliding-coupling clutch, actuated by a small lever mounted on the left of the transmission casing. This was the substance of the Ferguson patent 421983 mentioned earlier. Drive from the output shaft of the gearbox was taken to a standard Ford truck final drive unit of semi-floating design, with a four-pinion differential and a final drive ratio of 6.66:1, the unit running in taper roller bearings. It will be noted the internal toothed ring reduction gear used in the Ferguson type A was dispensed with.

The PTO output shaft was mounted on the centreline of the tractor, with its height set at approximately the same level as the attachment points of the lower links. Strangely, the shaft diameter was 1.125in (29mm) rather than the normal SAE standard of 1.625in (41mm); maybe this was an attempt to ensure that only Ford or Ferguson designed implements were used. If so it was not a very bright idea, because adaptor splines could easily be made up, and were. A belt pulley attachment was made available, taking its drive from the PTO shaft through a 90-degree bevel gearing to a leather-faced pulley of 9in (229mm) diameter and 6.5in (165mm) width. This gearbox unit was totally enclosed, running in oil, with a speed of 1352rpm at 2000 engine rpm. The 14in by 2in (356mm by 51mm) internal-expanding twin-shoe brakes were of self-energizing type, with one simple adjuster for each brake, and were probably manufactured by Bendix.

The front axle was of a totally new design brought to the project by Ferguson's team. It was covered by patent 541220, filed on 8 July 1939, and again it is claimed that it was designed by Greer and Sands but patented by Ferguson. Like so many inventions, it was simple in that it enabled the width of the front axle to be altered without making adjustments to the drag link settings. This was achieved by making the front axle beam in three sections of forged steel pierced with 0.6785in (17.7mm) diameter holes set 2in (51mm) apart. The centre section pivoted on a pin attached to a bracket mounted forward of the engine, allowing for front axle articulation. Bolted to each end of this centre section were the outer forgings, which carried the housings for the kingpins and the attachment points for the radius rods. The latter, made of forged steel, had a yoke at the forward end to fit over the axle beam, and a ball at the rearward end which engaged with a socket bolted to the bell housing. Further adjustment of the front track was possible by turning the front wheels inside out. The overall range of adjustment was from 48in (1219mm) to 76in (1930mm) in 4in (102mm) steps. Fore and aft movement of the front axle beam was restrained

Ford Ferguson 9N with earth scoop attached and in the dump position.

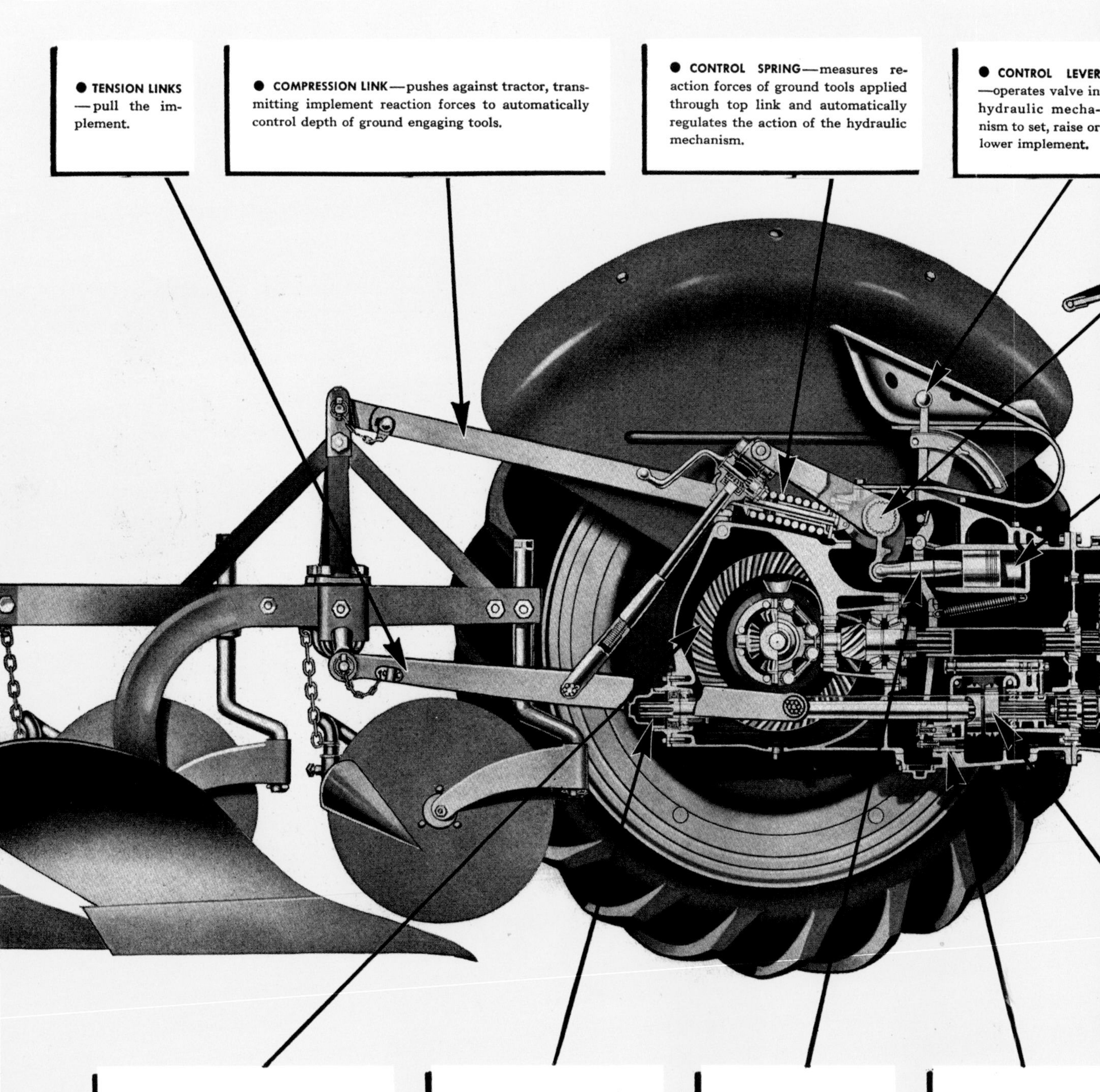
The inside story of the FORD TRACTOR
● TENSION LINKS —pull the implement.
● COMPRESSION LINK—pushes against tractor, transmitting implement reaction forces to automatically control depth of ground engaging tools.
● CONTROL SPRING—measures reaction forces of ground tools applied through top link and automatically regulates the action of the hydraulic mechanism.
● CONTROL LEVER —operates valve in hydraulic mechanism to set, raise or lower implement.
● SPIRAL BEVELED GEAR DRIVE—a sturdy and highly dependable design, quiet operating.
● POWER SHAFT—runs on roller bearings and has an oil seal at rear of housing. Standard equipment.
● PISTON AND CONNECTING ROD—transmit force to hydraulic lift shaft.
● CONTROL VALVE—controls flow of oil into or out of ram cylinder.

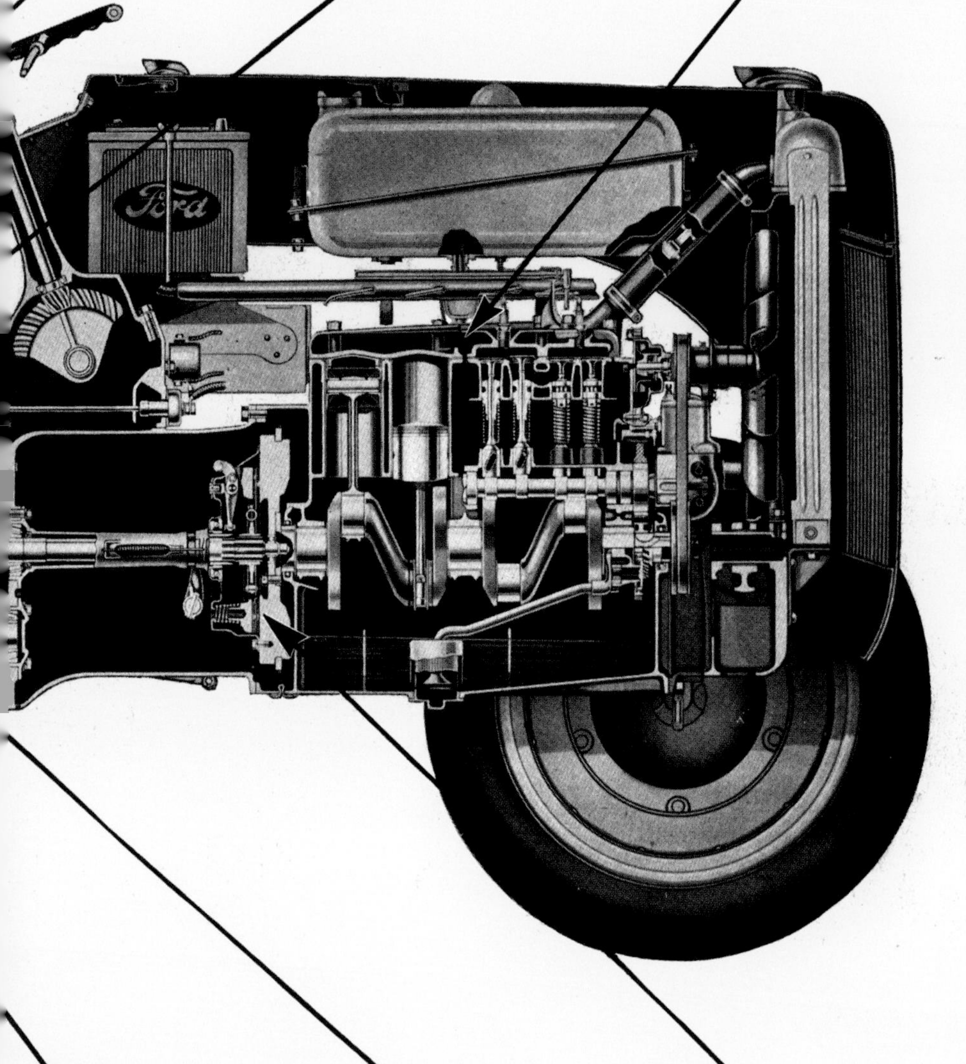

Sectioned view of the Ford 9N, from a 1945 American publication, Flexible Farming, *issued by Harry Ferguson Inc.*

by the radius rods.

Steering was by a centrally-mounted 18in (457mm) diameter steering wheel mounted at an angle of about 20 degrees from horizontal. The wheel was connected via a shaft to a bevel pinion in the steering box which engaged with twin bevel sectors on either side of it. These sectors moved drop arms mounted either side of the box, which in turn were connected to a drag link on either side of the tractor. Thus the steering spindle arms were either pushed or pulled, according to the movement of the steering wheel. The geometry of this was dependant on the adjustment of the front axle sections and radius arms, following an arc from the centreline at the front of the tractor. The fact that the axle sections were straight and not curved to a radius of that arc meant that the pin in the pivot point at the centre of the axle was made longer than if the axle sections were curved, which allowed the slight dimensional discrepancy to be taken up without further complications. This was a particularly neat and simple solution.

To align with the front wheel settings, the rear wheels were also made adjustable in 4in increments, by having offset and reversible wheel centres, rims that were similarly reversible, and fixing brackets that were offset. The range of adjustment was the same as the front wheels, 48in to 76in (1219 to 1930mm).

The final styling for the bonnet was obviously based on the then current America automotive aesthetic. The tractor was painted in Forest Grey and displayed the famous Ford blue oval logo on the nose of the bonnet, with another plate below reading "Ferguson System". By June 1939 the first production models were coming off the assembly line, priced at $585 including rubber tyres, electric starting and PTO, but no lighting system. These early examples were fitted with cast aluminium bonnets, grille and dashboard, which by their very nature were rather fragile. According to Harold Brock, this material was used as a stop-gap prior to the presses being completed to stamp out the steel version. It should be noted that both the aluminium and the early pressed steel assemblies featured almost horizontal slats to the radiator grille, like the later British-made TE20. Later steel versions had vertical slats to the grille.

The Ford 9N tractor with the Ferguson System was launched to the press on 29 June 1939. In typical well-planned Ferguson style, several tractors were made available, each fitted with a different implement from the Ferguson-Sherman range. As one would expect, Ferguson had set up his fenced-off enclosure to show off the tractor's manoeuvrability. With about 500 guests present, the star of the show must have been eight-year-old David McLaren from the local Greenfield Village School. It is stated that he was lifted on to the seat of the tractor in order to show how easy it was to operate. According to one observer, his furrows were as straight as those ploughed by Ferguson himself! These tractors sold well until production ceased in 1942, when the 9N was replaced by the very similar 2N model, which remained in production until 1947, bringing the total produced to at least 296,131, though even higher figures have been quoted of 306,221 and 306,256. Henry Ford and Harry Ferguson must have been well pleased with that handshake agreement!

To round off this chapter, the following are some of the changes that took place during the production run from 1939 to 1947. The 2N model introduced in 1942 was initially produced

The early Ferguson trailer incorporating the concept of weight transference to the rear wheels of the tractor. This type was made in America for use with the Ford Ferguson 9N.

as an austerity model, bearing in mind the materials constraints imposed by America entering the War. Early 2Ns had steel wheels and no electric starter, so had to be cranked by hand; accordingly the choke control rod was moved to the front of the tractor and ignition was by magneto. During the first year of the 2N only 16,487 were made, compared with just under 43,000 9Ns in 1941. By 1943 production was up to 21,000, and by 1944 43,000. As production rose, electric starting and rubber tyres returned, in fact rear tyre size increased to 10x28, and yet another small change was the introduction of a three-spoke steering wheel. The cooling system became pressurised, a spring-loaded cap being fitted. In 1944 the forged radius arms were changed to a pressed steel design, and sealed beam headlights were fitted. Sherman Brothers introduced a step-up auxiliary gearbox, installed internally in the bell housing between the clutch and gearbox, which increased top gear speed.

For a while, the 9N was fitted with a Holley 295 vaporiser for export to the UK market under the lease-lend scheme of World War Two. This model was designated 9NAN. Later in 1942 a more utilitarian version was shipped to the UK, again designed to run on TVO (Tractor Vaporising Oil), and this was known as the 2NAN. Ford also produced industrial and military versions of these tractors. The aircraft tug tractor BNO25 had no hydraulic system, and a single brake pedal. Yet another variant was the BNO40, which was fitted with dual rear wheels and heavy steel front and rear mudguards; these tractors had a drawbar pull of 2500lbs (1135kg) and 4000lbs (1816kg) respectively.

While Ford was producing these models at the Rouge plant, Harry Ferguson and the Sherman brothers were designing and manufacturing a wide range of implements to suit the Ford Ferguson tractor. After all it was Harry Ferguson who said, "It is the implement that sells the tractor." Most of the implements developed from 1939 to 1947 were carried over to be made by other firms, and marketed by Harry Ferguson Ltd, albeit with some modification, in the UK from 1946 onwards. These later implements are covered fully in Chapter 11, but for further reading and some excellent photographs, refer to the book *Ford Tractor Implements* by Peterson and Beemer.

The "Hydro-Fourche", made in France under licence from JCB, mounted on a 9N at a 1950 exhibition.

A later development of the same concept, again made in America, The coupling design predates the Mark I trailers made in England in the 1946-47 period.

Chapter Three

The First TE20

In 1945, Lord Perry, head of Ford in Britain, announced that the Ford-Ferguson tractor would not be built at the company's Dagenham factory. Harry Ferguson was at this time still in America, and sent his right-hand man Trevor Knox to England to search for a suitable manufacturing site for the proposed TE20 (Tractor England 20hp) to be built in large numbers. Knox established contact with Sir John Black of the Standard Motor Company in Coventry. Standard had a production facility of 1,000,000sq ft (93,000sq m) in Banner Lane, which had been built in 1938 as one of a series of "shadow factories" for armament production. It was owned by the Government and leased to the Standard Motor Company who, during the war years, produced aero engines and aircraft components for the war effort. It now lay unproductive and dormant.

As soon as it became clear to Ferguson that a suitable site had been found, he moved back to England and found himself and his family a very nice 600-acre (243 hectares) parkland estate near Stow-on-the-Wold in the heart of the Cotswolds, handy for travelling to Coventry. The house, Abbotswood, had been built around

Harry Ferguson stopping for a chat, or perhaps inspecting the state of a TE20 pulling a Mark I 3-ton trailer on the approach to the garage yard at Abbotswood in 1948.

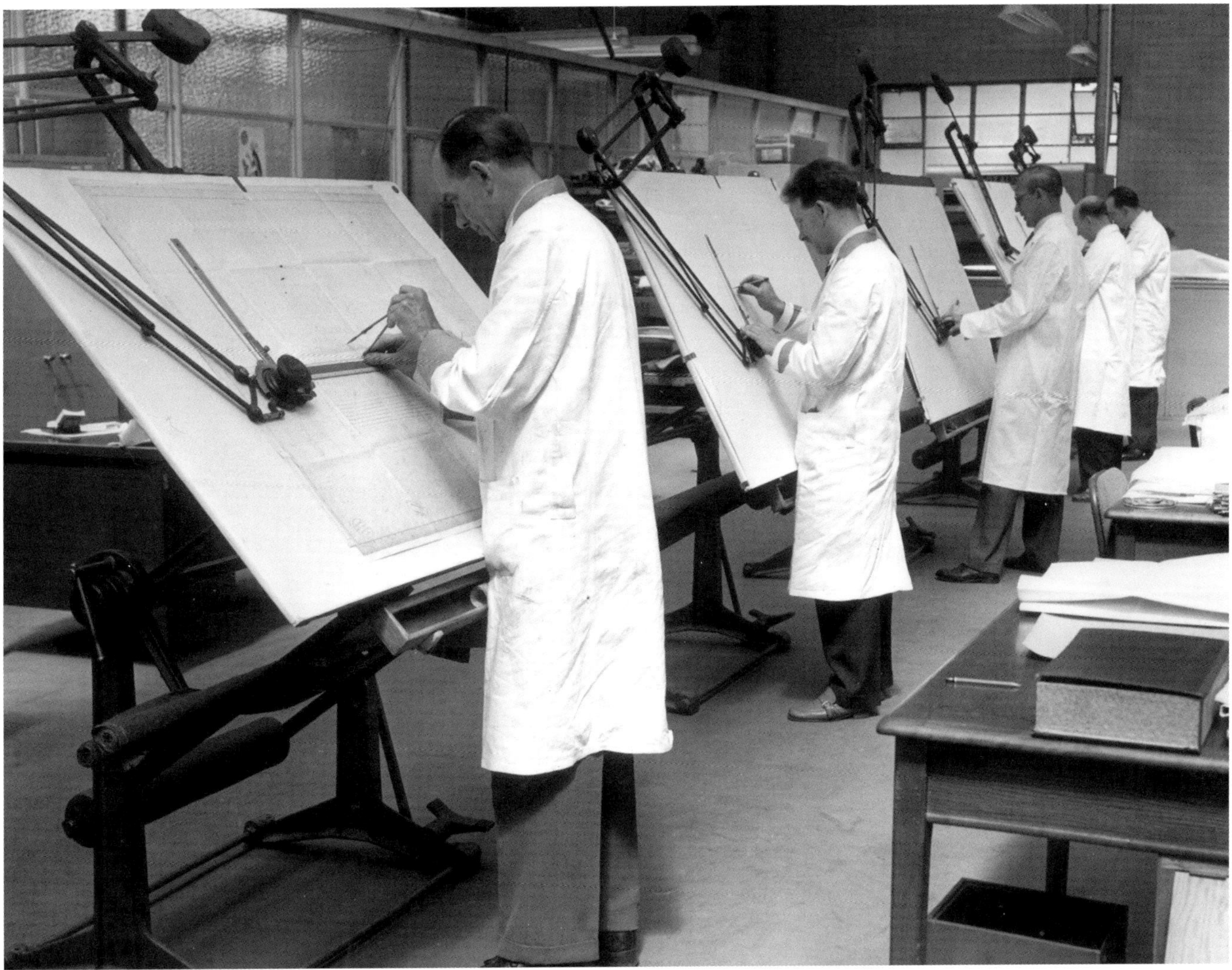

The Harry Ferguson Ltd implement design office in 1958. From left to right are Tom Wall, Steve Kenneth, Jim Campbell, Terry Grey and my friend Alan Stanley.

1870 in a typically flamboyant Victorian style. Around 1896 it was bought by Mark Fenwick, who did not find the house to his liking but was captivated by the possibilities offered by the garden and employed his friend the young Edwin Lutyens to modify the house by adding touches of the Arts and Crafts style. Mark Fenwick had come from Northumberland and was a director of the London Midland & Scottish Railway, so the house now passed from one captain of industry to another.

Work on the design and production methods for the new tractor got under way in 1945. Archie Greer, Willie Sands and Alex Patterson moved from Northern Ireland to be near Coventry, where Harry Ferguson Ltd set up its headquarters and an engineering department in a factory on Fletchampstead Highway leased from Standard. The new tractor was very much based on the Ford-Ferguson 9N, and with that experience behind them, Ferguson and his team, headed by John Chambers, had a real opportunity to refine the design of their beloved tractor system. At the time the Standard Motor Company was working on the design for a new car, to be launched in 1948 as the Standard Vanguard. It featured the American styling that was fashionable at the time, independent front suspension, hydraulic brakes and a four-cylinder overhead-valve engine, originally intended to be of 1850cc, although all production Vanguards had a 2088cc version. Later this engine would be used in the TE20, in its original 1850cc form, but before it became available from the Standard factory at Canley, the Ferguson design engineers had to import an engine made by Continental Motors of Muskegon in Michigan, USA.

The Continental unit was a four-cylinder

A 1947 petrol model, no. TE20 5148, fitted with the American-made Continental engine type Z120. These engines had a capacity of 120cu in (1966cc) and a compression ratio of 6:1. The trailer is the Ferguson 3-ton tipping model type F-JE-40, generally known as the Mark I. A non-tipping model was also made available.

One of the most striking characteristics of the Continental engine installation was the set in the downswept exhaust pipe. Also shown are the Marvel-Schebler carburetter and the early type oil bath air cleaner.

The carburettor, fitted to the combined induction and exhaust manifold.

overhead-valve petrol engine of 120cu in (1966cc) designated Z-120 and fitted with a Marvel-Schebler carburettor. The engine had wet liners of 3.1875in (80.96mm) bore and 3.75in (95.25mm) stroke, compression ratio was 6:1, and it developed a maximum of 23.9bhp at 2000rpm. This was an automotive-type engine but was fitted with a centrifugal governor with a speed range of 400-2000 rpm. Like all Ferguson's designs from the Black Tractor onwards, the TE20 was built on the unit principle, with the engine, gearbox, and rear axle forming one load bearing unit, and had no conventional frame. As the Continental engine was designed for automotive application, the Ferguson engineers had to overcome the inherent weakness of its pressed steel sump. This is often done by replacing it with one of cast steel or aluminium, which has much better load-bearing qualities. However, for speed and cheapness they chose the expedient of using a pair of 0.75in (19mm) diameter steel tension tie bars, fixed on either side of the sump and anchored at the rear to steel plates bolted to the bell housing; at the front they were secured to the front axle support bracket. This was a short-term fix to get tractor production under way until the Standard engine became available for tractor installation, with a sump in high-quality cast aluminium. One drawback to the American-made engine was that the camshaft journals ran directly in the block, without bearing shells. Hence, as they wore, the engine became quite rattly.

The upgrading of the basic Ford-Ferguson design into a new tractor was a painstaking job. The perfectionist Harry Ferguson insisted that "Beauty in engineering is that which performs perfectly the function for which it was designed, and has no superfluous parts." Progress was slow but meticulous. Ferguson insisted on high-quality materials, which at the time were scarce, so this must have slowed progress.

One of his prime considerations was reducing, where possible, the weight of the tractor. When he and his team were contemplating designs for the Ferguson Type A, he had wanted to keep the weight of that tractor approximately to that of a pair of horses. It weighed in at 16.5cwt or 1848lbs (839kg). The early TE20 weighed 2500lbs (1135kg), but was a larger and more powerful tractor. The weight was kept within bounds by the use of high-grade aluminium alloys, Elektron metal for the clutch and gearbox housing and the steering box. Ferguson was very conscious that every unnecessary pound of material not only added extra cost but also cost the farmer more fuel.

The oil filter was of replaceable type, located in the sump on the Z-120 engine. The six-volt starter and dynamo were supplied by Lucas of Birmingham, and Exide or Lucas supplied the thirteen-plate 75Ah battery. The operation of the starter switch was controlled by the gearlever, so there was no possibility of the starter being engaged with a gear selected - a nice safety feature and the logical development of the system employed on the Ford-Ferguson, which

The oil bath type air cleaner; later models had the air intake ducted from the dashboard.

The oil pressure gauge was the only instrument fitted to the petrol models. A blanking plate on the other side of the dash covered a a hole later filled with a temperature gauge on TVO and lamp oil models.

As these Continental engines had a pressed steel sump it was necessary for rigidity to reinforce the connection between the front axle and the bell housing. This was achieved by placing a steel bar either side of the sump. Later Standard engines had a cast aluminium sump, so this arrangement was deleted.

had a mechanical interlock between gearlever and hand-operated switch, patented by Ford.

On the early petrol TE20s, the only instrument fitted was an oil pressure gauge made by Smiths. Interestingly, a second 2in (51mm) diameter hole was provided on the dashboard, but fitted with a metal blanking plate: was this in readiness for the fitment of the water temper-

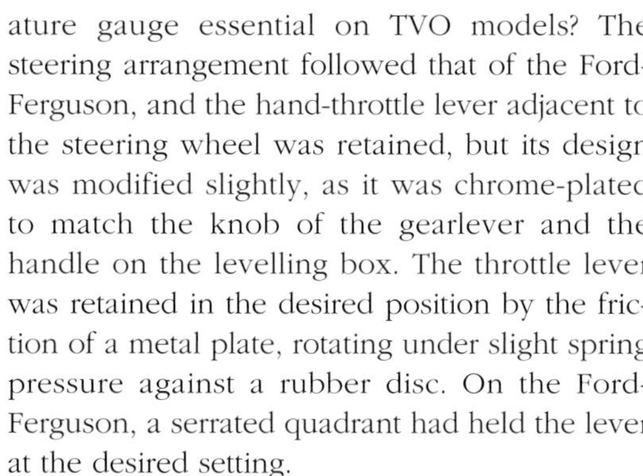

ature gauge essential on TVO models? The steering arrangement followed that of the Ford-Ferguson, and the hand-throttle lever adjacent to the steering wheel was retained, but its design was modified slightly, as it was chrome-plated to match the knob of the gearlever and the handle on the levelling box. The throttle lever was retained in the desired position by the friction of a metal plate, rotating under slight spring pressure against a rubber disc. On the Ford-Ferguson, a serrated quadrant had held the lever at the desired setting.

A 9in (229mm) Borg and Beck clutch was fitted, the same dimension as on the 9N. Ferguson insisted that the operator should not have to exert more than 35lbs (16kg) of foot pressure to release the clutch. The gearbox was completely redesigned, with four forward speeds and one reverse; the extra forward gear improved the tractor's operating efficiency greatly. The main changes to the gearbox design were that the gears were of helical-cut profile and were in constant mesh, with gear selection by sliding internal toothed couplings. All the bearings in the gearbox were of taper roller design, except for the reverse gear idler, which was phosphor bronze, as were the selector

forks. This represented a strong refinement of the straight-cut gears and sliding mesh selection used in the 9N. The final drive used was virtually the same as on the 9N, with same basic layout and the same ratio of 6.66:1. Likewise the brakes were of the same dimensions, 14in by 2in (356mm by 51mm), of internal-expanding fully energised design. The PTO gearing ratio was 2.75:1, so at an engine speed of 1500rpm the PTO speed was 545rpm which met the SAE standard of the time. The hydraulic system and draft control were again very similar.

No doubt the features of the 9N that were already proven were considered right for the next generation, and as time was of the essence during the development programme, there was no reason to modify the designs for the sake of it. The similarity between the 9N and the TE20 can be judged from the table opposite.

	9N/2N	TE20
Type of engine	Ford sidevalve	Continental overhead-valve
Compression ratio	6:1	6:1
Displacement	119.7cu.in (1962cc)	120 cu.in (1966cc)
Bhp	17.5	23.9
Clutch	9in (229mm)	9in (229mm)
Gears	Three and reverse	Four and reverse
Tyres, front	400x19	400x19
Tyres, rear	1000x28	1000x28
Brakes	14in by 2in (356 by 51mm)	14in by 2in (356 by 51mm)
Wheelbase	70in (1778mm)	70in (1778mm)
Track, front (normal)	48in (1219mm)	48in (1219mm)
Track, rear (normal)	48in (1219mm)	52in (1321mm)
Turning circle, using brakes	16ft (4.9m)	16ft (4.9m)
Overall width	64in (1626mm)	64in (1626mm)
Overall height	52in (1321mm)	52in (1321mm)
Overall length	115in (2921mm)	115in (2921mm)
Ground clearance under centre	13in (330mm)	13in (330mm)
Ground clearance under axle	21in (533mm)	21in (533mm)

Once the TE20 was in production, the basic design was changed very little over the years from 1946 to 1956 and a production run of 517,651 tractors, but there were naturally modifications. The Standard engine with cast aluminium sump was gradually phased in during 1947-48 from tractor number 8710 onwards, and the model designation was changed to TE.A20. The Standard engine, like the Continental unit, had wet liners, and an 80mm bore was used on petrol engines up to tractor number 172598 in 1950. After that point the bore was enlarged to 85mm, while the stroke remained the same at 92mm, increasing capacity from 1850cc to 2088cc. This brought the tractor engine into line with the Vanguard car unit, and the bigger bore had actually been introduced a year earlier on the TVO version (see Chapter 4). The early Standard petrol engines had a compression ratio of 5.77:1, later increased to 6:1, and their power outputs were 23.9bhp and 28.2bhp respectively.

Scalloped rear wheel centres were introduced to simplify changing track settings, while the introduction of 12-volt electrics coincided with the launch of the TE.F20 Diesel model in March 1951. Other minor modifications concerned the steel used for the exhaust valves, and the fitting of larger foot pads to the two independent rear brake pedals. Another minor change related to the Tecalemit external oil filter with replaceable felt cartridge and combined pressure relief and safety valve, which enabled oil to continue circulating should the filter become completely blocked due to neglected maintenance schedules. The earlier TE.A20 tractors up to number 56339 had the filter mounted vertically, whereas tractors from number 56340 onwards had the filter mounted at an inclined angle. Slight modifications were made to the valves. The later engines standardised the Zenith carburettor type 24T-2 with fully variable main jet. At tractor number 134001 an oscillating control valve was introduced to the hydraulic pump to minimise the possibility of it sticking, a simple refinement thought up by Alex Patterson.

At tractor number 200001, two additional

Nearside of the Continental Z120 engine showing the 6-volt Lucas starter motor, which is controlled by the gear lever.

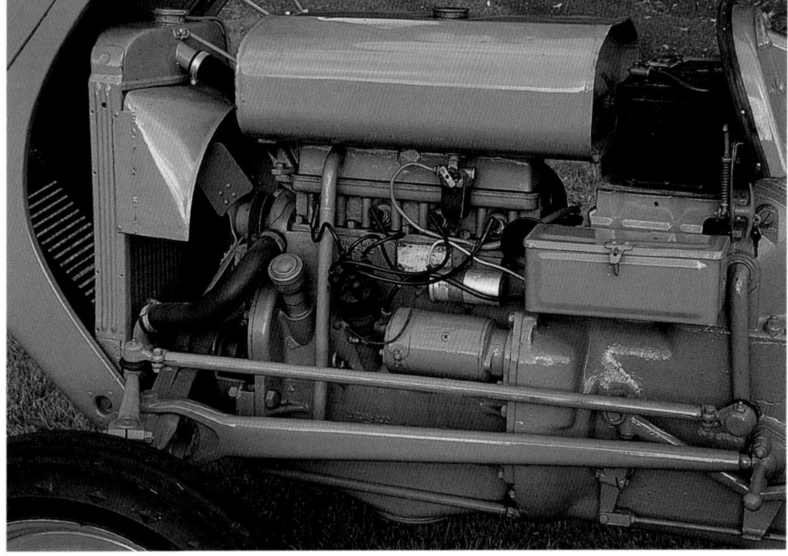

TE.A20 no. 57082 of 1948 fitted with the Handy Loader manufactured by Cameron Gardener of Reading. This was not part of the Ferguson implement range but did work very well because the weight was kept on the rear wheels and a second auxiliary contracting ram assisted the tractor's built-in hydraulic linkage to lift the fork or bucket.

tapping points were introduced for the hydraulic take-off. Also at this point, the design of the top link was changed to provide an additional range of adjustment, effected by locating the centre bolt in different pairs of holes in the two members. At tractor number 268153, the hydraulic ram cylinder was redesigned and strengthened. At tractor number 286543, the hydraulic pump inlet and transfer ports had "O" rings introduced into the joint, to improve the sealing between the pump base and the valve chambers.

At tractor number 330044, an improved safety valve was introduced. This valve was positioned in the left-hand side of the oil gallery drilling in the hydraulic lift cover, deleting the oil tapping point. A feature of the valve is that when it discharges all the working parts of the internal linkages and the valve itself are drenched in oil to eliminate possible corrosion from condensation. It is desirable for the valve to discharge at intervals. At this point the thread size on the RH take-off connection in the lift cover was changed from 0.375in (9.5mm) by 18 NPTF (National Pipe Thread Fine, an American standard) to 0.5in (12.7mm) BSP (British Standard Pipe), and the socket screw was replaced by a flanged hexagonal nut and sealing washer. The lift cover was also strengthened around the ram cylinder (again), so four longer bolts were needed.

At tractor number 374948, the longitudinal grooves in the central valve bush were re-introduced; they had been deleted at tractor number 134001. The steering wheels of earlier tractors had a dished design with three spokes of exposed steel; later steering wheels were flatter, and all the metal was heavily coated with a plastic material. At number 424591 (Diesel) and 427233 (spark ignition engines), a modification was introduced to the front axle pivot pin in order to reduce wear on this, and to provide a more positive method of fixing, together with other detail changes in this area. While on the front axle, it should be mentioned that at tractor number 459956 grease lubrication of the front hubs was introduced, as opposed to the oil previously used. The Girling brakes used on early tractors were of kidney cam type up to tractor number 200001, when the floating cam type became the standard fitment.

Very early TE20 tractors had a push-and-turn filler cap to the petrol tank, but early on in production this was changed to the brass threaded type with a cork sealing washer. The cap had a short length of chain attached to it, terminating at the other end in a sprung wire fork that entered the tank filler, thus preventing loss of the cap – a nice bit of attention to detail. There may well be other modifications that have slipped through the net, so beware when buying or using secondhand parts, as they might not always fit and function as expected.

An important factor behind the success of the TE20 was the amazing machinery and production facility the Standard Motor Company had installed at their 1,000,000sq ft (93,000sq m) factory at Banner Lane by November 1947, just two and a half years after the end of the War. This factory employed about 3500 people. It comprised three main buildings each 706ft (215m) long and 250ft (76m) wide. They housed two machine shops and one assembly shop. Other buildings housed the experimental shop, design and research departments, the laboratory, carpenter's and millwright's shops, the machine tool repair department, boiler house, offices and canteens. 1600 machine tools were needed to gain full production. By November 1947, 1200 were in place. Extensive use was made of conveyors, which were supplied by Knight of Hitchin, Hertfordshire; their total length amounted to between 7 and 8 miles (around 12km)!

The first machine shop was concerned largely with the production of gears and shafts, whereas the second was divided into two parts, one part dealing with the machining of castings, and the other with the production of small parts on lathes. Each machine shop had its own materials store and heat treatment and plating facilities. In the materials store provision was made for five continuous annealing furnaces used to heat-treat stampings, the whole heating, soaking and cooling process taking ten hours. Eight Kason-type cyanide furnaces were installed in No. 1 shop for heat-treating and could deal with about 2 tons of material per hour. In the materials stores of No. 2 shop, larger castings were shot-blasted to remove scale prior to dip painting and baking at 350°F

One of the testing booths, with a load of 600lbs being lifted. In five minutes the load must not fall by more than one inch.

Engine mounting section at the Banner Lane factory.

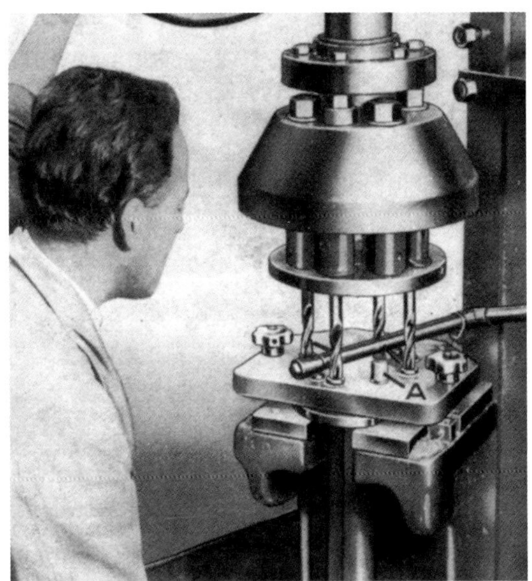

Drilling the bolt holes four at a time in the flange of the rear axle shaft.

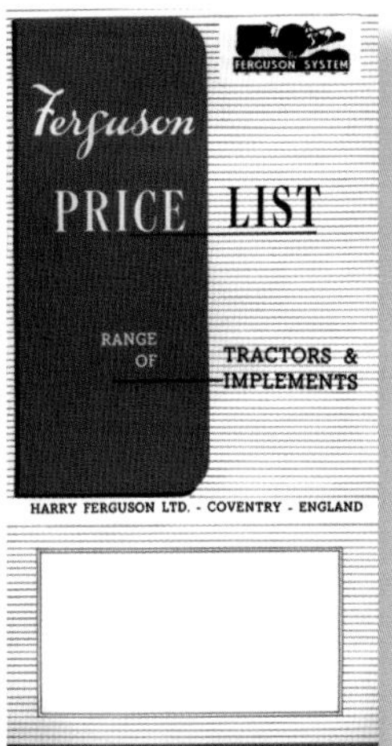

Part of the 1949 Ferguson price list.

Ferguson

TE-A-20 TRACTOR

(PETROL ENGINE)

£325 EX-WORKS

4 Cylinder Petrol engine, wet sleeve, variable speed governor.

Fuel tank capacity, 8 gallons with 1 gallon reserve.

TE-D-20 TRACTOR

(VAPORISING OIL TRACTOR)

£335 EX-WORKS

4 Cylinder special overhead valve type vaporising oil engine developing maximum engine torque between 1,000 and 1,500 r.p.m. Manifold enclosed by easily detachable shield. Thermostat setting for optimum cooling water temperature. Dashboard type thermometer with a coloured dial.

Two compartment tank holding 7 gallons vaporising oil of 50 octane and 1 gallon petrol.

THE FOLLOWING FEATURES ARE INCORPORATED IN BOTH TRACTORS

Constant mesh gear-box giving four forward speeds and reverse.

Speeds	Ratio	Speed at 1,500 rpm m.p.h	Speed at 2,000 rpm m.p.h.
First ...	78.5 to 1	2½	3⅜
Second (ploughing) ...	57 to 1	3½	4⅝
Third ...	41.3 to 1	4¾	6⅜
Fourth ...	19.8 to 1	9¾	13¼
Reverse ...	68 to 1	3	3⅞

Battery and coil ignition. Safety starter switch operated by gear lever.

Sturdy dust-proof type carburetter.

Internal expanding 14" × 2" fully energised brakes operating together or independently.

Power take-off.

Pneumatic tyres. Front 4 × 19. Rear 10 × 28.

Hydraulic System with control of implement from the driver's seat.

Easily adjustable wheel width from 48" to 76" in 4" steps.

Adjustable type drawbar **for use with non-Ferguson implements.**

ALSO AVAILABLE SPECIAL NARROW TRACTORS FOR CULTIVATION IN VINES, HOPS, ETC.

TE-C-20 TRACTOR
(Petrol Engine)
£360 Ex-Works

TE-E-20 TRACTOR
(Vaporising Oil Tractor)
£370 Ex-Works

ASK YOU
DEMONSTRATIO

3-SECTION SPIKE TOOTH HARROW £31

WOOD SAW £26 10s.

JACK £3 15s.

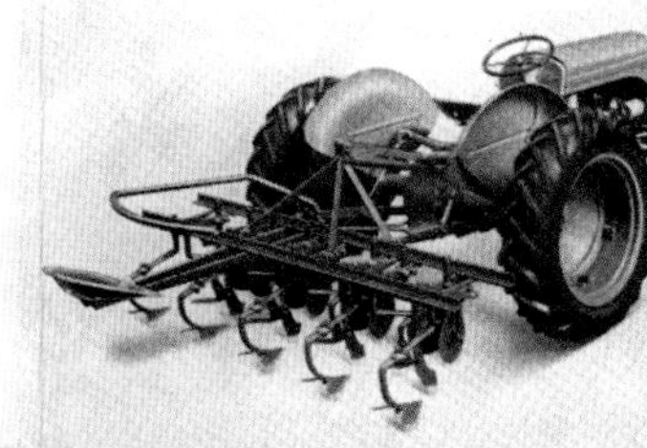

MOWER £74
Stabiliser Unit if required £2

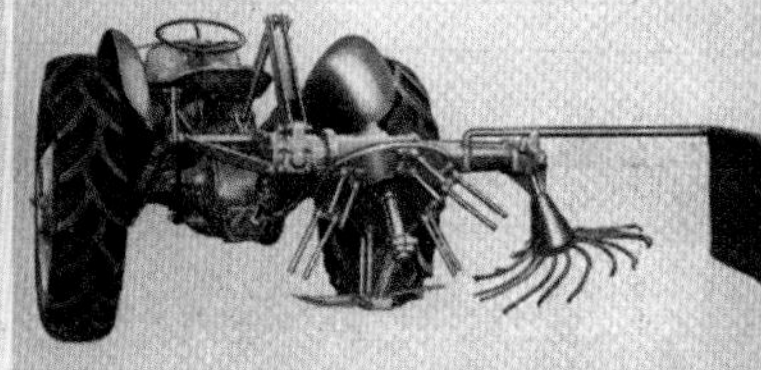

POTATO PLANTER £58 10s.
Attachment only £24 10s.

POTATO SPINNER £62
Stabiliser Unit if required £2

ALER FOR A
N *YOUR* FARM

THE FERGUSON SYSTEM OF *COMPLETE* FARM MECHANISATION

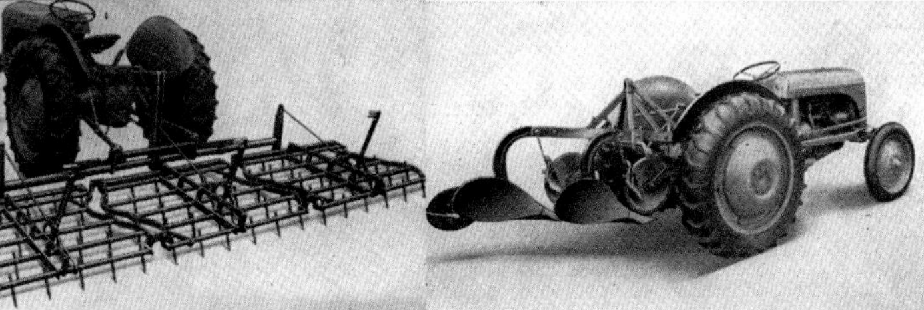

£40 10″ 2-FURROW PLOUGH
(10″ 3-FURROW Plough Conversion Set, Cast Iron share £23 10s. Fabricated steel share, £24 5s.)

3-SECTION
£28 SPRING TOOTH HARROW

12″ 2-FURROW PLOUGH £40

£33 16″ PLOUGH
(With Fabricated steel share)

£13 EARTH SCOOP

9-BE TILLER £41

£34 3-ROW RIDGER

STEERAGE HOE
£70 (with discs)
£50 (without discs)

9-NKE CULTIVATOR £41

£41 9-SKE CULTIVATOR

£23 SUB-SOILER

6ft. DISC HARROW £61
Complete with road wheels

ACCESSORIES

WHEEL GIRDLES, per pair	£19 10 0
STEEL WHEELS, FLAT 10″ TYPE, per pair	£26 0 0
STEEL WHEELS, OPEN TYPE, per pair	£24 0 0
SWINGING DRAWBAR ASSEMBLY	£6 0 0
DRAWBAR CLEVIS	£1 10 0
BELT PULLEY ATTACHMENT	£12 18 0
TRACTOR COVER	£2 10 0
TYRE PUMP	£1 5 9
STANDARD LIGHTING SET (Front lamp, rear flood-lamp, 2 side lights, brackets, rear lamp, number plate, wiring and switch.) Less fitting.	£12 0 0
SIDE LIGHTING SET (2 side lights, brackets, rear lamp, number plate, wiring and switch.) Less fitting.	£6 0 0
UNIVERSAL COUPLING	£2 2 6
TRAILER CONVERSION SET (Converting Mk. I to Mk. II. Trailer)	£7 10 0
HITCH ASSEMBLY (Used in conjunction with the Trailers and Manure Spreader)	£6 0 0
STABILISER UNIT (Used in conjunction with Mower, Manure Loader and Potato Spinner)	£2 0 0

ALL PRICES, EXCEPT WHERE MARKED EX-WORKS, INCLUDE CARRIAGE PAID TO DEALER ON MAINLAND OR F.A.S. MAINLAND PORT

FERGUSON TRACTORS ARE MANUFACTURED BY THE STANDARD MOTOR CO. LTD. FOR
Harry Ferguson, Ltd. Coventry, England

A page from a 1947 leaflet illustrating the advantages of the System.

Exclusive advantages of THE FERGUSON SYSTEM

PENETRATION WITHOUT WEIGHT

The forward motion of the tractor pulls the plough into the ground without the use of excess weight.

FINGER - TIP HYDRAULIC DEPTH CONTROL

The working depth of the plough is set from the driver's seat by finger-tip control lever.

FRONT END KEPT DOWN

Even when ploughing up-hill the front end of the tractor is kept down.

TRACTION WITHOUT BUILT-IN WEIGHT

The weight of the implement, plus the weight of the soil on it, plus the suck of the implement —automatically provides the traction required for the job.

AUTOMATIC PROTECTION OF TRACTOR AND IMPLEMENTS AGAINST HIDDEN OBSTRUCTIONS

Striking a hidden obstacle, the impact is carried to the automatic hydraulic control. It instantly releases the weight of the implement, decreases the traction and allows the wheels to spin.

(175°C). The bell housing and gearbox and steering box casings were made of Elektron, a high-quality cast aluminium alloy, and were treated similarly. A plating facility in No. 2 shop dealt with small parts, first in a tumbler-type shot blaster and then plating in zinc, copper or nickel.

The assembly line was completely conveyorised, and was set up to reach scheduled production of 200 tractors in an eight-hour shift. The build-up of the tractor started with the rear axle housing assemblies being mated to the main transmission housing (made of high-grade cast iron) and the insertion of the differential. The sub-assembly of the gearbox was bolted-on, and the engine was then installed. The engines were made at Standard's Canley works closer to Coventry. Following the engine fitting, the front axle, steering gear, radiator and cowling were fitted, together with the seat and its spring. Spray painting came next, in special booths, then oven drying at 210°F (100°C) for 30 minutes. Sheet metal parts already painted were added at this stage, followed by the attachment of the steering wheel. The tractor was now lowered off the conveyor on to a hydraulically-operated jacking cradle which allowed operators to fit both front and rear wheel assemblies conveniently. The cradle was then lowered, bringing the tractor on to its wheels, and it was started and driven away under its own power to the testing stations, which featured acoustic dividing panels. There the hydraulic linkage was tested by raising a 600lbs (272kg) block, concealed in a pit below the floor, in five seconds. The engine was then stopped for five minutes, during which the load must not drop more than one inch (25mm).

This 1949 publication promotes the company's hire-purchase facilities. This must have been frowned upon by lots of farmers of the day who believed that one should only buy what one could afford. Hire purchase was an American concept that took a long time to become accepted in Britain.

TE20 tractors which failed any of the final inspections and tests had their bonnets removed to identify them: a simple but effective way of ensuring that they did not inadvertently reach the dispatch bay. When faults had been rectified

Helping the Export Drive? Or off to dealers around the country? With nine bogie wagons each carrying three tractors, one wonders how long the train was.

How the Ferguson System fights hunger & poverty

The world's population is increasing faster than food production. And dear food—scarce food—is causing high living costs and world unrest. Slow, laborious farming with power animals or inefficient machinery can never solve this food problem. But a solution has been found—with the Ferguson System of *complete* farm mechanisation.

In 4 years Harry Ferguson Ltd., Coventry, have sold 150,000 tractors and the implements to work with them. These represent not merely new machinery but a new farming system. A system that is working successfully in 76 different countries.

The Ferguson System combines all the advantages of light and heavy machinery. It costs less to buy, less to run, and less to maintain. It enables old men and women, boys and girls to do a strong man's work — faster, better, more cheaply than ever before. This system has already produced up to *ten times more food* in some areas. It is helping farmers *everywhere* produce more food at less cost from every available acre.

GROW MORE FOOD — MORE CHEAPLY — WITH Ferguson

Ferguson tractors are manufactured for Harry Ferguson Ltd., Coventry, by The Standard Motor Company Ltd.

An advertisement from the 1951 Festival of Britain Handbook, highlighting Harry Ferguson's concern with the production of cheap food.

and the re-testing procedures satisfactorily completed, the bonnet would be re-fitted and the tractor pronounced ready to proceed on its way to a farm in this country or abroad. Tractors for export were at this point drained of oil, petrol and water. It is a tribute to the TE20, the assembly line technology, the engineering and not least the amount of human endeavour that went into the Banner Lane factory, that between 6 July 1946 and October 1956, 517,651 TE20s were produced and sold worldwide. Number 1 was given to Harry Ferguson and number 2 was presented to Sir John Black.

As noted in Chapter 1, Ferguson was not just concerned about tractors, for high on his agenda was his desire to help feed the starving thousands of the world and to cut food production costs globally. Likewise, sixty-odd years ago a large number of horses were still used for draught work in the UK, so he sold his tractors on the basis of the acres that would be freed up from the production of horse fodder and thus made available for the cultivation of saleable crops. Ferguson badgered people like Winston Churchill, Sir Stafford Cripps, as President of the Board of Trade, and other politicians with his World Economic Plan. His promotional material around the time of the TE20's launch and subsequently was aimed not only at the British market but also at world markets, where subsistence farming and draught animals were the norm. Ferguson was a great salesman who never missed an opportunity to promote his TE20.

On 18 September 1946 the launch took place

A nice period shot of a TE.A20 in a well-bedded stock yard Note the interesting centres on the rear wheels.

The launch of the TE20 at Coventry in 1946. Harry Ferguson in pensive mood, and John Chambers with his back to the camera.

Harry Ferguson on TE20 No. 1 with a 9-BE-20 a twin spring-loaded tiller attached.

in Coventry, on land adjoining Banner Lane. Another classic example of Harry Ferguson's salesmanship was the press conference held at Claridges Hotel in London in 1948, before an audience which included international agricultural officials. The management of the hotel was not keen on the idea of having a tractor in their venerable institution, but the persuasive Irishman leaned on their sense of patriotism: sales of his tractors would foster Britain's export drive and boost gold and dollar reserves. Eventually, the hotel management capitulated on the understanding that the TE20 and implements be brought in through a side entrance, which by the way meant partly dismantling it and then reassembling it in the ballroom, where it stood on a slightly raised platform.

Ferguson gave a long speech, pointing out all the advantages of his system and what it could do for mankind. A Russian delegate suggested that some of the claims for the manoeuvrability of the tractor were exaggerated. This was just what Ferguson was waiting for. He got on the tractor, started it up (although the engine had had to be drained of oil), drove it around the elegant ballroom, just missing getting the plough's landside caught in the brocade curtains, through a hallway and down the front steps into the street. It is clear that this had been planned and set up in advance as the staircase is well protected with dust sheets: bear in mind this was a top-class hotel where one would

Mrs Walters, a former member of the Woman's Land Army, on a TE.A20 at Banner Lane in 1948. She drove the tractor in the Coventry Victory Parade through the city.

expect to meet with royalty, heads of state and foreign dignitaries, not an eccentric Ulsterman driving a farm tractor with plough attached. This event made for big press coverage of the day. *The Guardian* pointed out in its editorial that "only presenting the thing at court could have had a greater impact." I have recently been told by Alex Patterson that two tractors were used – one in the ballroom and one out through the front door. Recent, on 10th May 2006, this stunt was re-enacted by AGCO but they had to use my narrow TE 20 because a standard model would not fit through the doorway.

Again highlighting HF's crusade for the mechanization of agriculture is this booklet, Freed from Bondage. *It describes the experiences of many farmers who have taken to the Ferguson System. It is five years since this farmer bought his first Ferguson tractor. He now has two and his farm has increased from 26 to 81 acres. He has reconstructed his house, built a new cow byre, his family has grown to seven, and he claims to earn £100 per year!*

From a slow start in 1946 - production was only 314 tractors to the end of that year - 1947 saw production of 20,580 units, so it is little wonder that Fordson salesmen began to refer to the TE20 as the "grey menace". It really had no competitors: plenty of firms did endeavour to produce small and handy tractors but as none of them had draft control of the implements they were no match for the Ferguson TE20. Some of the makers to enter the arena were Oak Tree Appliances with their Monarch tractor powered by a Ford 10hp sidevalve petrol industrial engine, BMB with their President powered by a Morris sidevalve petrol engine, Trusty with their Steed powered by an 8hp JAP engine, the Crawley 8hp Lister Diesel, and the Wingate powered by a Petter Diesel. None of these makers could capture what Ferguson had achieved with the TE20 and its draft control system and huge range of purpose-built implements, all designed with close attention to detail and made to high engineering standards. Equally obscure were the Bristol crawler tractor with Jowett's Bradford flat-twin engine, and the Kendall from Grantham, a short-lived pipedream by Denis Kendall MP, the would-be car manufacturer.

Harry Ferguson was keen that staff selling the TE20 and its implements should be thoroughly conversant with the Ferguson System – even, it may be said, indoctrinated in its merits. Likewise personnel involved in the servicing of tractors and equipment needed a clear understanding of the unique benefits of the Ferguson system. To this end, a training school was set up, in the first instance at the Packington Hall estate nearby. After a short time, however, the location was moved to Stoneleigh Abbey and the surrounding parkland, now the home of the National Agricultural Centre and of the European Operations Headquarters of AGCO, the company which now incorporates Massey-Ferguson.

All of those people who worked as instructors at Stoneleigh and virtually all who

Students, and their overalled instructor, on a factory and field course at Stoneleigh Abbey in 1956. My friend the late Erik Frederiksen is standing on the far right.

received instruction there speak highly not only of the standards of perfection achieved but also of the team spirit that was generated on the courses. These people felt privileged to be involved with products of fine engineering excellence. They also felt themselves to be pioneers with a sense of purpose, not just to make money but also to help feed the people of the world. In a typical touch, Ferguson insisted that all demonstrations of the TE20 and its equipment should be carried out with military precision, with the operators dressed in clean white overalls and the equipment presented to the assembled gathering in pristine condition.

Page 21

Each of a family of eight own a Ferguson

It is five years since Mr. David Kirk of Drumaglea, Cloughmills, bought his first tractor incorporating the Ferguson System. He now has two Ferguson's, and he himself, who does most of the work, weighs $14\frac{1}{2}$ stone, instead of being a lean 12 stone. His acreage has grown from 26 to 81, which includes another farm that he bought $3\frac{1}{2}$ miles from his first place. He has also reconstructed his house, and built a new cow byre, and his own family has grown to seven. Mr. Kirk comes from a large family, and his rapid expansion has caused five of his brothers and three husbands of his sisters also to farm the Ferguson way, for he declares that he always lost money in trying to farm with two, and sometimes three, horses. Moreover, he will tell anyone that he earns over £100 a year on contract. He will also ask "how could I profitably work a farm $3\frac{1}{2}$ miles away without a Ferguson ?"

Mr. David Kirk of Drumaglea, Cloughmills, ready for work with his Ferguson.

My friend the late Dick Dowdeswell (wearing tie) giving instruction in the tractor yard at Stoneleigh.

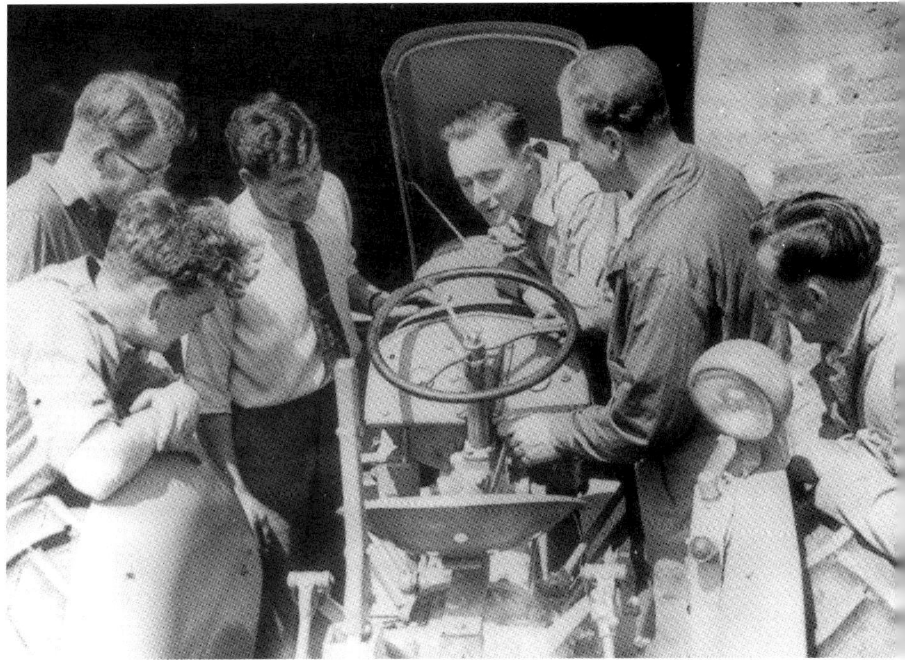

Chapter Four

The TVO TE.D20 and Lamp Oil TE.H20 Versions

By 1948, the Ferguson sales people were under pressure from customers for a version of the TE.A20 that would run on Tractor Vaporising Oil (TVO). Harry Ferguson himself did not like the idea of producing a TVO option and offered numerous reasons for not making one, such as the loss of power from a less efficient engine, and the risk of oil dilution due to operators changing over to TVO before the engine had reached its correct operating temperature. The need for more frequent oil changes to offset this risk would lead to higher operating costs, he said. Customers thought differently, and outside manufacturers of TVO conversion kits were vying with each other for this expanding business. These firms are mentioned in Chapter 12, including details of Ferguson's own comprehensive conversion kit introduced in 1950.

The modest showroom of West Regional Autos in Barnstaple, North Devon, with a smart new TE.D20 registered and ready for delivery.

So Harry Ferguson had to be cajoled into producing a TVO model rather against his wishes, bowing to customer pressure and the threatening presence of the companies who were marketing what in some cases were poorly engineered conversion kits. Undoubtedly Ferguson realised that these conversion kits might well compromise the reliability of his beloved TE20, so the engineering department were set the task of producing a well-engineered solution to allow the TE.A20 to run properly on TVO, a fuel of a lower octane rating than petrol.

The design team was headed by Alex Senkowski, and a serious effort was made to produce a satisfactory modification. The compression ratio of a spark ignition engine is related to the octane rating of the fuel used. In the late 1940s the tax-free petrol sold for commercial use was dyed red (a wartime legacy) and had an octane rating of around 72, whereas TVO had an octane rating of only 50-55. It is interesting to note that TVO typically produces 150,000 British Thermal Units (BTUs) per gallon, whereas petrol produces less at about 140,000 BTUs, but because higher compression ratios can be used with petrol,

The front cover of a simple fold-out brochure of 1949 extolling the benefits of the TE.D20 tractor.

L.E.C. CONVERSION SET

FOR THE

FERGUSON TRACTOR

The Unit fitted to Ferguson Tractor with Standard Engine
(Registered Design No. 862992)

Report from a Customer

16/11/51

I have received my Tractor from Messrs.—— on Tuesday. The state of the land does not permit much work just now, but I have made two tests of approx. I hr. each with pitchpole harrows on some old pasture. As a result, and knowing the tractor and the carburetter, I have no hesitation in saying your Vaporiser is an outstanding success. I think the pitchpoles to be a heavier load than a 2-furrow plough. The tractor pulled so well on T.V.O. that I got down once to verify that I had changed over from petrol. I have no blind spot and the jet setting is about the same as on petrol.

LATER

I have now had an opportunity to test the Vaporiser on heavy work for a period of several hours. I find it entirely satisfactory, and knowing fuel requirements for various operations per acre, I can say that the consumption of T.V.O. is little, if any, in excess of petrol.

LATER

I can now say finally that the Vaporiser is an unqualified success.

Supplied through your own Agricultural Agent, but full details from

Loddon Engineering Co., Ltd. - Loddon, Norfolk

Among outside manufactures to produce TVO conversion kits was L.E.C The kit included a slightly modified carburettor, a decompression plate, a temperature gauge, a small petrol tank and a new thermostat. Special sparking plugs were an extra on top of the £22.00 for the kit.

typically between 5:1 and 6.5:1 in engines of this period, the output is generally more or less the same in terms of brake horsepower. Tests carried out by the National Institute of Agricultural Engineering in the mid-1950s show specific fuel consumption figures in the region of 11.5 to 13.5bhp-hours per gallon at maximum output for both petrol and TVO. As an aside, Diesel engines were achieving 17bhp per hour per gallon of fuel!

These basic physical factors were taken into account by the design team. The first change to be made to the engine was to increase the bore size from 80mm to 85mm as used on the Vanguard car, a year before this happened to the petrol tractor engine (see Chapter 3). The stroke remained the same at 92mm, so the capacity went up from 1850cc to 2088cc. The compression ratio was lowered from 5.77:1 to 5.1:1 for the new TVO engine. To quote power outputs, the petrol engine with 80mm bore produced 23.9bhp, whereas the TVO version with 85mm bore produced 25.4bhp. Other modifications to the engine devised by the Fletchampstead engineering team included the fitting of hotter Champion N7 sparking plugs. The carburettor remained the same updraught Zenith 28G or 24T2, with a main jet of 105 on the TVO engine compared to the 100 jet on the

Offside of a TE.D20 engine showing the heat shield fitted to the induction and exhaust manifolds on TVO models. This expedient was thought up by Alex Senkowski and worked very well. This tractor has a four-wheel drive conversion.

Dashboard of a later TE.D20 with 12-volt electrics and the modified air intake position with adjacent temperature gauge.

petrol version. The inlet and exhaust manifold were the same, but Alex Senkowski thought up the idea of the aluminium heat shield so characteristic of the TVO and lamp oil engines. Most test drivers confirm that this expedient to retain

The two-compartment fuel tank with a pair of brass screw-on filler caps. The neat three-position fuel tap is within easy reach of the driver.

heat around the inlet manifold worked extremely well, in fact a lot better than the more traditional vaporiser system. Another change to enable the engine to reach working temperature quicker was the installation of a later-opening thermostat in the cooling system. This now started opening at 75-80 degrees C and was fully open at 95 degrees C. The thermostat on the petrol version began to open at 56-64 degrees C and was fully open at 77 degrees C.

In an attempt to mitigate the possibility of oil dilution, the number of rings fitted to each piston was increased from four (petrol) to five (TVO version). A more obvious change was the fuel tank with two compartments, and therefore the provision of two brass screw filler caps. The overall physical dimensions remained the same, with a total capacity of 8 gallons (36 litres) of fuel, being divided between 7 gallons (32 litres) of TVO and 1 gallon (4.5 litres) for starting petrol. A three-position fuel tap and sediment bowl was conveniently positioned near to the rear of the tank, within easy reach of the driver, so he could first turn on the petrol with the lever of the tap sensibly pointing to the petrol tank, start the engine and when it reached its correct operating temperature for running on TVO, simply turn the tap the other way, with the lever pointing to the main TVO tank.

The Smiths temperature gauge mounted on the dashboard was calibrated in degrees Centigrade with a brown sector up to 75 degrees, the temperature at which the driver could safely switch to TVO, whereas the remaining sector was coloured light blue. It was considered good practice to turn the fuel tap back to petrol about one minute before switching off the engine. This ensured that when the tractor was restarted the carburettor was fully charged with petrol. If it was not, the float chamber had to be drained by unscrewing a small valve in its base. The price of petrol being about four times that of TVO, the author can well remember the bailiff on the 1000-acre (405 hectares) Oxfordshire farm where he started work as a student being extremely parsimonious with the petrol issue. The risk of not having enough petrol to re-start the tractor from cold was always scary, as was the thought of a long walk back to the farmyard, coupled with the embarrassment of having to ask for extra petrol! It was in September 1949 that rebated or Red petrol for commercial use was abolished, with the result that all petrol now carried a duty of 9 old pence per gallon, or 3.75 new pence. The new TVO model was launched in May 1949 with the designation TE.D20 for the basic agricultural tractor, and was in production by July. Other versions soon followed, designated TE.E20 for the narrow model, TE.L20 for the vineyard model, and TE.R20 for the industrial model.

Introduced a year later in April 1950 was a range of tractors designed to run on lamp oil, paraffin, some times called "zero octane fuel". These were produced for export only, to countries where this low-grade fuel was the norm. As lamp oil has an even lower octane rating the TVO, the compression ratio was further lowered to 4.5:1, which reduced power to 22.9bhp. Later lamp oil engines had a water distribution tube in the head, and the water pump mounted on the cylinder head. Tractors fitted with the lamp oil engine were designated TE.H20 (normal agricultural), TE.J20 (narrow), TE.M20 (vineyard), or TE.S20 (industrial). The TE.S20 by the way is the rarest of all Ferguson variants, as only one was made!

As far as I know the lamp oil range was never sold in the UK, but the TVO type TE.D20 was by far the most favoured choice for many farmers until the advent and establishment of the Diesel version in 1951. Field test drivers claimed that the lamp oil engines would even run on Diesel fuel, but the black smoke was horrendous!

Ferguson instruction book for the lamp oil tractor TE.H20. It points out that the cooling system holds 17 pints while the petrol and TVO versions hold 15 pints. This was due to the fitment of a different type of cylinder head.

What appears to be a TE.D20 in the aftermath of the Lynton and Lymouth flood disaster of August 1951. The gentleman with a tie could be a rep from West Regional Autos, who were Ferguson dealers in Barnstaple, North Devon at the time. It is understood that the tractor was recovered and repaired!

Chapter Five

The Diesel Version TE.F20

Harry Ferguson was not a lover of the Diesel engine, as his preference was for the quieter-running petrol engine of the day. This is not surprising, as generally speaking Diesel engines of the 1940s were expensive, heavy, slow-running, noisy, and produced a fair amount of black smoke when pulling hard, which however they did very well. Their other positive attributes were intrinsic reliability, and very good fuel economy because of their high compression ratio, which gave rise to their higher thermal efficiency. Rudolf Diesel invented the four-stroke engine bearing his name and patented it on 3 December 1892; it was ready for production in 1897. Its development and use had been more or less confined to heavy marine, industrial and railway applications. For these types of usage, weight was not of prime importance. However, the German Junkers company developed a lightweight high-speed two-stroke Diesel engine for aircraft during the 1930s because of its excellent economy when running at constant speed over flights of long duration, and it was used on the early transatlantic Dornier flying boats.

Radiator grille of a 1947 TE20 fitted with a Perkins P3TA Diesel engine conversion. The Perkins badge was part of the installation kit.

In Britain, Frank Perkins was one of the first people to realise the potential of the "high-speed" Diesel engine. Prior to 1932 he had worked for Aveling-Barford, who produced Diesel engines for their road rollers among other types of municipal equipment. He saw a future for the high-speed Diesel, and with the help of Charles Chapman started out to design and produce an engine that would not only meet the needs of plant and light marine applications, but could be uprated to become a direct replacement for petrol engines installed in medium-sized lorries. In 1937 he successfully launched the famous P series of engines, with indirect swirl chamber head design. This series of engines could, with slight modification, be adapted to a wide variety of applications. He

Offside of the same tractor. The raised bonnet line was necessary because the Perkins engine was taller than the petrol engine. There is very little clearance for the driver's hands between the bonnet and the steering wheel.

even experimented with and used on his own farm a Ford-Ferguson 2N fitted with a P4 engine.

A later prototype was an early TE20 using a P3 engine. This proved to be a worthwhile conversion, and was to lead Perkins of Peterborough to produce a full conversion kit for the TE20 and the Ford-Ferguson. The bonus for users was that the Perkins engine produced 32bhp compared to the 24bhp of the Standard petrol engine. This, together with more pulling power, and more economical running on the cheaper Red Diesel which was available for agricultural use, made the conversion an attractive proposition, and many thousands were sold. Today, these conversions are easily recognised by the raised bonnet line that was necessary when the P3TA (TA for Tractor Application) engine was installed in a TE20.

When Harry Ferguson eventually conceded that it would be prudent to offer customers the benefit of Diesel power as an alternative to the petrol and TVO factory-built units, much debate took place in the engineering department of Ferguson's headquarters at Fletchamstead Highway, and it was eventually decided to ask

Nearside of the Perkins engine, showing the raised fuel tank and the three fuel filters.

A TE.F20 fitted with the Freeman-Sanders designed Standard 20C Diesel engine. It is coupled to a Ferguson reversible plough T-AE-28, and is owned by Brian Whitlock. The starter motor is on the right-hand side of the engine; on petrol and TVO models it would be fitted on the left-hand side.

The small auxiliary fuel tank is placed to the rear of the main one.

three manufacturers to produce engines of suitable size for fitting to the TE20 for field testing and evaluation. The Standard Motor Company were one of the obvious contenders for this project. They sought out the services of Arthur Freeman-Sanders who was an expert on small Diesel engine design; he lived and worked at Penzance in Cornwall. He had already developed a fairly lightweight six-cylinder indirect injection high-speed automotive Diesel engine, and had had two made. One he installed in a Studebaker Dictator which was the subject of an extensive technical write up in *The Autocar* on 28 April 1950, with a further article the following week. The other engine he installed in an Alvis TA21 saloon, which was normally powered by a 3-litre petrol engine. This vehicle was bought new from Alvis less engine, and still exists today (see David Culshaw's book *Alvis Three Litre in Detail*).

The general layout of the Freeman-Sanders six-cylinder engine is remarkably close to that of the four-cylinder unit he eventually helped to develop for Standard Motor Company for installation in the Ferguson TE20 tractor, and which was subsequently designated the Standard 20C engine. Production TE20s fitted with this engine carried the prefix F on agricultural versions and T on industrial versions, thus TE.F20, and TE.T20. The engine was also briefly offered in Standard Vanguard cars and light commercial

Nearside of the TE.F20 opposite showing the CAV injection, the two fuel filters and the engine breather.

vehicles between 1954 and 1956, and was sold for installation in London taxis.

It is worth comparing the specification of the 20C Standard engine installed in TE20 tractors with those two prototype six-cylinder engines developed by Freeman-Sanders.

	Freeman-Sanders 6 cyl.	**Standard type 20C 4 cyl.**
Bore and stroke	76.2mm x 101.6mm	80.9mm x 101.6mm
Capacity	2780cc	2089cc
Compression ratio	16:1	17:1
Power output	55bhp at 2700rpm	25bhp at 2000rpm
Weight	396 lbs (180kg)	

Dashboard of the TE.F20 showing the Ki-Gass pump and the starting instruction plate. Below that is the decompression lever, with the tractormeter adjacent to it. The large black knob on the left operates the heater plug; the small knob above is the light switch.

Nearside of the Standard 20C Diesel engine. Its installation in the TE20 added 224lbs of extra weight when compared to the petrol version.

When the Standard engine was installed in a road vehicle, the pneumatic governor allowed it to run up to 2200rpm.

On the 20C engine, various devices were fitted to aid cold starting. Indirect injection engines do not have the good cold-starting characteristics of direct injection, but on the other hand they do have more efficient combustion of fuel – or so some say! An excess fuel button was fitted to the in-line CAV fuel injection pump which overrode the governor by allowing the metering rack to extend the full length of its travel. A heater element was fitted in the inlet manifold, controlled by a substantial switch on the dashboard, and often working in conjunction with a Ki-gass pump which was also mounted on the dash. This drew fuel from a small auxiliary tank under the bonnet, and metered it into the inlet manifold, to create a hot burning vapour that aided starting.

Also fitted to the engine were two decompression levers, one at the front and one at the rear of the engine, which operated with a choice of three positions:

(1) Not operating
(2) Decompression on three cylinders
(3) Decompression on all four cylinders

On the dashboard was also fitted a brass instruction plate on "Cold Start Procedure", this

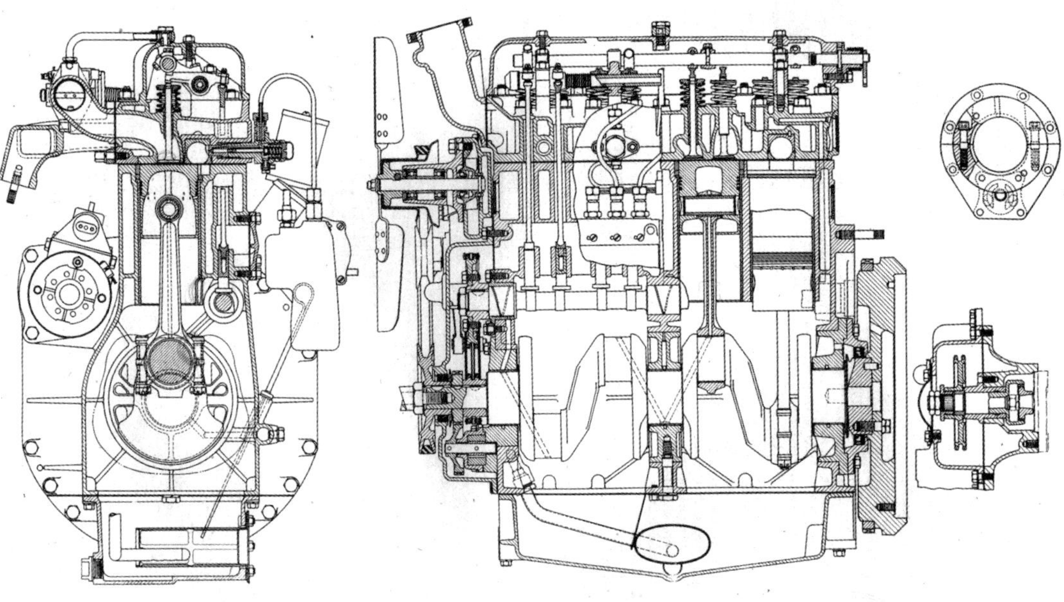

Sectional views of the 20C engine

must have been either reassuring or confusing to novice drivers. It is worth mentioning that it was possible to start this engine by hand! A certain mechanic at North Devon Autos, formerly the Ferguson dealers of Barnstaple, was known to show off his strength and mechanical prowess to his mates: having rebuilt a TE.F20 engine, he proceeded to start it by hand. Those were the days when men were men!

The Lucas starter motor M45G was of the mechanical pre-engagement type, and was controlled by movement of the gearlever into the start position. As an added safety feature, a spring-loaded mechanical button, fitted to the top right-hand side of the gearbox casing, had to be depressed by the driver's calf muscle before the gearlever could be moved into the start position. Another feature of the Diesel engine installation was the 12-volt system with two Lucas 6-volt batteries of 115Ah capacity connected in series, and mounted on brackets either side of the driver's seat. This necessitated a modification to the draft control lever, which had to be moved slightly forward, with a simple linkage to connect it to the hydraulic control shaft. This in turn gave rise to the need to modify slightly the profile of the pan seat on its off-side to give sufficient clearance. Since the 20C engine had its starter on the right-hand side, whereas on the petrol or TVO

Offside of the 20C Diesel unit.

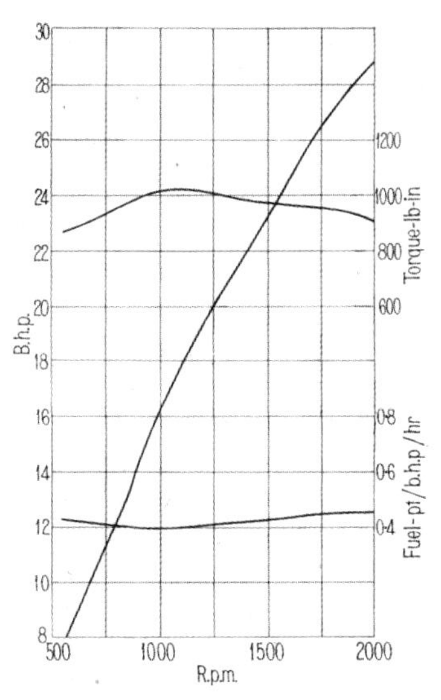

Engine performance curves.

The 20C engine with head removed to show the air cells in the side of the block, intended to give more efficient combustion - a halfway house between power units with direct injection and those with swivel chamber designs.

The three-cylinder Perkins P3TA Diesel engine.

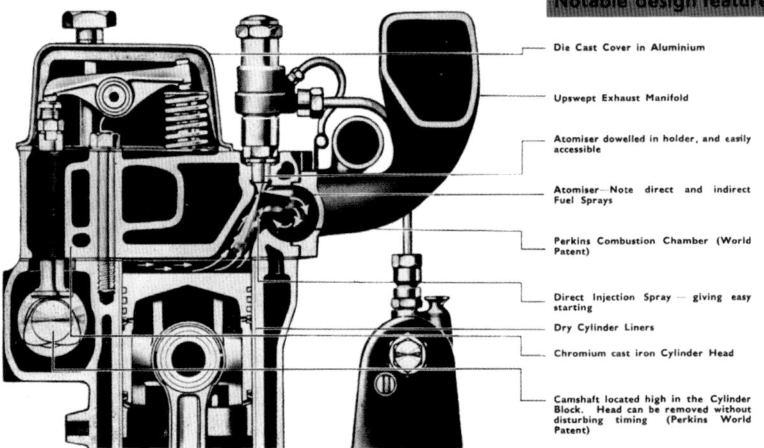

The patented Perkins combustion chamber design. Note the twin spray from the injector into the swivel chamber and to the top of the piston.

Standard engine it was on the left of the bell housing, and the gearbox casing was different, it was not possible to fit a 20C engine retrospectively to a petrol TE20. That must have pleased Mr Frank Perkins!

The next engine to be offered for evaluation purposes came from Perkins of Peterborough, in the form of their successful three-cylinder indirect injection engine with swirl chambers, of 2360cc capacity and with a rated power output of 32bhp at 2000rpm. The engine was of course their type P3TA. Although this was a proven engine, the higher bonnet line needed to accommodate the fuel tank raised the centre of gravity of the tractor, with potentially dire results. Nigel Liney had a taste of this, when the tractor which he field-tested in 1950 for evaluation purposes turned upside-down after a high-speed manoeuvre. The only cold starting aid fitted to these engines was a heater plug in the inlet manifold, and no excess fuel device was fitted to the CAV inline injector pump.

The final offering for field testing and evaluation came from the engine manufacturer Meadows of Wolverhampton. This old-established company must have thought they had a very good chance of securing a contract with Harry Ferguson Ltd to supply Diesel engines for the TE20 production line at Banner Lane. As they did not have an in-house Diesel engine of suitable size for fitting to the tractor, they built a small batch to the required parameters, so as not to lose out on a possible contract. One of these tractors survives to this day and is part of the Coldridge Collection.

The Meadows engine type 4DC 1/35 was a four-cylinder unit with overhead valves and direct fuel injection. With bore and stroke of 80mm by 110mm, capacity was 2212cc, and while the power output was not known, it would appear to be around 35bhp. The engine with number BXA 105 was fitted to tractor number TE.D 124939 which came off the line on 22 March 1950 and was registered in Coventry under KDU 559 on 14 September 1950.

Looking at the cast-iron block, it is clear that the shape of this engine was tailored to fit the line of the front axle mounting bracket, and the rim of the clutch bell housing. The sump and oil strainer are direct from the TE.A20 petrol engine, as is the water pump. The pistons were Petter AV-series, as were the valves and springs. A direct injection system was used, with a CAV A-series pump. There was a pneumatic governor and a 6-volt starter on the left-hand side.

Nigel Liney tells how these three Diesel Fergusons, each fitted with a different make of engine, were extensively tested by the field test team including himself, Jack Bibby, Dick Dowdeswell, and Colin Stevenson. On some winter nights, the tractors were left in the open fields of Warwickshire in freezing conditions so that their cold starting characteristics could be assessed in the morning. Nigel recalls having to light a small fire under the Meadows to warm up the oil before it would start - perhaps the 6-volt electrical system was to blame! Now restored, it starts well on a 12-volt battery and its original 6-volt starter.

The net outcome of these trials and tribulations was that Harry Ferguson Ltd made what perhaps was the obvious choice, and decided on the 20C Diesel engine designed by Freeman-Sanders, which was to be manufactured by Standard at their Canley works. After all, it would have been strange for Standard to buy in engines from an outside manufacturer when they had their own available, even though it was less powerful than the Perkins engine. The production model was launched in March 1951, with tractor number 200033.

Ferguson tractors powered by Diesel engines were designated as follows: standard agricultural type TE.F20, and industrial version TE.T20. Narrow and vineyard version were never produced at Banner Lane, but only in France (see Chapter 7). It has come to light that Banner Lane did produce a total of 1996 TE20s for export to Yugoslavia fitted with the Perkins P3 engines, the first one being made on 15 November 1955, and the last on 23 March 1956. These Perkins-engined tractors were designated TE.Y20.

It is fair to say that although some users have complained of the bad starting characteristics of the 20C engine, this is usually due to excessive wear of pistons, liners and valves, or lack of service attention to the injection equipment. These tractors were deservedly popular in their time, and many thousands were sold worldwide. In 1954 a TE.F20 on 10in tyres was priced at £525 ex works, while a petrol TE.A20 on 10in tyres cost £395. Fifty-odd years later the TE.F20s are very sought-after by smallholders, hobby farmers, the horse keeping fraternity and road run enthusiasts alike.

A prototype Meadows-engined Ferguson TE.D20, no. 124639, made 22 March 1950 and first registered 14 September 1950. Note the 6-volt Lucas starter motor on the left-hand side, as on the petrol and TVO engines.

The neat installation of the Meadows engine into the TE.D20. The sump comes direct from the Standard petrol engine. The air cleaner is by Donaldson, who was the supplier of the oil bath air cleaners from the Ferguson-Brown.

On the Meadows prototype the normal Ferguson water pump was used. The battery carrier, fuel tank and oil filler were all specially made and the routing of the exhaust system is unique. Photos by courtesy of Tim Bolton.

Chapter Six

The American-built Ferguson TO20

The American company, Harry Ferguson Inc, had been in existence since the 1939 handshake agreement with Henry Ford. Ferguson was marketing the Ford 9N tractor, together with a range of matched implements. When this product range came to an end in 1947, Harry Ferguson Inc had a large and loyal following of customers, an extensive dealer network, and an efficient marketing team, but no tractors to sell. As a stop-gap arrangement, Continental-engined TE20 tractors were imported from England into the USA, until an

A TO20 with loader and manure spreader.

The Ferguson Corn Planter D-PO-A21 with fertiliser attachment, developed for the American market, shown here coupled to a TE20.

Detail of the mechanism of the same machine.

alternative manufacturer willing and able to take on making the Ferguson could be found, or, as eventually proved to be the case, the company could set up its own factory. Until then, Harry Ferguson had never shown any great interest in manufacture, and had always contracted out this

important aspect of his business.

Horace D'Angelo (Harry Ferguson's right-hand man in America) had made contact with Willys-Overland, the Jeep manufacturers, and General Motors, to ascertain if they would be interested in taking on the manufacture of the Ferguson tractor. Both firms declined. So the alternative was for Ferguson to build their own manufacturing facility. D'Angelo eventually found a 72-acre (29 hectares) site on the outskirts of Detroit which was to become known as Ferguson Park. Harry Ferguson's interest in the development was quite remarkable. He insisted that the chosen architects design the most modern of factories, to the

A preserved piece of American Ferguson service equipment.

A TO30 with subsoiler in 1953. Note how use was made of the 11-hole draw bar very similar to those made in South Africa. To the rear is fitted the pipe or cable laying attachment.

The Ferguson agricultural mower 6F-EO-20 with 6-foot cutter bar and (right) the drive mechanism for the same mower. The photographer has ensured that the name Ferguson on the pulley is correctly orientated!

highest standards of design and appointment, on a tight budget and to an incredible timescale. Both architects and contractors balked at these constraints, but Harry Ferguson stuck to his programme.

The site was purchased in January 1948. Work started in February, and the building works were completed by the end of June. The internal fitting-out took a further nine weeks, so that on 11 October 1948 Harry Ferguson was able to drive the first TO20 (TO for "Tractor Overseas") off the assembly track. This tractor was basically the same as the TE20 produced at Banner Lane in its early form, fitted with the American-made Continental Z-120 petrol engine, producing a maximum of 23.9bhp. It should be remembered that by now the British version had become the TE.A20 and was fitted

with the Standard Motor Company's own engine, which produced the same power output, but had a smaller capacity. American-built Fergusons used locally sourced componenets, so instead of Lucas electrical equipment the TO20s used Delco-Remy, likewise Borg-Warner supplied the clutch, the hydraulic pump, and the gears used in the gearbox and rear axle. Brakes were supplied by Bendix, and the air cleaners were supplied by either Vortox or Donaldsons.

In 1949, the first full year of production, 12,859 TO20s were made at this brand new, state-of-the-art facility. 1950 saw production double to 24,503. In August 1951, an improved model was launched on the American market, known as TO30. This featured a 29bhp Continental Z-129 petrol engine (of 129 cu in or 2114cc), and was fitted with modified tinwork. The rear axle was strengthened to take account of the increase in engine power. By 1952, Massey-Harris and Ferguson had reached a draft agreement for Massey-Harris to build a combine harvester for the Ferguson. Harry Ferguson himself was meanwhile undertaking his own development work on combines at the Fletchampstead headquarters in Coventry.

With a downturn in profits which eventually became a loss in 1953, Harry Ferguson held a meeting with James Duncan of Massey-Harris, ostensibly to discuss the combine project, but in reality to offer the Massey-Harris organization the chance to purchase his American factory. Concurrently Ferguson was producing tractors in France (see Chapter 7), where the small Massey-Harris Pony tractor was very popular, and it had become known to Massey-Harris that Ferguson had developed a higher horsepower tractor that was almost ready to go into production, the LTX or TE60 (see Chapter 13). This would certainly have challenged their model 744. Apparently James Duncan went with two of his senior people to tour the factory at Ferguson Park, and they were most impressed by the quality of production they saw. As a result of this inspection, Massey-Harris offered to merge the whole of the Ferguson organisation worldwide with their own. The final outcome of this is dealt with in Chapter 1.

The Ferguson side-mounted pickup baler B-EX-A20, fitted up to a TO20 in August 1951.

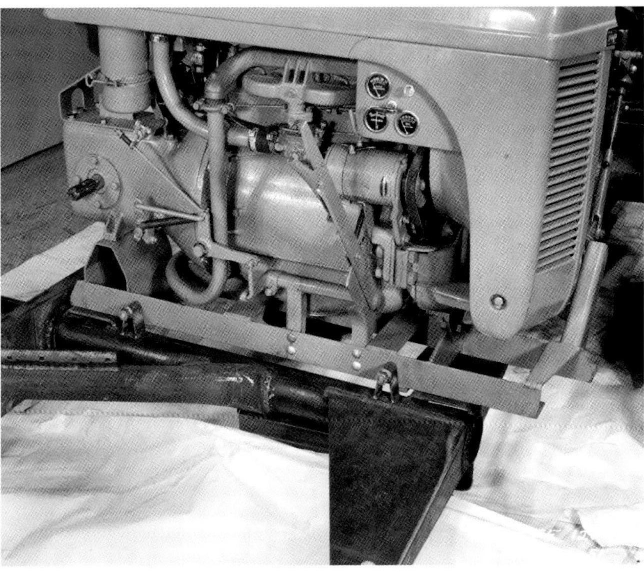

The Ferguson forager F-HX-A20. Note the auxiliary drive engine mounted at the rear of the machine. The auxiliary engine was used to drive the forager, the combine and some balers. The linkage to the clutch control lever incorporates a facility to slow down engine speed when the clutch is disengaged.

Chapter Seven

Ferguson in France

It is unclear whether Ferguson ever marketed the Ferguson-Brown Type A in France as he did in the Scandinavian countries, but there are certainly a few examples there today. According to the writers Jean Cherouvier and Jean Noulin in their joint book *Tracteurs Ferguson* (1999), the Ford-Ferguson 2N was imported from 1945 under the Marshall Plan, but was fitted with rubber tyres as found on the 9N.

At the Paris Fair in September 1946, the Ford-Ferguson 2N cost 16,000ff, including a two-furrow mounted plough and an eleven-tine cultivator, but because of inflation, by July 1947 the price of the tractor alone had increased to 23,000ff. These Ford-Fergusons imported into France just after the end of the War were supplied by Harry Ferguson Inc of Detroit, and Ferguson took it upon himself to ensure that each tractor was supplied not only with a maintenance handbook, as one would expect, but also with a leaflet titled *To Win the Battle of Food Production*. Strangely this was produced with an American-English text, but was apparently so well laid out that the French user could grasp the basic ideas dealt with.

A Ferguson side-delivery rake made by Matrot of Poissy, France.

The imported Ford-Ferguson 2N series were equipped with Marvel-Schebler variable-needle type carburettors, but were considered by their French users to have excessive petrol consumption, as at times this reached 7.5 litres (1.65 gallons) per hour. This was not a problem in the American home market at the time, but in a fuel-deprived France recovering from the ravages of war it was not acceptable. To get around this problem, French farmers found that by fitting their native Solex carburettor, fuel consumption could be dramatically reduced, albeit at the cost of a slight reduction in power output. It is understood that approximately 5000 2Ns were imported into France between 1945 and 1947, with a final one in early 1948.

Only a few of the 2Ns were fitted with lighting systems at the factory, and these had headlamps of the American sealed-beam type. The majority remained without lights, but French-made lights such as Marchal were fitted retrospectively, no doubt with yellow bulbs as was required by French law at the time.

It is fair to say that the Ford-Ferguson endeared itself to French farmers, no doubt

A Ferguson TE.F20 attends an address by the Reverend Father Dom Felicien Jacques at the abbey at Rémy, Rochefort, in 1951. The sharp-eyed will notice the outsize starting handle on the transmission casing. Perhaps this allowed two men to attempt to turn the engine.

A Ferguson vineyard plough, with fore-and-aft, width and depth adjustment of the shares available.

because it was a very light tractor, very capable with its purpose-designed implements, and providing high reliability and good performance overall. So it is no surprise that, when production of the 2N ceased in 1947, Banner Lane received an order from France for 5000 TE20s. At the time, the French arable acreage was about three times that of England, and this, together with the state of the country following the German occupation, created a huge demand for tractors, especially ones that were light and fuel-efficient. A company called Compagnie Génerale du Machinisme Agricole – COGEMA for short – was appointed by Harry Ferguson Ltd as French distributor in 1947.

At around this time, the French government had devalued the Franc and placed severe restrictions on imports, with the result that the quantity of 5000 tractors ordered by COGEMA in February 1947 was cut by the government, which licensed the importation of only 1000. The following year saw the restrictions relaxed to some extent, with the licensing of 6465 imports from Banner Lane. Upon the introduc-

Nearside of a recently imported FF-30DV French-made diesel vineyard model. Note the rather crude extension to the rear of the bonnet and the side-mounted battery.

On the offside there is provision for a second battery. Note the rather contorted shape of the drag link on this narrow-track model compared with the standard tractor.

tion in 1948 of the narrow petrol version TE.C20, later followed by the narrow TVO model TE.E20 and the lamp oil version TE.J20, these immediately proved popular with French farmers, especially those with orchards and vineyards to cultivate. Later in 1952, Harry Ferguson Ltd started to build the special vineyard models at Banner Lane, designated TE.K20 (petrol), TE.L 20 (TVO) and TE.M20 (lamp oil), and these too proved popular in France, although total production of the vineyard models only reached 1350 units.

To overcome the French government's restrictive measures, negotiations took place between the government, Harry Ferguson and the Standard Motor Company, with the result that a production facility was set up at St Denis

The French-made two-furrow reversible plough FF76 and FF77. Turnover was achieved by hydraulic ram and rack.

near Paris. As part of these negotiations, the Standard Motor Company set up a subsidiary company, Societé Standard-Hotchkiss, in affiliation with the established (but ailing) French car manufacturer. They were to be the manufacturers of the French Ferguson tractors. At more or less the same time, Harry Ferguson Ltd took over the distributors COGEMA, which became Harry Ferguson de France SA, under the direction of Jacques Boilliont-Linet, with François Kauffman as the senior executive.

In his book *Harry Ferguson and I*, Michael Winter recounts how in the spring of 1948 he collected for Ferguson a brand-new Bentley with the registration number JLX 73 from Jack Barclay, the Bentley dealer in London. This coincided with Harry Ferguson, his wife Maureen and daughter Betty travelling by train to Paris, where they stayed in the Hotel Ritz on the Place Vendôme, for a meeting with the directors of Harry Ferguson de France, as well as meeting with Paul Hoffman who was the

Marshall Aid administrator. After the Paris meetings, the Ferguson family would go on to Aix-en-Provence for a short holiday. Their journey was by the *Golden Arrow* out of Victoria Station in London to Paris. Michael Winter travelled by train from the Cotswolds to London to collect the Bentley, and then drove on to Dover to catch the cross-channel ferry to Boulogne. He was met there by François Kauffman, and they proceeded towards Paris, "stopping en route for a most enjoyable lunch which included a fair measure of vintage wine." On the outskirts of Paris in the rush hour, Michael pranged the new Bentley, as he said "in an embrace with a French lamp post." He arrived at the Ritz where the Ferguson family was staying, and then had the unenviable task of telling Ferguson what had happened to the new car. Michael Winter recounts that the conversation went something like this:

Ferguson: "Hello Michael, have you got the car?"
Winter: "Yes Mr Ferguson, but it is not quite the same car as the one I collected from Jack Barclay yesterday."

He was later told that his position in the company had been seriously jeopardised, and that the question of his future employment would be given serious thought! That evening Michael Winter spent a most enjoyable time at the Folies Bergère and Maxim's with the top crew of Harry Ferguson de France SA. He thought he was on his way out of Harry Ferguson Ltd, and no doubt had a ball at the company's expense.

The next two days were spent acting as Ferguson's interpreter at board and technical meetings, where the main topic was how to modify the TE20, together with its implements, to make it more suitable for the French agricultural market, and particularly the narrow-tracked versions for vineyards. Another meeting took place between Harry Ferguson and the American Paul Hoffman, the administrator of the Marshall Plan, and Michael Winter recounts that Harry Ferguson was a fantastic salesman and negotiator, with more than his fair share of Irish blarney. He progressively convinced Hoffman that Marshall Aid funds should be used to buy Ferguson tractors, and thereby achieved his objective. All the while, Michael Winter listened with ever-increasing amazement to their dialogue. This experience caused him to coin the phrase, "one can slide much further on flannel than on gravel!"

Winter eventually set off on his lonely return to England, expecting to be fired when Ferguson and family returned from Aix-en-Provence. He treated himself to the best suite on the *Golden Arrow* for the trip, at the expense of Harry Ferguson de France SA! Two days later, back at Abbotswood, he received a phone call from daughter Betty to say that she too had pranged the new Bentley on the way to Aix-en-Provence, that as far as Daddy was concerned all was forgiven, and that Michael's future with the company was secure.

A French Ferguson poster of the Massey-Harris-Ferguson era.

A French-made Diesel FF30 Ferguson owned by Colin Guard, of Devon. This colour scheme is unique to the French-built models.

The following New Year's Eve, Winter and his wife Pam spent a wonderful time in Paris, with François Kauffman and his vibrant wife. Starting out at 6pm in François's old Citroën, they stopped off at six or seven parties, and ended up dancing and drinking until 5am at the home of the Michelin family, who were the tyre suppliers to Harry Ferguson de France. On the way back to their hotel, the radiator of the Citroën boiled over and desperately needed liquid refreshment. This was provided by the remains of a bottle of champagne and some other liquid, the French name of which Winter could not remember.

Back to French tractor production. September 1956 saw the launch of a new range from the St Denis factory, the FF30, which was available in petrol and Diesel variants, both rated at 29bhp. This improvement in power output was achieved by subtle tuning of the engine and using the maximum governor setting. A colour scheme of red and grey was used to set the FF30 apart from previous models, and possibly to indicate the Massey-Harris connection. Harry Ferguson had taken a wise decision to have a 1/16th scale model of the FF30 produced by Erica Toys, complete with plough. It was an opportunity to attract the interest of the younger generation in the new tractor family. Although the French-made tractors were very similar to their Coventry-built counterparts, all the proprietary components were of French manufacture, including Diesel fuel injection equipment by Lavalette or alternatively, on petrol and TVO models, Solex carburettors, electrical equipment by Duçellier or Paris-Rhône, but an SEV distributor, Fulmen batteries, and headlamps by Marchal or Clinterache, while tyres came from Michelin.

Other details unique to the French range were the fitting of a suspension for the driver's seat made by Houdaille, while some examples had a crude passenger seat on the left-hand rear mudguard, as was common practice in European countries at that time. Harry Ferguson

The compactness of the original design is evident in this side view.

The headlamps, with yellow bulbs, are fitted directly to the bonnet side panels.

The ammeter, temperature gauge and oil pressure gauge are on the left of the dash.
The black knob operates the heater plug in the induction manifold.

The cold starting pump, starting instructions plate and lighting switch are on the right.

The commission plate is in the centre of the dash.

The injectors and injector pump, made by Lavalette.

The front mounting for the driver's seat.

de France SA did produce a narrow *(Etroit)* model and a vineyard *(Vigneron)* model, in both petrol and Diesel versions, as well as the standard agricultural model. The designations of the various models were as follows: FF30 for Ferguson France 30bhp, followed by a suffix G for petrol or D for Diesel, followed by S for standard, E for narrow and V for vineyard. On either side of the bonnet there was a chromed metal badge with a red background, reading Ferguson 30, very similar to the badges later used on the Coventry-produced FE35 tractors. Another improvement incorporated in this new model was larger tyres, 11x28 at the rear and 6.00x16 at the front.

By 1957, production was running at just under 20,000 tractors per year, of totally French manufacture. Although the St Denis plant had been expanded, by 1957 it was at bursting point, so a new production facility was planned on a 45-acre (18 hectares) site at Beauvais, 40 miles (64km) from St Denis. By 1958 this plant was fully operational, and the St Denis plant was closed. Production of the FF30 tractor ceased in June 1958, to make way for the introduction and production of the Massey-Ferguson 835. On this model, the prefix 8 related to French production, and the 835 was the French version of the Coventry-built FE35.

Judging by the seat spring, French users demanded more comfort than their opposite numbers in Britain!

Gear positions are cast into the top cover of the gearbox. Note the brass push-in button that had to be depressed prior to moving the gear lever to the start position.

Chapter Eight

The Ferguson TE20 Overseas

It is not surprising that once the Banner Lane production facility was well established, with output at times exceeding 300 tractors per day, the marketing department would begin to look for export markets to expand their sales. The British government of the day was keen to encourage manufacturing firms to export a high percentage of their production, and every help was given to those firms to foster the "Export Drive". Allocations of materials were granted more readily to firms with strong export trading. The Export Drive was necessary to help offset the huge deficit Britain had incurred as a result of the War.

For these circumstances the TE20 was an ideal product; a lightweight tractor whose production would not unnecessarily waste or consume precious raw materials, and which offered an efficient design for applying power to land cultivation, especially when it was coupled to one of a wide range of purpose-designed implements, mostly made of quality alloy steels which ensured weight was kept to a minimum and thus matched the tractor's performance. The Ferguson TE20 and its implements made up a unique system. Farmers and users liked the tractors as they were nice to drive, handled well, and were economical on fuel. It was also possible to attach a huge range of implements, designed to do almost any job on any farm anywhere in the world. So from every possible angle, the Ferguson was a natural export product, suited to the needs of many countries recovering from the devastating human and economic losses of the War, as well as countries like India, struggling to build an agricultural system to support a fast-growing population, and then still a part of the British Empire.

I shall concentrate here on the countries which either imported tractors directly from England or were supplied with tractors in CKD (Completely Knocked Down) form for local assembly. Around 1952, Paul Spencer was Export Sales Manager for Harry Ferguson Ltd, and his prime role was to promote the export drive for the company.

Since America had its own Ferguson factory producing its own line of TO20s and related implements (see Chapter 6), that facility met the needs of the countries within the Americas. France was close to England, and had a huge agricultural and vineyard economy that needed rebuilding following the War, so it was natural for French farmers to look favourably on the early TE20s which arrived in their country. They fitted in well with the small-scale family farms found in France in the 1940s and 1950s, but it was not all plain sailing for Ferguson, as there were plenty of locally-produced tractors vying for sales, especially Massey-Harris with their Pony model. Another factor which had a restricting effect on Ferguson sales was the French government's reluctance to grant import licenses for all types of machinery. Eventually Ferguson by-passed this constraint by arranging

The Swedish Ferguson club has over 5000 members. "Gralle" is the nickname of the little grey tractor.

for TE20s to be assembled in France and later to be manufactured under license by the French car company Hotchkiss, in co-operation with the Standard Motor Company, as discussed in Chapter 7.

Moving further away from Britain, another part of Europe which bought Ferguson tractors and implements in large numbers was Scandinavia, including Sweden, Norway, Denmark and Finland. For the story of Ferguson's success in Sweden I suggest buying a copy of *Ferguson i Sverige 1947-1957* by Sture Tufvesson, which has 300 pages of photos and dense information, although being able to read Swedish will be a great help! My friend Hans Göran Persson tells me that over 40,000 Fergusons were sold in Sweden between 1947 and the end of production in October 1956, when the FE35 was launched in the showroom at Fletchamstead Highway.

He also tells the story of how TE20 number 2 came to Sweden. This tractor stood at the Banner Lane works alongside number 1 from 1946 until 1956. Harry Ferguson's wife Maureen and their daughter Betty kept both tractors clean and tidy. In 1956, Lennart Cassler, the manager of the Swedish Ferguson agency, celebrated his fiftieth birthday, and Harry Ferguson decided to give him TE20 number 2 as a special birthday present, to be used on his hobby farm. While number 2 had originally been given to Sir John Black, he had by now been ousted from the Standard company! This historic TE20 was duly shipped to Sweden, with a consignment of new Fergusons.

In Norway, little information is to hand. My Norwegian friend, the late Erik Fredriksen, who had graduated in agricultural engineering, made his way to Britain and found employment at first with Midlands Industries Ltd, which made loaders suitable for the TE20 and in fact manufactured several other implements for Harry

A cutaway transmission used by Nordisk Diesel in Denmark for training purposes.

Rear view of the cutaway transmission model. The very substantial crownwheel is visible in the differential casing.

A dockside scene from Denmark, with a Ferguson on road-sweeping duty.

Preparations for a Danish Christmas: logs for the fire and a tree to decorate.

Ferguson Ltd. He soon moved to Harry Ferguson Ltd, and completed the rest of his working life with Massey-Ferguson on product design. I can remember him telling me that somewhere in the region of 23,000 TE20s were sold in his home country and about 12,500 in Finland. Again it was the TE20's efficiency that had an immediate appeal to small farmers and industrial users in the cold and beautiful country of Norway.

My Danish friend Merethe Hansen, herself a Ferguson enthusiast and the driver of a council-owned MF20, the industrial version of the MF135, tells how these small, handy and efficient tractors soon endeared themselves to the Danish farming community. The Danes generally like good design as do most Scandinavian people; in the late 1950s the effects of their house design and architectural achievements spread to England. But they liked our grey

A Danish photograph showing how the rear-wheel girdles are positioned before attachment.

Recording the arrival of Denmark's 15,000th Ferguson.

Ferguson TE20s! Merethe recalls that there were about 40,000 new TE20s imported to Denmark, and about 30,000 second-hand ones, starting in 1947. The agent was Nordisk Diesel, which also imported cars, including Standards. The Fergusons were mostly petrol-engined in the early years, when petrol for agricultural use was duty free in Denmark. Later, when petrol became subject to duty, the TE.F20 Diesel obviously became the more popular choice. The famous Danish toy manufacturer Lego made first wood and later plastic models of the TE20, and the Tekno toy car maker brought out a die-cast Ferguson model, complete with a range of implements.

Moving to Holland, the Ferguson collector and enthusiast Piet Mooij recalls that, as in France, the first Ferguson tractors came to Holland under the Marshall Plan aid scheme after the War. They were very well received by the farmers and growers of Holland for exactly the same reasons that farmers in England were attracted to them, and that included the wide range of implements that were available for them.

Norman Tietz from Germany reports that the first TE20 tractors were imported into Germany in 1947 or 1948 by individuals buying from dealers in England. In 1948, LMV GmbH (Landwirtschaftliche Maschinen Vertriebsgesellschaft mbH) became the general importer for Western Germany. This is related by Erich Lutz, who became a Ferguson salesman in 1950. Some months earlier, the Ferguson System had been demonstrated at the university where Erich was studying process engineering. By the early 1960s, he worked in the product development department at the German Massey-Ferguson headquarters at Kassel, before becoming responsible for the company's forestry programme.

This resourceful Danish owner has rigged up an innovative child seat.

An exhibit from Denmark's Ferguson Museum gets an outing - a fascinating device.

LMV had their first Ferguson display at the DLG Show (today known as Agritechnica) in Hanover in early 1949, and this was considered to be excellent. At around the same time, demonstrations were held throughout West Germany, but in his report, G H Thomas, the managing director of Massey-Harris UK, considered this to be a strange effort, in view of the fact that at the time it was impossible to import tractors into Germany. Thomas was advised by Ferguson's representatives that although imports of tractors were forbidden, the Ferguson company felt it desirable to show the German people the most modern developments in tractors (see E P Newfeld, *A Global Corporation*).

LMV was owned by Josef Deppert, and had their offices at Hannover Landstrasse 223 in Frankfurt-am-Main. They moved to a new building in Friesstrasse some time later. Erich Lutz worked with Josef's brother Willi, who became the Ferguson main dealer for the area south of Frankfurt, and also had a dealership for Henschel lorries. Other well-known dealers were Max Walk in Munich and Willi Lehmann in Hamburg.

After Ferguson's merger with Massey-Harris in August 1953 the distribution rights were transferred to the new Massey-Harris-Ferguson GmbH based at the Massey-Harris plant at Westhoven near Cologne. E P Newfeld mentioned in his book *A Global Corporation* that LMV had been a distributor of "indifferent quality". However, it has to be said that it was very difficult to sell British tractors in Germany so soon after the War. Apart from that, German farmers were aware of the advantages of the Ferguson System, since many of them knew the Ford-Ferguson 9N and 2NAN tractors from their time as prisoners of war working on British farms. But there were many prejudices against this new concept: it had not been made in Germany, no metric bolts were used, and what would happen if spare parts were needed? This was an important question in the days before the overnight express service. However, importation got easier, and LMV managed to sell many hundreds of Ferguson tractors. Against all the difficulties, Ferguson became the first foreign manufacturer to enter the top twenty in the German tractor registration statistics in 1953. In 1955, 1123 Ferguson tractors were sold, which was a 1.1 per cent market share. In total, several thousand are thought to have been sold in Germany.

According to Erich Lutz, only a few TE.A20s were sold in the first few months, because LMV then opted for the TE.D, which had cheaper running costs, as pointed out by Hermann

Kreim. His father, Georg Kreim, from Büttelborn near Frankfurt, became the first Ferguson dealer in Germany in 1948, and Hermann Kreim states that his father sold the very first tractor that was imported by LMV. The TE.D was sold together with the narrow TE.E, and the lamp oil TE.H is also mentioned in some German sales literature, but it is not certain if any were actually sold. The TE.F became the most successful TE-series tractor. From 1952, the TE.L vineyard model was also offered. There is no information that any industrial versions were sold in Germany. The tractors were fitted with German lighting equipment made by Bosch or Hella, and with a German-style towing hitch for two-axle trailers, made by Martens & Co KG, the Ferguson main dealer for the South Hannover and Brunswick areas, if the new owner did not want, or was not able to use the Ferguson trailer.

Ferguson tractors were imported into Switzerland from 1946 onwards, by the Service Company Ltd in Zürich. The first tractor sold in Switzerland was a TE20 with Continental engine, tractor number 267. This was also the first TE20 tractor to be exported anywhere, according to Hans Klaesi, the former managing director of the Service Company. The boss of the Service Company, Dr Amsturz, was a good friend of Sir John Black, chairman of Standard, and Amsturz already imported Standard and Triumph cars under the umbrella of the Neue Amag company. Due to that relationship, he also became the importer of Ferguson tractors in Switzerland. Tractor imports were restricted to protect the Swiss tractor industry. Annual quotas were approximately 150 units, and it is thought that in total 800-900 Ferguson TE tractors were sold. The Ferguson TE20 with Continental engine, and later the TE.A, TE.D and TE.F, with their respective narrow and vineyard versions, were offered. In 1954, 95 tractors were sold, including 33 TE.A, 30 TE.D and 32 TE.F models. The Service Company remained the importer for Switzerland for nearly sixty years until 2003.

Norman Tietz has provided information on Ferguson in Austria. J Athardjieff, a businessman born in Rumania, founded a company called Agrartraktor Vertriebsgesellschaft in Vienna, and imported the first Ferguson in 1953, but his company went into liquidation in late 1954. In the spring of 1955, Gebrüder Schöller, also of Vienna, took over the distribution rights, but only imported the Diesel TE.F 20 model. To protect the local tractor manufacturers such as Steyr, tractor imports to Austria were strictly limited to approximately twelve tractors per month in the sub-40bhp class, which was far below the demand, and it is thought that in total

Four Sigmund pumps powered by Standard 20C Diesel engines on irrigation duties in Rangoon, Burma.

A Ferguson of India trailer being painted at the Balmer Lawrie factory in Calcutta.

only 800-900 Ferguson TE20s were sold. This figure was remembered by Dr Othmar Grössl, the sales and later managing director of Gebrüder Scholler, who worked for the company from 1955 to 1991.

Turkey was a good customer for Ferguson TE20s for two basic reasons. Firstly the tractor's size, economy and versatility were well suited to the requirements of small Turkish farmers, and secondly the Turkish Agricultural Bank positively encouraged farmers to invest in tractors and equipment by making very attractive loan packages available.

A B ("Sandy") von Behr remembers that the sub-continent of India proved to be a very successful market for the TE20, especially in the northern grain and arable areas. The market for the TE20 in India was opened up by chance in 1949 when Mrs Vijayalakshmi Pandit, (Pandit Nehru's sister) who was the Indian High Commissioner in London, happened to attend a Ferguson demonstration somewhere in England. The story goes that she immediately ordered twenty TE20s with implements to be shipped to the Ministry of Agriculture in Delhi. Before the arrival of the first eight tractors, Harry Ferguson Ltd had set up an office for Harry Ferguson of India Ltd in Bangalore, the centre of the southern plantation area, under the directorship of Roland C ("Roly") Heath, aided by his charming Polish wife Ella, and the able Scot John Armstrong, who recalled that this was the only part of India where the climate was suitable for Europeans.

On the arrival of the first consignment of eight TE20s, an impressive gathering had been arranged by the Ministry of Agriculture in Delhi to launch the tractors to the Indian public. Included in the gathering was of course Nehru himself, and as Roly Heath was a man of great charm and wit, he persuaded the Pandit to pose for the photographers while ploughing. From that small beginning, the TE20 spread over most of India during the period from 1950 to 1956, and it is claimed it had 85 per cent of the tractor market, with 10,000 TE20s sold. It was Peter Boyd-Brent who developed the paddy disc harrow, which worked well where underlying soil could support the weight of the tractor. Here is his account of his time with Harry Ferguson Ltd in India.

"In 1950 I was working for Harry Ferguson Ltd. of Coventry when I was seconded to their subsidiary company in Bangalore, Southern India. My job was to arrange local sub-contracting of certain basic farm implements which could be used to fit Ferguson tractors imported into India. At that time, the Standard Motor Company assembled these tractors at their plant in Madras. The first of the implements to be produced in India were Ferguson trailers made by Messrs Balmer Lawrie, a manufacturer in Calcutta well equipped to carry out the work. These trailers were followed by earth scoops, transport boxes, portable irrigation pumps, and tractor jacks made locally.

"In keeping with Harry Ferguson's ideal of 'feeding the world', the concept of mechanised rice cultivation was mooted, and soon prototype paddy wheels (to cultivate rice fields prior to

The finished trailer has steel side boards.

planting) were produced. These wheels, not unlike 'water wheels' in form, were fitted to the tractor's driven wheel hubs, and extended by about 3ft (0.9m) on each side. We also fitted a 'levelling board' to the tractor's three-point linkage, behind its wheels, and this copied the Indian method of levelling the wet and churned-up ground after cultivation.

"My business journeys took me as far north as Assam and Delhi and, on one occasion, accompanied by Dick Chambers who was the manager of Ferguson's farming school in the UK at the time, we caught the night-train from Bombay to Gwalior, with the object of carrying out rice cultivation trials in the differing conditions there. Unfortunately we did not bargain for the food offered on the train, and made the mistake of choosing roast beef etc., instead of the more freshly-cooked 'Curry of the day'! The result was three days in bed for both of us when we arrived in Gwalior! This delayed the start of our trials a bit, but our hosts, a kindly Dutch couple, soon had us on our feet again.

"On another occasion, I travelled as far south as Cape Comarin, the southernmost tip of India – on the very edge of the world – with its golden sunrise and Biblical fishing boats. On these travels by road, our staple diet was eggs, baked beans and soda water – easy to prepare, but not inspiring for the stomach! My journeys were mostly by Air-India Dakota 'planes and, where possible, by Standard Vanguard company cars.

"On the west coast, near Cochin and Alleppey where the landscape is mostly water and shallow lakes extending for miles and used extensively for rice growing, we sank and lost a tractor in the nearly liquid sub-soil. There were sluice gates to control water levels, and the local people would fish for food using large seine nets. Up the east coast, towards Madras, the land is less waterlogged and therefore easier for the tractor. Generally the roads consisted of single tracks with rough edges for passing vehicles, and embankments in places to prevent wash-aways.

"Sacred cows abounded, and a drama occurred to us when a young bullock bounded across the road and hit the front of our car, smashing the radiator. The bullock escaped unhurt, but our Hindu driver's face turned a pale shade of grey, with shock and religious fear! The car was badly wounded, and we had a stop-start journey to the nearest town, constantly having to refill the leaking radiator from the supply of bottled drinking water we kept in the car.

Peter Boyd-Brent in a rice paddy field in Gwalior, India, demonstrating the Ferguson flotation drums fitted inside the tapered paddy wheels. Peter's comment on the back on the back of the photograph reads "excellent idea - but it did not work."

"Subsequent visits to Ceylon and Malaya were made to study local methods of rice cultivation, and in Malaya we came up against the insurrection problems that were then hitting the country, and this meant that many of our local Ferguson dealer personnel had to carry guns in self-defence.

"We experimented with our paddy wheels at length, and came to the conclusion that the level and condition of the sub-soil in the paddy field was all important. When land has been puddled-up for generations past, the sub-soil becomes unsupportive to the weight of a tractor, and simply sucks it in – resulting in a very wet

The opening of Harry Ferguson of India Ltd's new offices at Cunningham Road, Bangalore, in 1953. The staff are flanked by a pair of Standard Vanguards, with their drivers.

driver! Land at higher altitudes was easier to work with the tractor and, by the end of 1953, when I left India, a small number of paddy wheels had been produced and used. However the tractor and paddy-wheel combination does not seem, today, to have replaced the bullock – and the old traditional methods of rice cultivation still largely prevail.

"Working in the Bangalore office in the early 1950s was an enthusiastic group of Brits – the 'Ferguson Boys', who were mostly wartime ex-servicemen – they were Roland Heath the managing director, John Armstrong, Charles Calder, Tony Cox, David Perrot, the writer and John Roberts who was based in Delhi as our Northern India representative. All these people had been fully trained in the Ferguson System in the UK. There was also an equally keen and able Indian staff working on administration, and the all-important dealer liaison. We all belonged to the "B.U.S. Club" (British United Services), and this was a haven of relaxation after our frequent tours in hot and dusty conditions 'up-country'.

"The partition of India took place in 1947, and in 1953 there had been little change at the Club. Antlers and guns still adorned the walls, together with faded photos of past British military dignitaries. The badminton court still functioned for the benefit of Indian ladies in their colourful saris, and there was a fine outdoor swimming pool, where we frolicked after the many parties and dances.

The original office of the company was at 10 Palace Road, Bangalore, and it was housed in a colonial-type bungalow, where Winston Churchill had been billeted when visiting India around 1896-97. I like to think that his pioneering spirit lived on in the enthusiastic attempts of the Ferguson Boys to 'feed the world'."

Soon after the successful introduction of the TE20 to India, it became clear that the tractors should be exported in CKD (completely knocked down) form, with tyres being sourced locally from Goodyear India. These kits were assembled at the Standard Motor Products (India) Ltd plant in Madras. As the export of tractors was expanded, service training schools were set up in Bombay, Delhi and Bangalore, under the control of Harry Ferguson of India Ltd headed by Roland Heath. By the time the production of the TE20s came to an end in 1956, almost 10,000 units had been sold. Peter Boyd-Brent indicated to me that some lamp oil versions were exported to Ceylon - presumably TVO was not available there - and over 2000 tractors were supplied to the island.

Sandy von Behr recalls how he was seconded by Paul Spencer, Ferguson's export sales manager, to go out to Japan at the beginning of 1954 to open up the market for Ferguson products in that country. As an agricultural graduate with four years in Africa behind him, Sandy was well equipped for this new role. Having joined Ferguson about nine months earlier, he spent that time undergoing intensive tuition at the Ferguson training school at Stoneleigh Abbey.

His route to Japan took him through Rangoon, where he met up with those involved in marketing Fergusons in Burma and looking at the possibility of serious exports to China. Eventually this objective was achieved direct by Paul Spencer in Coventry, who through skilful negotiation and diplomacy was able to conclude a deal with the Chinese government to the value of £1.5 million for several thousand tractors with implements. From Rangoon, Sandy went on to the Philippines for a week, meeting the Massey-Harris sales people. Finally he arrived in Japan to meet up with the directors of Tokyo Motors, the distributors for Japan and Okinawa. Sandy and the Tokyo Motors directors decided that an extensive series of field demonstrations would be required to persuade the omnipotent agricultural co-operatives and the Japanese Ministry of Agriculture that the little grey Fergusons would suit the farming fraternity of Japan.

Sandy and his demonstration team travelled the length and breadth of the country. They had at their disposal two TE20s and 26 implements. It is difficult to imagine that in those days Japan had virtually no motor industry. Much training and fine tuning of drivers and machines was achieved in three weeks from the end of January 1954, prior to the first demonstration to Japanese Ministry of Agriculture representatives, held at Zama near Tokyo in February. This demonstration proved to be effective, and the team was given an order for a few tractors and implements, to be shared around various government agricultural establishments. This was at least a foot in the door, but while sales eventually reached reasonable numbers, they were never at the hoped-for level. Most sales came later in the Massey-Ferguson era. It is interesting that the paddy disc harrows designed for the Indian market by Peter Boyd-Brent were marketed successfully in Japan.

Angus MacLeod-Henderson from South Africa told me that the TE20 was first introduced to this market in 1948, and by 1956 over 20,000 tractors had been imported. At first, South African farmers thought they were toys, but as demonstrations got under way the farmers soon realized the unique capabilities of the Ferguson System, and eventually huge numbers were sold. One unconventional use of the TE20s, related by Angus when he visited the Coldridge Collection in 2004, was to use one of the tractor's rear wheels with the tyre removed as a winch drum, the wire hawser being anchored to the rim. With the tractor mounted on a suitable frame, the tyre-less rim was free to rotate, first or second gear was selected, the clutch engaged, and the wire rope wound in, pulling its load, usually bundles of sugar cane. The load could be held by depressing the clutch and brake pedals together, and could be paid out using gravity or reverse gear.

Another country to import Fergusons in sizeable numbers was Australia, and over 51,000 were sold in the period from 1949 to 1956. These tractors were shipped out from Banner Lane in a part-knocked down condition.

Squadron Leader Keith Base had left the RAF as a wartime Spitfire pilot; at one point he was shot down over the Sussex coast. He went on to train at the Harper Adams College of Agriculture in Shropshire, and on completing his studies took a teaching appointment with Harry Ferguson Ltd at their training school at Stoneleigh. Having gained a wide range of experience there, he was asked if he would go to New Zealand to help set up a training school alongside the New Zealand dealership, C B Norwood of Palmerston North. It must be remembered that in the 1940s and 1950s quite a few British ex-servicemen were emigrating to New Zealand to start farming careers, with British Government support.

Again it was the innovative concept of the Ferguson System and its efficient operation that appealed to the farmers of New Zealand, whether they were dairy, arable, or vegetable producers, and sales to New Zealand reached 17,190 tractors. It was Keith Base and his team, based for this purpose on the South Island, who helped to develop and prepare Ferguson tractors for the Antarctic Expedition to the South Pole (see Chapter 14).

Obviously many other countries imported TE20s, where their small size and efficiency fitted in well with the local needs. Local agricultural engineers and blacksmiths were quick to make up special implements where the need arose. All in all, this demonstrates how a British invention fostered food production throughout the world. Harry Ferguson's dream became a reality.

Chapter Nine

Industrial Fergusons

As TE20 tractor production got into its stride, with output in the peak year of 1951 reaching approximately 1500 per week, Ferguson and his sales team looked for other avenues to extend their sales. Not that the agricultural marketplace had reached saturation point, far from it, but with a successful assembly operation it would only be natural to keep the pressure on production, personnel, and sales directors to capitalise on the full output potential of the Banner Lane factory. However, the actual number of the industrial models made was relatively modest, only 992 industrial Fergusons of all types being made until 1956. These included the TE.P20 (Standard petrol engine), TE.R20 (TVO), TE.S20 (lamp oil, but only one made), and TE.T20 (Diesel engine).

A very busy montage of transport, construction and industrial subjects illustrates the front cover of this brochure.

The municipal, construction and industrial sectors were the obvious areas to target and, to a lesser extent, the military, whose Fergusons were designated "tractor, 4x2, Ferguson". As in agriculture, wages were beginning to rise in the industrial and construction fields, so there was pressure to cut down on labour costs, and to mechanise. Ferguson tractors were no new phenomenon in industry. Harry Ferguson was quick to recognise this back in the late 1930s when the Ferguson-Brown Type A was launched. By looking at the illustrated price list of 1938, it can be confirmed that an industrial model was offered. This was listed with 9x24 tyres and without hydraulics at £244, whilst the agricultural version, with hydraulics and slightly smaller 9x22 rear tyres, was priced at £270. Likewise, when the Ford-Ferguson was in production at Dearborn during the war years, several thousand of the tractors produced were turned out to meet industrial and military requirements.

The compact dimensions and good power-to-weight ratio of the Ferguson, together with its built-in hydraulic system and good turning circle, lent themselves readily to industrial applications. As the basic agricultural tractors were

TE.T20 no 350692, 1953, a Diesel industrial model fitted with the basic lighting kit and coupled to a 3-ton industrial tipping trailer of the Massey-Harris-Ferguson era. The trailer is fitted with overrun brakes, a sprung axle and small mudguards to the rear of the wheels. A special latching device operated by a chain reached from the driver's seat prevented the brakes coming on when reversing.

being produced in large volumes, unit cost was at an economic level, despite the high standard of engineering. By March 1951, with the introduction of the Standard 20C indirect injection Diesel engine, the sales team could offer industrial and municipal users the choice of three fuel options, petrol, TVO and Diesel. However, although the TE20 range was an attractive vehicle for highway use, certain modifications had to be made to meet the legal requirements of the Road Traffic Act of 1947. Highway tractors like other road vehicles had to comply with the legal obligation to have two independent braking systems, wheel fenders or mudguards, a horn, and a rear view mirror.

To meet these requirements, the braking system required a complete re-design, while the other areas mentioned were relatively straightforward. Eventually the engineering department at Fletchampstead Highway came up with a neat solution for a dual braking system. The standard diameter of 14in (356mm) for the brake drums was retained, but by re-designing the backplates and increasing the drum width, they came up with the simple expedient of mounting two sets of shoes side by side. The outer set of shoes were of 2in (51mm) width and were operated hydraulically by Girling brake cylinders connected to a master cylinder bolted to the left-hand side of the transmission casing, just above the footboard level. This was controlled by the normal footbrake pedal on the right-hand side. The inner sets of shoes were slightly reduced in width to 1.5in (38mm) and were operated mechanically, either together by the handbrake lever mounted on the top of the gearbox cover, or independently by the steering brake pedals mounted either side of the rear axle housing. This gave the best of both worlds: good forward and reverse braking hydraulically operated for road work, and a positive mechanical system for parking and manoeuvring in tight spaces, while meeting the requirements of the law. A Lucas HF XYZ high-frequency horn and a Weathershields rear view mirror were fitted. The protection of the wheels by mudguards came in several variations. The industrial kit A-TE-120 had extended rear mudguards, and front wings

The tractor was once used by Surrey County Council.

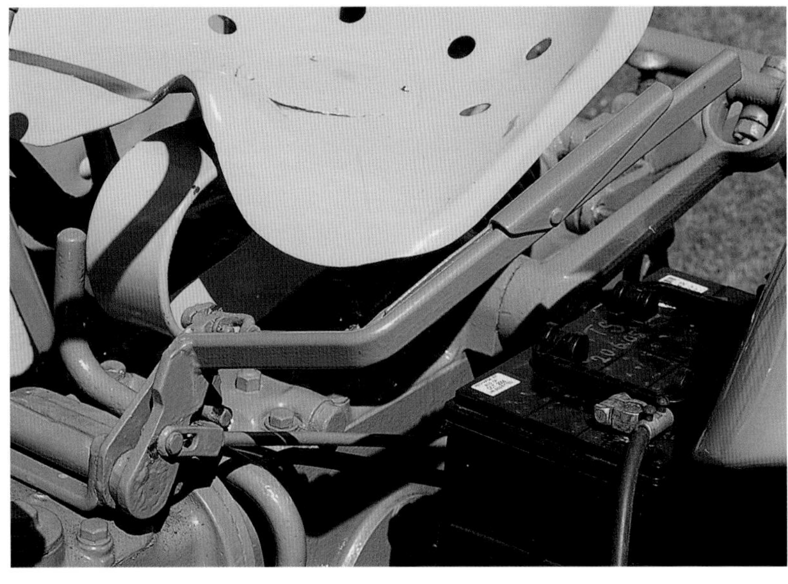

The seat in its normal position with parking brake lever conveniently positioned alongside.

The wide Girling brake drums fitted to industrial models. Each houses two pairs of brake shoes. The inner pair is mechanically operated either singly by the independent brake pedals or together by the parking brake lever. The outer pair is operated by the normal footbrake pedal via two hydraulic cylinders.

that were hinged to the front of the bonnet on the bumper, and could be lifted off for maintenance. These more or less covered the engine sides, leaving a gap where the driver could step up on to the seat. The author can only ever remember seeing one of these full industrial variants; it was on display at the Commercial Motor Show at Earls Court in 1952.

Type A-TE-116 was a rear wing of extended width, whereas type A-TE-115 was a wide front wing that was bolted with special brackets to the radius arms. These front wings had rubber mud flaps. If lighting equipment was fitted, it was slightly more sophisticated than the single central headlamp found on some agricultural versions. To meet the lighting requirements of the Road Traffic Act, two headlamps were fitted, having twin-filament bulbs and integral side-

The dashboard of the industrial model, showing the heater plug switch, lighting switch, oil pressure gauge, ammeter and Ki-Gass pump with operating instruction plate, below which is fitted a Tractormeter A-TE-F93 calibrated to read engine rpm and speed in mph in top gear. The built-in hours counter would advance one hour with the engine running at 1500rpm.

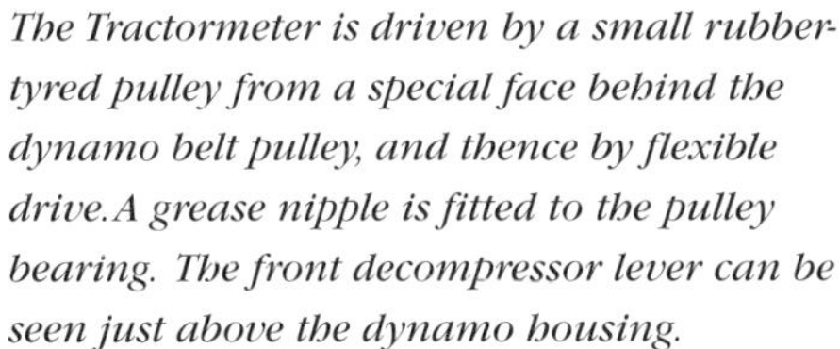

The Tractormeter is driven by a small rubber-tyred pulley from a special face behind the dynamo belt pulley, and thence by flexible drive. A grease nipple is fitted to the pulley bearing. The front decompressor lever can be seen just above the dynamo housing.

The combined brake master cylinder and reservoir and its mounting bracket adjacent to the PTO lever on the right-hand side of the tractor.

lamps, together with a standard single tail lamp of 2in (51mm) diameter, twin Lucas reflectors of 1.5in (38mm) diameter, a rear floodlight, and a two-pin trailer light socket.

Other modifications outside the scope of legislation included a tip-up seat pan, full step boards, sometimes a front bumper, and a radiator protection grill that was designed to fold down to allow the bonnet to tip forward for fluid level checks. For highway use, the standard 3-ton Ferguson Trailer, whether fixed or tipping, made by Joseph Sankey Ltd at their Hadley Castle Works, Wellington, Shropshire, had to be modified to meet the requirements of the Road Traffic Act. The areas needing attention were the fitting of an over-run braking system to the draw bar. This was no mean feat, when one remembers that the draw bar of a

An industrial model on the front cover of a brochure, dating from around 1952, aimed at local authorities.

The subsoiler D-BE-28 shown in more detail. In addition to tearing up road surfaces it was used for laying cables or subsoiling playing fields for better drainage.

fully loaded trailer bears down on the tow hook with a force of 1 ton. Also fitted to this draw bar was a latch which prevented the brakes coming on when the trailer was reversed. This latch was conveniently operated by the driver, by reaching around to the handbrake lever support bracket, where a length of light chain was stowed that connected to the reversing latch.

These highway trailers were fitted with leaf springs to the axles, and unlike the agricultural version did not have the two axle position facility because of the length of the springs. One

A subsoiler being used to pull up the wood block surface of a Scarborough street.

other modification was to fit quarter mudguards to the rear of the wheels; these were made of tough rubber, a sensible expedient bearing in mind their vulnerability! Most of these trailers had hinge-down sides and tail boards. As far as the author is aware, the 30cwt (1525kg) trailer, although ideally suited for municipal and industrial duties with its low loading height, was never adapted to meet the requirements of the law – perhaps users were happy to take a chance and plead innocence if questioned, which one would hardly dare to do today!

Some of the standard agricultural implements in the Ferguson range quickly found a place in municipal and industrial usage. The sub-soiler D-BE-28 was an excellent piece of equipment for ripping up the wood blocks used in some road construction at the time. It was also handy as a mole plough, for drawing in alkathene water pipes, and plastic coated telephone and electricity cables, which were being used for the first time early in this period. Likewise a use was found for the trailed fertiliser spreader type 721. This would be hitched up behind the 3-ton trailer, with a hard-working man on the trailer shovelling salt or grit into the hopper for spreading on the road. This must have prevented many accidents in icy conditions.

The Ferguson low-volume crop sprayer S-LE-20, with a little modification, could be turned into a useful roadside weed killing outfit. The rear-mounted agricultural mower 5A-EE-B1320 was offset to the right, and therefore not suited for highway work, where it would have operated against the flow of traffic. This was remedied by the introduction of the Dynobal-

A TE.F20 fitted with a 25cu ft/min Hydrovane compressor A-UE-20. My Norwegien friend, the late Erik Fredriksen, is holding the Marples Shearomajor hedgecutter often used by municipal authorities.

ance mid-mounted mower type 736 from America, which was left-hand mounted and could work from vertical for hedge trimming, to 20 degrees below horizontal for verge trimming.

Yet other agricultural implements that found a use on small earthmoving jobs were the earth scoop type B-JE-A20, and the front-mounted earth mover, which in reality was a small bulldozer blade. Another implement for earth works was the blade terracer B-FE-20. The mounted winch type W-UE-20 manufactured by The Scottish Mechanical Light Industries Ltd of Ayr in Scotland, with a rated pull of 7000lbs (3178kg) and a rope speed of 50ft (15m) per minute at 1500 engine rpm, could be used for light recovery jobs such as winching cut timber and uprooting small trees.

Ferguson marketed two sizes of compressors, both in the Hydrovane range made by Binks Bellows. These advanced rotary compressors were quiet and smooth running, and did not require a pressure vessel, unlike the conventional piston type. The 25cu ft (0.708cu m) per minute A-WE20 was used mainly to power hand-held reciprocating hedge trimmers, made by Marples of Parkstone, Dorset. These were available in two different sizes, the smaller, lighter model being suitable for yew and privet hedges, where cutting was on a regular basis. The larger model had a nice additional facility in that there was a short saw blade built into the end of the reciprocating knife that could be used to cut branches which were beyond the

This 65cu ft per minute rotary compressor was manufactured by Hydrovane and is mounted in a cradle which is attached to the tractor's three-point linkage; again this machine is belt driven from the belt pulley attachment. It was necessary to fit a speed control unit to the tractor's engine. This slowed the engine down to idle speed when there was no demand for air. When air was needed the engine control allowed the engine to run up to maximum governed speed. Maximum operating pressure is 100psi at full load, the unit absorbing about 15bhp. A safety valve was fitted, with a small over-centre lever that could be manually lifted; otherwise it blew off at 125psi.

capacity of the knife. Unlike today's flail hedge cutters, these hand-held machines could be used selectively. Other small air tools such as paint sprayers, drills, sanders and grinders were well within the capacity of this compressor.

A larger compressor of similar design, again made by Hydrovane, with an output of 65cu ft (1.7cu m) per minute, was claimed, optimistically, to be capable of operating two road

A TE.A20 fitted with the early-type Ferguson forklift. Note the hook for trailer attachment and that weights are fitted to the front wheels.

breakers. The larger machine required the fitment of a speed/response governor to the engine. Both these compressors were mounted in a frame that was attached to the three-point linkage, and were driven by a flat belt from the PTO on the tractor via the reversible pulley attachment type A-TE66.

The Ferguson fork lift attachment made by Fewster of Hexham, Northumberland, with a 12cwt capacity and a lift height of 147in (3.73m), was again suitable for many industrial applications, and in fact was probably the precursor of today's rough terrain fork lifts. It could be fitted with a pick-up hook, thus enabling trailers to be towed. To facilitate this, the tines had to be folded back and stowed, and the towing weight on the trailer restricted to 1.5 tons because the hitch point was now some 24in (610mm) from the centre of the rear axle, whereas the normal under-belly hook was only 9in (229mm) away.

Yet another piece of Ferguson equipment that was widely used in construction and industry was the dump skip type R-JE-20, which in reality quickly transformed TE20 into a small dumper truck, its rear-mounted self-tipping hopper capable of holding 10cwt (508kg) of material. This combination could travel at 14mph (22.5km/h) on smooth roads, and at slower speeds would take rutted building sites in its stride.

The post hole digger type D-FE-20 was available with detachable augers in four sizes (6in, 9in, 12in and 18in – 152mm 229mm, 305mm and 457mm), and found use with fencing contractors and tree-planting landscapers alike. The Ferguson irrigation pump manufactured by Beresford, mounted and driven in a similar way to the compressors, would have its uses in fire-fighting, emptying ponds, dealing with emergency flooding, and of course irrigation of arable and vegetable crops, as well as sports fields, in dry weather.

The wood saw A-LE-20 would no doubt have

A nice factory shot of a TE.D20 fitted with a Ferguson dump skip R-JE-20, which would have been used perhaps to deliver parts or collect rubbish on site.

been used by foresters and park superintendents to clear up fallen trees and broken branches.

The crane attachment type C-UE-21 was also fitted to the three-point linkage. This ingenious device had its linkage designed so that as the hook was raised, the load was drawn in slightly closer to the tractor for added safety. The maximum height of lift was 7ft 4in (2.24m) under the hook, and the length of the jib adjustable in 5in (127mm) increments from 4ft 2in (1.27m) to 6ft 11in (2.11m), with lifting capacities of 650lbs (295kg) to 350lbs (159kg) respectively. It was a very handy piece of kit to have around on any construction site or in a works yard.

Probably the widest industrial usage of what was a basic agricultural design was the manure loader M-UE20 which, in addition to its eight-tine fork attachment with hydraulic push-off facility, could be equipped with a hydraulically controlled earth bucket of 0.33cu yd (0.25cu m) capacity. This loader had a maximum working height of 11ft (3.3m), making it ideal for loading tipper lorries with sand, gravel, coal, etc. Scottish Aviation, who produced simple aluminium cabs for the TE20, developed a special cab for use with this loader which enabled the cab to tilt back when the loader reached three-quarters of its lifting height. The cab then went back and up with the loader arms for the final length of the travel!

For jobs not catered for by the existing Ferguson implement line-up, other manufacturers were quick to capitalise on the popularity of the TE20. Twose of Tiverton produced a field or road roller, where the TE20 was driven up a ramp on to the framework above the rollers. The rear wheels were jacked clear of the decking and sprockets bolted to the eight studs of the drive wheels were connected by roller chains to each half of the rear roller. The front roller, with its own steering wheel, was placed adjacent to the driver, and enabled him to take charge – even if the position was a bit awkward. Twose of Tiverton also offered an offset verge plough, using a special framework but where possible standard Ferguson plough parts.

Another firm used the basic TE20 as the running gear for a 1-ton dumper truck. Whitlock developed their Dinkham Digger back-hoe for use with the TE20 – this must have been a huge advance on hand trench digging. Atkinson of Clitheroe put into production a salt, grit or lime spreader, which was towed behind the TE20 and had a slow moving floor that fed material to the rear spreading mechanism. This dispensed with the hardworking man in the trailer.

The 3-ton tipping trailer could be fitted with a specially made curved-top cover with sliding access panels that enabled it to be used for refuse collection. Yet another attachment, developed this time by Studilux, was a front-mounted road sweeper, driven through a drop gearbox fitted to the PTO, with a lower shaft taking the drive forward under the belly of the tractor to a right-angle gearbox on the sweeper unit. The raising and lowering of the brush was activated by a system of rods and cable linkage connected to the rear three-point linkage.

A 3-inch Beresford pump mounted in a cradle for attachment to the three-point linkage. This centrifugal pump, driven from the tractor's PTO through the belt pulley attachment, can raise water from a depth of 25ft and has a capacity of up to 16,500 gallons per hour. It absorbs about 18.75bhp at maximum capacity.

A tipping refuse trailer in use by the Royal Borough of Leamington Spa.

Chapter Ten

Conversions

This photo shows well the reduction in width to just over 44 inches overall that was achieved by Reekie. This is a late conversion based on a TE.F20 Diesel, produced after the date when Reekie agreed with Harry Ferguson not to produce any more conversions. Angus Fruit farm of Blairgowrie, who commissioned this tractor from Reekie, were adamant that they wanted a Diesel version, and despite the agreement the tractor was supplied.

By the late 1940s the TE20 was becoming a widely used and respected tractor. Its sound design and good engineering ensured that it was nice to drive, as well as reliable and fuel efficient, all endearing characteristics. Its usage extended far and wide, so it is not surprising to find that berry farmers in the north-east of Scotland were soon asking Reekie of Arbroath, the local Ferguson distributor, to reduce the track width of the standard TE20 tractor to make it suitable for operating between the rows of raspberry canes that were at that time such a feature of the area. In 1947 Reekie rose to the demand by cutting out a piece of the rear axle housing on each side and welding the inner and outer parts together again. By treating the half shafts similarly, the rear track was reduced to a minimum of 32in (813mm). Dealing with the front axle was a bit more tricky, and it was found necessary to put a set in both the radius arms and the steering drag links. A crude modification was done to the bonnet side panels to enable a reasonable

The badge Reekie fitted to the tractors modified by him. On early examples it was placed above the Ferguson one. Harry Ferguson was not impressed and ordered the arrangement shown here!

The same tractor showing the 12-volt battery repositioned below the air cleaner.

The nearside radius arms and drag link on the Reekie conversion needed to be heavily modified to cater for the narrow track.

The Reekie conversion is wearing Allman 36-inch rear wheels.

The drop arms on the steering box were also modified and the lift arms were altered too.

steering lock to be maintained.

Gavin Reekie had started his business at the end of World War Two after he was demobbed, having served in the Royal Electrical and Mechanical Engineers. He began by doing agricultural repairs and eventually took on the Ferguson dealership for that part of Scotland. His modifications resulted in a tractor 44in (1118mm) wide. It is believed that about 200 of these conversions were produced; they cost around £250 on top of the price of a new tractor, which was around £325. When Harry Ferguson got to know about these modifications to his tractor he was not impressed, and it is recorded that he visited Gavin Reekie in person. As the Reekie conversion was much narrower than the standard tractor but retained the standard size wheels of 10x28 rear and 400x19 front, it was inherently more unstable. To add insult to injury, Reekie had added his own name plate to the bonnet above the Ferguson badge, and painted a blue line along the sides of the bonnet on some tractors. John Reekie found himself in an awkward situation; he had a dealership for Ferguson tractors, which were selling very well in a prosperous farming area of Scotland, but he had also established a niche market for his modified tractors.

Harry Ferguson's solution to this situation was to make John Reekie a cash offer to take over the manufacture of narrow tractors. Reekie refused, and in 1948 Harry Ferguson Ltd started producing their own narrow version of the TE20. This was the TE.B20 with the Continental

A Ferguson TE.E20 Narrow TVO tractor fitted with the Ferguson low-volume sprayer S-LE-20. Note the Allman 400 x 36-inch rear wheels and the hub caps fitted to the front wheels.

The modified brake pedals fitted to the Narrow version.

The sliding bar lever fitted instead of the cranked handle to Narrow models.

engine, later the TE.C20 with the Standard engine (petrol), TE.E20 (TVO) and TE.J20 (lamp oil). The TE.G20 was a Diesel version but was only made in France. The track of all of these was 42in (1067mm) whereas the Reekie conversion had a track of 32in (813mm). Later an even more modified tractor, the vineyard model, was produced. Despite this hiccup, Harry Ferguson and John Reekie continued to enjoy a good friendly relationship, and Reekie's dealership flourished. The Ferguson-designed Narrow tractor was an altogether better engineered product than the Reekie conversion. Gone were the crude cutting and welding that Reekie had employed, and the modified parts were purpose engineered and manufactured. This resulted in a properly designed and made product which carried the maker's (Standard Motor Company's) full warranty.

The front hubs which were covered by car type press-on hub caps. These necessitated welding to the front wheel centres three equally spaced lugs to secure the hub caps, which were intended to ensure that crops did not become entangled with the hubs or wheel nuts. At the rear, standard mudguards were used, but if for example a sprayer was used with the wheels on a narrow setting, special brackets were needed to inset the mudguards. The levelling lever was modified to a tommy bar type, and the lower links had a set in them. The point of attachment of the check chains near to the PTO was a sliding arrangement, to allow the chains to rise slightly as the lower links moved upwards. The two independent brake pedals were changed from the elliptical shape with a serrated surface for foot grip, to a flat bar turned up at the inside end; this modification was needed because of a lack of space.

The Vineyard tractor was introduced by Harry Ferguson Ltd in 1952 in three versions, TE.K20 (petrol), TE.L20 (TVO), or TE.M20 (lamp oil), while the Diesel version TE.N20 was made only in France. This was a properly designed and engineered modification to the TE20 tractor, supplied by the factory, and carrying the normal warranty. To retain stability with the track at the narrowest setting of 37in (940mm) front and 32in (813mm) rear, with an overall width of 46in (1168mm), smaller diameter tyres were fitted both front and rear, being 500x15 and 900x24 respectively, but the wheel tracks could be set

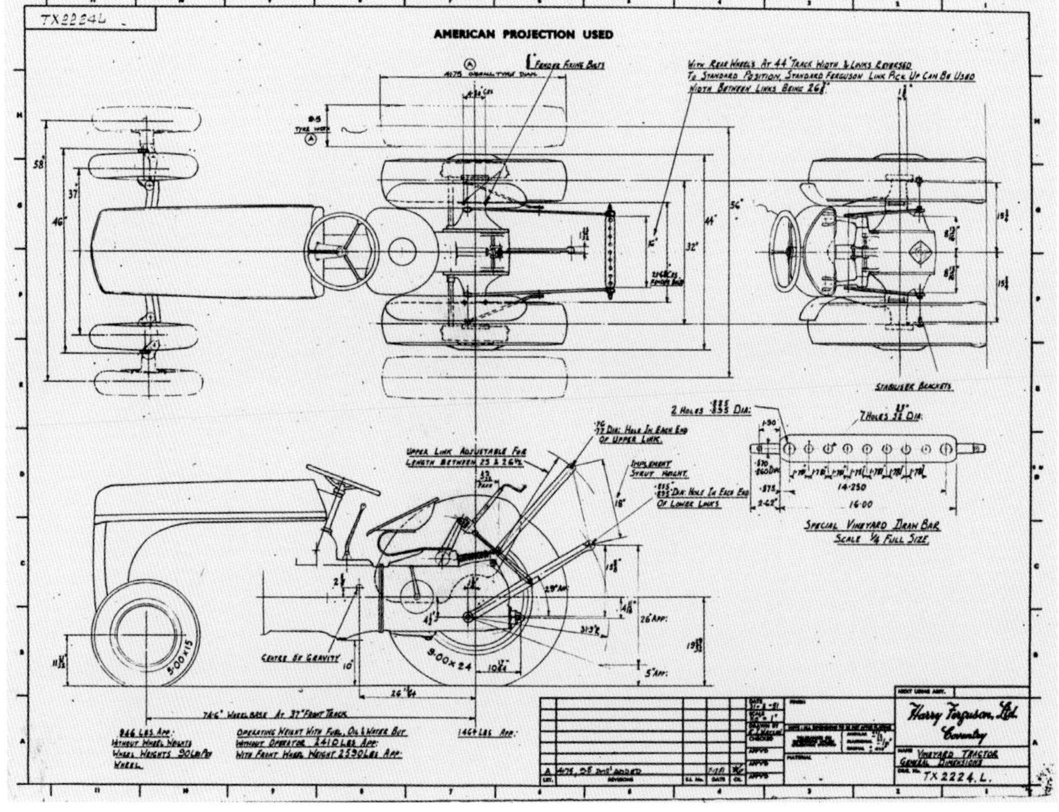

Dated 31 August 1951, this drawing shows the general layout, with dimensions, of the proposed vineyard tractor. It was drawn by the product engineer C J Watson, but it was not until February1952 that Alex Senkowski approved the design. Production started in early May 1952.

A Vineyard model alongside a standard tractor. It is not only narrower but also rides lower owing to its smaller wheels.

A Ferguson TE.L20 Vineyard model running on TVO

out to a maximum of 58in (1473mm) front and 56in (1422mm) rear, which was adequate for most other applications.

Apart from the track modifications, other aspects of the design had to be revised. To enable the front wheels to attain sufficient lock, the radiator was moved forward on a special bracket by about 3.75in (95mm). This in turn necessitated extending the bonnet by a similar amount, achieved by welding an extension piece to the rear end where the bonnet met the dashboard. The heat shield on the TVO and lamp oil version had to be cut away to prevent fouling by the dynamo, which was repositioned to give clearance to the right-hand swivel arm. The fan cowling was made deeper by 3.75in (95mm). Apart from a shorter centre section to the three-part front axle, the axle stub assemblies were also shorter and featured a different hub cap design which did not protrude to the same extent as the standard type. Pressed steel type hub caps were not generally fitted to Vineyard models. To deal with the narrow front axle, special curved radius arms were fitted, and likewise the drag links had a set at each end. For some strange reason the foot rest position changed from the normal, where it was cast integral with the rear ball joint end of the radius arm, to a position about 4in (102mm) further forward, where it was welded to the radius arm, so your feet wobbled a bit as the front axle articulated!

At the rear these tractors were fitted with smaller mudguards in keeping with the reduced

The compact arrangement of the Vineyard model's rear end. Note the 9-hole draw bar, the 10 x 24 rear tyres, and the extended levelling-box crank handle.

diameter of the wheels. They were mounted on special brackets that could be used to adjust the width between the mudguards. The mudguards extended down to foot level, giving good protection from the rear wheels. The independent brake pedals were of similar design to those fitted on the standard tractors. The lift shaft arms were redesigned to be more or less straight, and the lower links had a set at the implement attachment end when used on the narrow setting. The levelling control lever was extended by 10in (254mm), to clear the rear mudguard. Special stabilizer links were made available which connected to a special plate bolted to three of the rear hub retaining bolts. The hydraulic control lever was moved forward by about 4in (102mm).

Off side of a TE.L20, showing the pronounced sets in both the radius arm and the drag link. The heat shield is modified to clear the repositioned dynamo.

Most Ferguson implements could be used with the Vineyard tractor but the following could not be used: 3-ton trailer, high lift loader, earth mover, manure loader, dump skip, potato planter, and fertilizer attachment. Although these ultra-narrow tractors are known as the Vineyard models, they found wide use in other locations, including sugar cane plantations, orchards, market gardens, even industrial situations, where their narrowness enabled them to negotiate restricted gangways. They were very handy in large gardens, and one could consider them the precursors of modern compact tractors. A special Ferguson jack was produced for the vineyard range. One drawback was that the tractor was slower because of the smaller rear wheels. Maximum speed in fourth gear was reduced to 11.875mph (19.1km/h), compared to the standard TE20 which could achieve 13.25mph (21.3km/h).

Ferguson never produced their own four-wheel drive conversion but the author can remember when at agricultural college in 1955 a Ferguson representative came to give a talk on the benefits of the Ferguson System, and a certain clever dick from the floor asked why did Ferguson not produce a four-wheel drive tractor? The answer, predictably, was "our tractors are so good they don't need four-wheel drive!"

If Ferguson deemed the option of four-wheel drive to be unnecessary on the TE20, Selene of Nichelino not far from Turin in Italy considered it worth their while to develop and offer a kit for sale. They named it the Converzione Emanuel Selene. The company submitted one of its conversions for test at The National Institute of Agricultural Engineering at Silsoe, Bedfordshire, on 9 December 1954. In test number R54033 it was claimed that the gain in draw bar bhp could reach 80 per cent, which seems rather optimistic. The real benefit of the four-wheel drive option became most apparent when working steep ground and when soil conditions were adverse. The system used for the TE20 tractors had a transfer gearbox inserted between the gearbox and the rear transmission. This lengthened the tractor by about 1.625in (41mm), aiding driver legroom! The drive was taken from the output shaft of the tractor gearbox, and transmitted by a train of gears to an enclosed sliding gear type of selector mechanism. Drive was then taken by an open propeller shaft to the differential in the front axle, which in this case was a modified Willys or Ford Jeep axle. This was modified to reduce the normal Jeep track to the standard Ferguson track of 49.5in (1257mm). The front brake shoes were discarded but the drums remained. Sadly one of the drawbacks of this conversion was the loss of the very good steering lock one associates with Ferguson TE20 tractors.

The universal joints in the swivel housings were of the constant-velocity ball type. The

A TE.D20 converted to four-wheel drive with the Selene conversion kit. The front tyres are 7.5x16 and the rears the standard 10x28.

The transfer box fitted to the rear of the gearbox for the Selene conversion which transmits drive to the propeller shaft via a dog clutch. The selector lever is clearly visible.

The modified Willys Jeep front axle used in this conversion.

The front wheel swivel hubs retain the original Jeep brake drums; unfortunately there are no brake shoes inside! The swivel hub encloses constant-velocity joints.

A TE.D20 fitted with a G Bryden Engineering full-track conversion.

front tyres were 7.50x16 traction type, and Selene must have got the gear ratios almost spot-on, because even travelling flat-out in top gear on a tarmac road it was possible to slip in and out of four-wheel drive with only very light finger pressure on the control lever. All in all this was a very nicely engineered conversion, but very few were sold in this country, no doubt due to cost.

This shot probably taken at a Smithfield Show in London, gives a clear view of the Cameron Gardener full-track conversion.

A few Ferguson TE20s were converted to high-rise, for use in vegetable fields and for crop spraying. One has survived in Lincolnshire; once part of the W Chafer fleet of tractors, it has been well restored and is owned by Hydro Agri (UK). These conversions raised the height of the TE20 by 6in (152mm), achieved by cutting the front steering spindles (kingpins) on each side, cutting the forged steel casing of the kingpin housing, welding in a piece of 2in (51mm) diameter heavy tube 6in long, and making up longer spindles, which were re-fitted in the normal way. The original 4.00x19 front wheels were used. For the rear the 10.00x28 wheels were exchanged for row-crop 6.50x44 wheels, which gained the necessary extra 6in in height at the rear end. The mudguards were raised on packing pieces, to ensure clearance to the wheels, and were extended to the foot boards to give protection to the driver. It seems that no modifications were made to the hydraulic linkage, so presumably these tractors were used solely for spraying purposes. It is claimed that these tractors were racers and could achieve 25mph (40km/h)!

One other interesting Ferguson conversion was produced by George Bryden Engineering of Seacroft near Leeds, who designed and produced a full crawler conversion with steel tracks. Two side frames were attached to the

Perhaps the idea for a wrap-around combine stemmed from this wrap-around binder fitted to an Allis Chalmers WC tractor.

rear of the transmission housing, and at the front to a heavily modified front location point. The drive to the tracks was from the existing rear wheel centres, to which were bolted a fabrication consisting of two circular rings spaced apart at about 8in (203mm) with round steel bars. These engaged with a tooth on the reverse side of each track plate, which was the opposite way round to the system used on most crawlers. The steering was by the tractor's brakes, which were ingeniously controlled via the steering wheel: movement of the drop arms either side of the steering box was transmitted to the brake operating linkage. Very few of these conversions seem to have been made.

The well-known firm of H Cameron Gardener Ltd near Reading produced a crawler conversion by the simple expedient of fitting modified outer sections to the front axle. There were stronger front hubs, larger front wheels and reverse traction tyre treads (7.50x16), while the treads of the rear tyres were also reversed. Strung around the front and rear wheels in an oval was what can only be described as giant snow chains, with heavy rubber cleats bolted to steel connecting links. These must have been difficult machines to steer.

Finally we need to take a close look at what was done in the mid-1950s to produce a number of prototype mounted combine harvesters for the Ferguson TE20. It is understood that in 1949 the concept of a self-propelled demountable combine harvester came from an instructor at the Stoneleigh training school, Michael Stoltenburg-Bloom. He showed his rough sketches to Harry Ferguson, who liked the idea and told him to build it. The first prototype of a wrap-around design combine was heavy and cumbersome, but it must have come up to expectation, because Harry Ferguson gave the go-ahead to build a second one of improved design.

Let us first consider the thinking behind this

Mike Stoltenburg-Bloom, who was the proponent of the wrap-around combine idea. He is seen here outside the Fletchamstead engineering shop in 1958 with an experimental model.

The same combine outside the engineering shop again. Apart from its wheels, the tractor has almost completely disappeared.

ambitious project, which was set in motion over fifty years ago. It would fit nicely with the general principles of the Ferguson System, it would extend the sales of Harry Ferguson Ltd, and it would hopefully provide farmers of the world with an affordable self-propelled grain harvester. The advantage these prototypes claimed over existing self-propelled designs was cost. The TE20 became the power plant and drive train for the combine harvester, which could be put on and taken off at will. This is, however, an over-simplification of what was actually involved in practice. To start with, the tractor had to be modified rather drastically. An epicyclic gearbox was fitted to the transmission to reduce forward speed to an acceptable

Mike Stoltenburg-Bloom on a suitably modified TE.F20 about to mount the combine. Note the battery repositioned close to his right knee.

level for harvesting and to provide live PTO for the belt drives to the threshing mechanism. The rear axle housing and half shaft on the right-hand side had to be changed for an extended unit bearing a special mounting cradle - not exactly a five-minute job. Harry Ferguson claimed that two men with spanners and a pair of pliers would take twenty-five minutes to mount the combine and fifteen to take it off. No mention was made of the basic modification to the tractor, which would make it pretty unsuitable for normal agricultural applications. The epicyclic gear would be most useful, but a lopsided tractor with 2ft 6in (762mm) of extended right-hand axle would not be much use!

After much development, eight prototypes and the huge expenditure of £1 million, the combine harvester never reached the production stage, although it was tested far and wide in the UK, France, Sweden, Holland, Germany, Australia and the USA. A tanker version was developed but the others were all baggers, which were more appropriate to the era. One was build around a TO35, imported from the USA, obviously in an attempt to gain some extra horsepower. I was told by a farmer near Crediton in Devon that a Ferguson-mounted combine was tested on his farm, driven by the late Dick Dowdeswell. It was apparently based around an FE35 grey and gold tractor; maybe he was confusing it with the American grey and green TO35, although I doubt it.

The Moffett self-propelled potato harvester was displayed at the Ulster Royal Show in 1996, the year that saw the celebration of fifty years of the TE20. The machine was very much based on the running gear of a TE.F20. The engine, clutch and gearbox were separated from the remainder of the transmission, turned through 180 degrees and lowered slightly, and reconnected by a heavy fabricated transfer box which must have incorporated a step-down multi-chain drive. The lifting of the single row feed roller was taken care of by the tractor's built-in hydraulic lift system, but try plotting the linkage and hydraulic lines! The use of a standard front axle shows to the full the kind of settings achievable.

Joseph Cyril Bamford of Uttoxeter, in the early days after he started in business in 1945, made a front loader to fit the TE20, but the better-known back-hoe loader which made the JCB company famous from its introduction in 1953 was based on the Fordson Major.

Moffett Self-Propelled Potato Harvester

Underside of a combine, showing the extension to the right hand rear axle and the fitment to the belt pulley attachment of a twin vee-belt pulley with built-in slip clutch.

The American version of the wrap-around combine fitted with a bulk grain tank. This combine was powered by its own engine, mounted at the rear of the machine.

Chapter Eleven

Implements

Ferguson developed and marketed a vast range of implements in the 1940s and 1950s and had them made by outside manufacturers. To understand this range better, it is worth going back briefly to trace their evolution from the Ferguson-Brown days of 1936-39. With the introduction of the Ferguson Type A tractor, a very limited range of implements for mounting on the three-point linkage was made available. These were the 10in (254mm) two-furrow plough and a tool bar frame which, depending on what tines were fitted, could become a nine-tine row crop cultivator, a seven-tine general-purpose cultivator, or, with three ridger bodies, a three-row ridger. Later, about 1938, a 16in (406mm) single-furrow plough was added. A distinctive feature of the early mounted implements was an upward-facing cupped bracket fitted next to the top link which was capable of holding the top link slightly rearwards when attaching the implements to the tractor. This useful feature did not appear on later models. The early implements set the trend for later designs in that they were made from high-strength steel, combining strength with light weight and good non-rusting properties. The early designs used BSF bolts and nuts, whereas in the Ford-Ferguson phase UNF bolts were introduced, continuing into the TE20 era. So it is no good trying to use your 1950 Ferguson spanner on Ferguson-Brown implements!

In the following text, the various implements are divided into tillage, plant cultivation, harvesting and others, leaving out in this chapter the various implements already described in Chapter 9 on the industrial models.

Transplanting young spruce trees using the Ledmore lining-out plough.

TILLAGE: PLOUGHS

Foremost among Ferguson engineers in the development of the range of ploughs was John Chambers, who returned from America in 1945. The outside contractor commissioned to manufacture the ploughs was Rubery Owen of Darlaston in Staffordshire. These ploughs, like the earlier Ferguson plough mouldboard designs, were based on those of the American firm Oliver.

For all types of plough, the front track should be set to 48in (1219mm). For 8in (203mm) and 10in (254mm) ploughs, the rear track should also be 48in, but for all other types of ploughs

A fascinating scene, full of life: Samuel Wilson & Son Ltd's stand at the Bakewell show in the early 1950s, with a wide range of Ferguson equipment on display – and a wide range of people.

the rear track should be 52in (1321mm). This is vitally important if good results are to be achieved. The 8in plough is of three-furrow design fitted with ley type boards, and is designed primarily for grassland ploughing where good covering is required. It is fitted with disc coulters and skimmers. The two- and three-furrow 10in ploughs can feature either general purpose or semi-digger mouldboards, and again these are fitted with disc coulters and skimmers. Two different types of shares were available, cast iron or cast steel. Bar point ploughs became available later for use in very stony conditions.

The chilled cast iron types are for general work, being the cheapest in the range. They are termed chilled cast iron because the underside, which is subject to the most wear, is hardened in manufacture. In use the softer top side wears hopefully at a similar rate, thereby maintaining for longer the profile of the share, with the slightly curved-down point that is essential to maintain suction and in turn traction. These chilled cast iron shares are not suitable for stony or rocky soil because they tend to fracture. For tough ground conditions the cast steel shares are much more resistant to damage, but they are more expensive.

The 12in (305mm) plough is a two-furrow design, with options of either semi-digger or

The classic two-furrow plough at work.

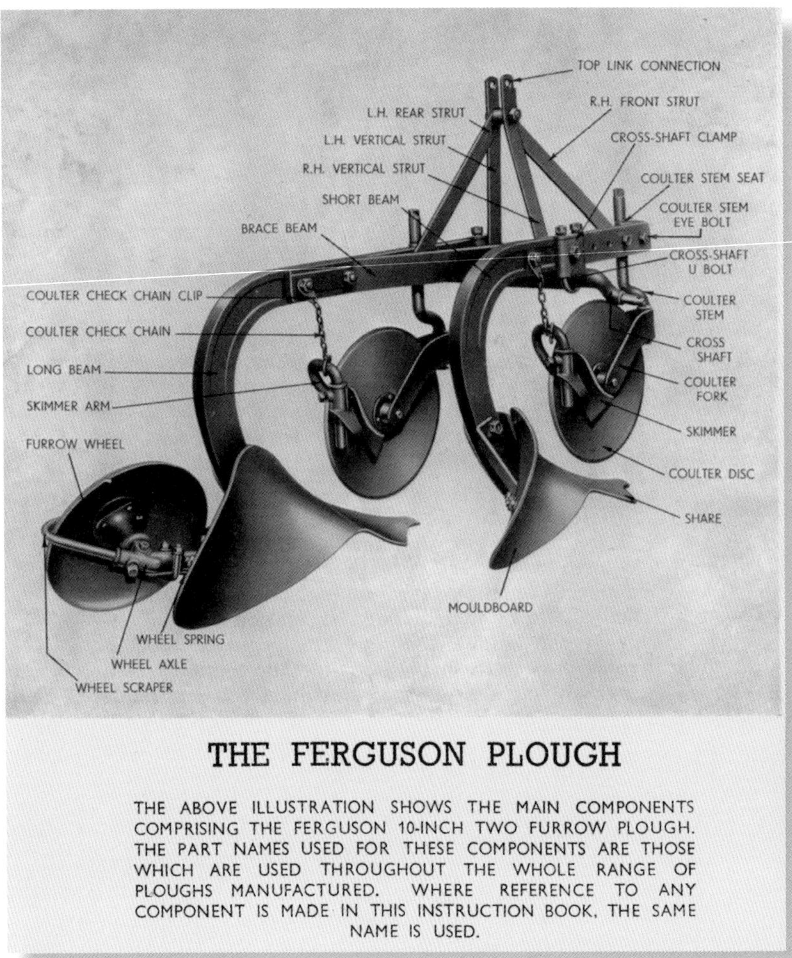

The 10-inch two-furrow plough explained in the 1951 Ferguson Plough Instruction Book.

deep digger mouldboards, again available fitted with either type of share. The 16in (406mm) plough is of single-furrow design, with only deep digger mouldboard available. The choice of shares in this case is limited to either cast steel or steel slip-nosed shears. These ploughs carry an 18in (457mm) diameter disc and 12in skimmers.

The 8-inch three-furrow plough 16CF-AE-28.

To complement this wide choice of plough types, various accessories were offered. These included a conversion kit to turn the two-furrow 10in plough into a three-furrow version. A furrow width adjuster AE-A7900 for hillside ploughing consisted of a serrated quadrant bolted to the plough's frame, and a hand lever with lock that firmly attached to the cross shaft. This gave a 5in (127mm) range of adjustment. It was a very popular accessory because it greatly simplified front furrow width adjustment, and one did not have to resort to the cumbersome business of slackening off and retightening the U-bolts on the cross shaft. Mould board extensions were offered which were useful for grassland or deep ploughing as they aided the turning of the furrow. Single arm coulters were available, which enabled the furrow wall to be undercut to produce crested furrows, which weather better and break down easily.

It may be prudent here to outline the exact procedure laid down by Ferguson for the efficient coupling of three-point linkage implements to a TE20 tractor. Harry Ferguson was most pedantic about this, and woe betide anyone he caught not following the exact guidelines.

Attaching the plough and tillage implements to the tractor.

1. Ensure top link is set in its central setting and in position on the plough. Back the tractor so that it is square with the plough cross shaft and that the tractor and plough top link are in line. The tractor must be correctly aligned before proceeding to attach the lower links. If it is not correct drive forward and try again. This is easier than attempting to manhandle the plough. Before dismounting from the tractor wind the levelling lever clockwise until three threads are showing on the lift rod.
2. Dismount. Attach left lower link to the cross shaft and insert linchpin.
3. Attach right lower link in a similar manner, using the levelling lever to bring the ball joint into line with the cross shaft. Insert linchpin.
4. Mount the tractor, start the engine and place forward end of top link in tractor top link connection, moving the tractor slightly backwards and forwards until the top link pin can be inserted. Secure with the linchpin.
5. To recap: 1. Lower left link.
   2. Lower right link.
   3. Top link.

To detach plough.

1. Level plough with levelling lever, lower slowly to the ground.
2. While seated on the tractor, detach front end of top link, moving the tractor slightly backwards or forwards if necessary to remove the pin. Replace pin and retain with linchpin.
3. Detach right lower link, adjusting levelling lever to free any tension on the ball joint.
4. Detach left lower link. Be sure to stow linchpins in their clips on the lower links to prevent them being torn off.

These words of advice are true for most mounted tillage implements.

Demonstrators of Ferguson tractors and ploughs, especially Dick Dowdeswell, used to amaze their spectators by pretending to get stuck with a two-furrow plough, and telling the assembled audience that it was no use continuing with the two-furrow, he would have to get the three-furrow plough. This must have seemed like complete lunacy to most farmers of the day, not being fully conversant with the Ferguson System, but it has to be remembered that, for all intents and purposes, traction on a TE20 is proportional to the draft of the implement. So this is why the TE20 could gain added traction with a three-furrow plough. There must have been some open mouths among the spectators at such a practical demonstration of the benefits of the Ferguson system.

There was one other mouldboard plough in the Ferguson range. This was the reversible plough T-AE-28, also known as the butterfly plough because of its appearance. It is a 16in (406mm) single furrow plough, fitted with left- and right-handed mouldboards of the deep digger type. The turn-over mechanism is purely mechanical in operation, and automatically turns the plough from left-hand furrow to right-hand furrow on lifting the implement out of the ground at the headland. The only special parts needed to be installed on the tractor were a special slightly longer cast steel PTO cover, with a groove machined on it into which slotted the lower end of the indexing chain bracket, the top of this bracket being retained by the long pin on the axle housing. The advantage of a one-way plough is that time and skill is not needed in marking out a field in the traditional way: just a shallow furrow drawn on the near and far headland, set 5 yards (4.5m) from the boundary if one chooses to do a short turn or 8 yards (7.2m) if one does a loop turn.

The final plough in the Ferguson range is the two-furrow disc plough 2-P-AE-20, for which a conversion kit was available to bring it up to three-furrow. These ploughs were primarily designed for export to countries with hard, dry, stony soils that could not be ploughed successfully with conventional mouldboard ploughs. A few were sold in the UK, presumably where a farmer was faced with having to plough hard and stony land. Because of their limited sales in this country they are hard to find today. The substantial tubular frame could be ballasted with lead weights to aid penetration of the discs, likewise the rear furrow wheel could be weighted with a special cast-iron ring bolted to it. The adjusters positioned between the discs and frame feature a large 1.625in (41mm) AF nut that was way beyond the capacity of the famous Ferguson spanner, and a special single-ended spanner 2ft (0.6m) long was supplied with the plough, so it was possible to get these nuts really tight.

The link between the ploughs and other tillage implements must be the Ferguson sub-

The Ferguson disc plough 2-P-AE-20 working at Stoneleigh.

Disc plough 2-P-AE-20 fitted to a TE.D20 with the Selene four wheel drive conversion.

soiler type D-BE-28, which can be considered as a massive single-tine cultivator used to create drainage slots in the sub-soil, or to break up a hard soil pan. It is fitted with an adjustable high-carbon steel 15.5in (394mm) diameter disc which is spring loaded to give protection if an obstruction is met. The main beam is constructed of high-strength heat-treated alloy steel. The sub-soiler will operate to a maximum depth of 18in (457mm). Like most Ferguson cultivators, it is fitted with a reversible wearing tooth. This implement sold well and is still a handy piece of equipment to have around for use today.

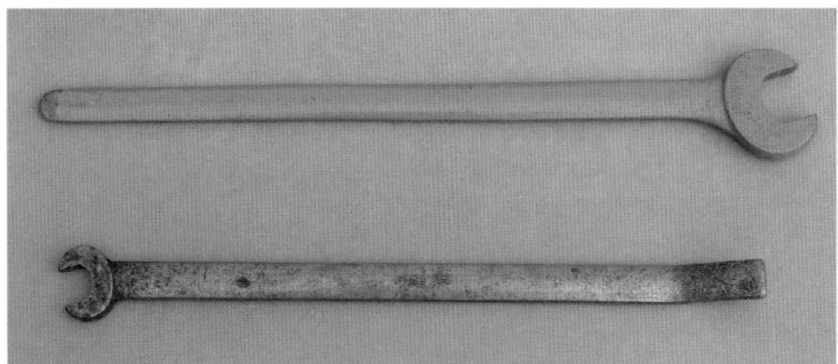

The single-ended spanner supplied with the disc plough is 1⅝"AF. The longer spanner with a cranked end was supplied with the Mark I 3-ton trailers. The open end fits the square bolt on the latching mechanism, while the cranked end could be used to lever the side boards out of their sockets.

TILLAGE: CULTIVATORS

Most of these were made by Steel's Engineering Products in Sunderland. They can be broadly divided into those that have tines of varying designs attached to a tool bar frame, which in turn is attached to the three-point linkage, and those that are of disc- or harrow-type designs. In the category of those that have tines attached to a tool bar frame is the cultivator with nine rigid tines, type 9-KE-A-20. The tines were fitted with points that had two wearing edges, so that when one became blunt, it could be turned around and the second face put to work, a nice economical idea. The nine-tine spring-loaded tiller type 9-BE-20 again featured reversible wearing points, with the option of four different sizes. The idea of spring-loading the tines was to offer protection to tractor and implement, in the event of hitting an obstruction. They were designed to be automatically reset.

The Ferguson three-row ridger R-DE-20 has it origins back in the Ferguson-Brown days, when it was part of the range of about five implements. Again it made use of the Ferguson tool frame, so that the ridger bodies could be set to the required spacing. Ridging had to be effec-

The independent steerage hoe with discs, B-KE-20. The driver has a tip-up seat whilst the poor chap steering the hoe must be getting a good dose of exhaust fumes!

tive, so to foster high standards of work an adjustable marker could be folded down on either side of the frame, to make a line in the soil for the driver to follow with the front tyre of the tractor on his return run. The implement was also fitted with a steerage fin which helped to maintain straight ridges. Special ridging bodies were available to produce flatter ridges, if that was required.

Another implement to use the tool bar frame was the nine-tine spring cultivator 9S-KE-20. Again the tines were fitted with reversible wearing points, and the curved spring steel tines were held in a serrated adjuster. The fact that they were of sprung steel gave a vibratory effect on the soil as they passed through it, with good effect to produce a good tilth.

Other implements that took advantage of the tool bar frame, but this time made by John Garington, were the steerage hoes. These were offered in two versions, the rigid B-KE-20 with or without discs, which was popular and priced at £86 in 1954, and the more sophisticated version, the independent steerage hoe, priced at £117 including discs. These implements were used extensively to weed crops such as kale, swedes, sugar beet and mangolds that were grown in rows. At this time, selective weed killers were only available for corn crops, so other crops demanded mechanical weeding or hand-hoeing. In the case of the simple version, it could be set to deal with three central rows and half of each of two outside rows. Fine steering of the unit 5in (127mm) either side of centre line was possible, with an operator sitting on the seat with a pivoted steering bar attached to a bracket on the right-hand lower link of the tractor. It was essential to fit a vertical exhaust pipe to prevent the poor person steering the hoe becoming overcome by carbon monoxide fumes!

The independent gang steerage hoe D-KE-20 with discs was a much more sophisticated development, in that each individual set of hoes could "float". This was achieved by having each set of hoes connected to small hydraulic rams, these rams being interconnected by a closed circuit which was quite independent of the tractor's hydraulic system. It has been suggested that there was an option to place an additional ram in the top link which was connected to this circuit. Both versions of this implement featured a tension spring, connected just below the top link pin on the implement, and fixed to a yoke attached to the long pins on the tractor rear axle housing. The top link connected in the normal way. All in all, these mechanisms achieved a fully floating effect and good work could be achieved, providing the discs and shovel blades were well set up, the tractor driver followed the crop line carefully, and the chap on the seat kept his concentration. Great clumps of young plants could be knocked out if these criteria were not met!

TILLAGE: HARROWS

The disc harrows were manufactured for Harry Ferguson by Thomas Blackburn & Sons Ltd of Preston in Lancashire. The earlier model was of tandem configuration, semi-trailed, and offered in widths of 5ft (1.52m) or 6ft (1.83m), both with 18in (457mm) discs. The model designation was 13A-BE-21 for the 6ft version. Scraper blades were fitted as standard, as were weight frames that could be ballasted for added penetration. A pair of cast-iron road wheels was offered as an accessory, to enable the disc harrow to be taken on the roadway without damaging the surface.

In 1953 the disc harrow became the 7ft (2.13m) wide 2A-BE-22, fitted with 18in (457mm) diameter discs. This implement was fully mounted on the three-point linkage, so it was not a problem to transport. Two separate levers within easy reach of the driver's seat altered the angle of the discs to the line of travel. A weight frame was provided for in the design of this implement, and the fact that it was fully mounted meant that it was impossible for the tractor to rear up. Two lower link positions were available, either for good road clearance when travelling light, or for sensitive hydraulic control in the field.

A variation of this was the heavy duty reversible disc harrow 4A-BE-22, either 5ft 6in (1.68m) or 7ft (2.13m) in width, fitted with 22in (559mm) diameter discs of serrated design. The main feature of this implement was the facility to turn and lock the disc gang through 180 degrees, thereby throwing the soil inwards or outwards, unlike the conventional disc harrow, which has one set arranged one way and the other the opposite way. This feature made it attractive to overseas buyers who needed to create irrigation channels, throwing soil outwards, or throwing the soil inwards to make

The tandem mounted disc harrow 4A-BE-22 was 7ft wide.

Reversible heavy duty disc harrow H-BE-20.

raised beds.

Another popular disc harrow, especially with vineyard, orchard and grove owners, was the mounted off-set disc harrow G-BE-20. Each of the two gangs was fitted with seven 20in (508mm) diameter discs, and could be set in a variety of configurations, normally in line with the tractor, or to the left or the right, to give the required amount of offset. They were fitted with heavy-duty white-iron bearings and adjustable scrapers to each disc. A hand-crank lever placed conveniently to the driver provided adjustment of the disc angle. It was normal practice to use a full stabiliser kit with this implement, and front wheel weights together with a top link balance spring.

Finally, while dealing with the range of disc harrows offered by Harry Ferguson, it is only right to mention briefly the wet paddy disc harrow system B-BE-20, although for obvious reasons these were not sold in the UK. Basically, the front of a tandem-mounted disc harrow is used with only one pair of gangs; trailed behind these are smoothing boards. Of the two control levers within easy reach of the driver, one adjusts the angles between the gangs, and the second controls the levelling boards to the rear of the discs. For safe operation Ferguson recommended that a tip-up seat be fitted, together with step boards, a vertical exhaust system, front wheel weights, and paddy cage extension wheels. It was also necessary to seal the drain holes in the clutch housing by drilling them out, tapping a thread and fitting brass plugs, a bit like the wading plugs on a Land Rover. It was necessary to fit a rocker extension to the top link connection to improve depth control sensitivity.

To round off the disc section, the disc terracer A-FE-20 was again designed with the overseas market in mind. A single 28in (711mm) diameter disc was mid-mounted on the right-

The Ferguson paddy disc harrow B-BE-20, possibly taken in India judging by the registration number.

A Ferguson three-gang spring tine cultivator with early-type hitch, K-BE-A31.

hand side of the tractor and was adjustable through 12 degrees, which was ideal for creating shallow drainage channels.

Another type of harrow marketed by Ferguson was the two- or three-section spring-tooth harrow K-BE-A21 or K-BE-A31, respectively giving a covering width of 6ft (1.83m) or 9ft (2.74m). Each gang frame was hinged to the next one, giving flexibility and allowing the harrows to follow the contours of the ground, and lever adjustment was fitted to each gang. The high-quality spring-steel tines, shod with reversible and replaceable points, gave a vibratory effect to clods of soil as the implement passed over. The implement was very efficient at collecting couch grass roots, which could then be dumped at the headland and burnt. This was before the days of chemical couch control.

The Ferguson spike-tooth harrow S-BE-31 was priced at £31 in 1953, and had an operating width of 13ft 4in (4.06m), with adjustable ridged tines set in three separate frames, each with its own lever to adjust the pitch of the tines. The centre section mounted to the three-point linkage, and the two outer side sections could be folded for transport, reducing the width to 64in (1.63m). The implement weighed 389 lbs (177kg). It was necessary to fit a rack to the top link and a spring-loaded yoke to control depth of penetration.

To complete the range of tillage implements marketed by Harry Ferguson, there is the spike tooth heavy duty harrow S-BE-41 produced by Thomas Blackburn Ltd. It used four traditional zigzags of heavy construction, suspended on chains attached to a linkage mounted on a folding frame of tubular construction. The fixed frame took care of two harrow sets, while the folding sections on either side accommodated one each, giving an overall working width of approximately 12ft 10in (3.91m). This implement necessitated the fitment of a ratchet on the top link to selectively engage with a yoke on the top, and a short length of chain attached to the mainframe of the harrow. As the setting of this determined the height of the frame from the ground, it gave some measure of control over the depth at which the implement would work. A couple of spring-tined versions were offered in two models, a three-section K-BE-A31 which folded for transport, and a two-section K-BE-A21 which was of a fixed width of 109.5in (2.78m); again all these implements were made of high-grade steel to withstand hard use.

At that time, fifty-odd years ago, these were very handy implements to have and a pleasure to use. Compare for a moment what had gone before: if a tractor driver was to go harrowing a field, first he would have to hitch up a trailer and load by hand three or four quite heavy zigzag harrow sections, the whipple tree that the harrows were connected to by chains, and a tow chain to join the assembled implements to the tractor. On reaching the field, he would reverse the process, unhitch the trailer, hitch up the harrows and charge on, providing the field he was cultivating was clean; if there was trash about, he would have to stop frequently, manually lift one harrow section at a time and with one leg kick the rubbish clear of the harrow. This can get very irksome in a dirty field! In stark contrast with this is the Ferguson tractor three-point linkage mounted harrow: the driver connects it up in the farm yard in one minute and off he goes down the lane, in through the field gate, stops, lowers the implement by fingertip control, folds down each outside section of harrow and goes to work. If trash builds up in the tines, all he has to do is stop, lift the implement on the hydraulic linkage, drive forwards for a couple of paces, lower the harrow and continue. What a revolution Harry Ferguson and his engineers produced!

Drilling corn at Stoneleigh Park with the Ferguson universal seed drill G-PE-A20, fitted with disc coulters. The tractor is a very early TE.A20 with vertical oil filter.

PLANT CULTIVATION: SEEDING AND PLANTING

As we move away from the tillage implements, I shall attempt a gradual progress through the different processes. Naturally, after preparing the soil we have to look at what Ferguson developed and sold to aid planting of seeds. The multi-purpose seed drill G-PE-A20 was a thirteen-row seed drill and was offered fairly early on in the TE20 era. It was available with either disc- or Suffolk-type coulters, and provision for fitting drag chains to the coulters. It was designed with one-man operation by the tractor driver in mind, not the norm at that time, when a second man was usually needed on a platform at the rear of the machine to check the flow of seeds. On the Ferguson drill, the thirteen fluted feed rollers were visible from the driver's seat. The machine was of course three-point linkage mounted but trailed on pneumatic tyres, the hydraulic linkage being used to raise and lower the coulters in and out of work, and to put out the wheel-driven feed mechanism. The seed hopper held 7.7cu ft (0.218cu m) of seed and the fertilizer attachment held 4.5cu ft (0.127cu m). This was a most versatile machine with a huge range of settings, making it suitable for green crops, grain crops, grasses and clovers. It was fitted with an acreage meter to help the operator ensure the machine was correctly set, and a most comprehensive instruction book came with it, running to thirty-four pages of useful information.

The fertilizer attachment G-RE-60, for use with the seed drill, enabled the farmer to place fertilizer adjacent to the drills of seed, thus ensuring a more effective utilization of the chemical fertilizer. The pressed steel hopper had a capacity of about 3cwt (153kg) of material and had a rotating-plate feed system, each plate being driven by bevel gears from a shaft running the width of the machine. This shaft was in turn gear-driven from the existing land wheel driven gears. Three possible combinations of gear speeds were available, and this, combined with the eleven gate-notch settings provided on the control shutters, gave a very wide range of application rates, from 110lbs to 1200lbs per acre (124 to 1347kg per hectare). A special gear wheel was available to reduce this output to the low figure of 56lbs per acre (62kg per hectare). An agitator was offered as an accessory, to help ensure the smooth flow of fertilizer material.

There were also seed planters designed for overseas application. For the potato grower there was the planter type P-PE-B20, which had to be used with the ridger R-DE-20 already mentioned. When this combination is used, a balance spring must be emplyed in conjunction with the top link. The planter basically consisted of a double hopper with open troughs at either

A posed shot of the Ferguson potato planter with fertilizer attachment, P-PE-B20 and P-RE-20 respectively.

side. A pair of operators sat either side of the hopper at 90 degrees to the line of travel, facing each other but screened from view by the hopper! A metal clicker wheel ran behind the offside ridger; it had a series of cams set on its side, arranged at different radii. A bicycle-type bell with a clanger was mounted on a slot adjacent to the cams, so that as the wheel turned, the bell struck, which was the signal for each operator to drop a potato down the chute into the bottom of the ridge just created – a repetitive task yet one requiring total concentration.

This simple but rather labour-intensive implement was fine for non-chitted potatoes, and Ferguson engineers then went on to develop a planter, D-PE-C20, suitable for chitted seed. The general arrangement was similar, but the hopper was dispensed with,and the two operators were seated facing forwards in line with the direction of travel. The chitted seed potatoes were carried in standard-size wooden trays on racks attached to the frame. A tray was positioned facing each operator, and a further frame was carried each side on an extended bracket for spare or empty trays. A fertilizer attachment, P-RE-20, could be added to the outfit, holding 190lbs (86kg) of material. The drive for this was taken from a special sprocket bolted to the nearside rear wheel of the tractor. Different combinations of sprocket sizes enabled application rates to be varied. If we do some quick sums, we find that the total rear-mounted weight of the machine plus seed potatoes, fertilizer, two operators (at say 168lbs/76kg each), comes to something like 900lbs (408kg), which is just about the lift capacity of the TE20 hydraulics, so front wheel weights were essential.

PLANT CULTIVATION: WEEDING AND THINNING

Moving on to the subject of growing crops and the implements that were offered by Ferguson for the purpose, the first to be considered is the weeder M-KE-A21. It is worth remembering that in the late 1940s and early 1950s selective weed-killing sprays were in their infancy. Selective hormone weedkillers for corn crops were available, and the manufacturers lost no time in advertising them and promoting their widespread use. Their use of course gained momentum over the years, but now, thankfully, people are questioning their long-term effects, not only on those who consume this chemically

Ferguson weeder M-KE-A21 in a fenland setting. The old battledress jacket and beret were common working wear at the time.

polluted food, but also on the ecology of the soil. This implement, which is 13ft (3.96m) wide and folds for transport to 9ft 7in (2.92m), is again three-point linkage mounted, with a balance spring fitted adjacent to the top link. The 71 delicately sprung tines are 21in (533mm) long and are set 2.5in (64mm) apart, flicking young weeds clear of the soil without damaging the more fully established crop. The weeds' roots, exposed to a dry atmosphere, soon die, and with the soil lightly aerated the crop is encouraged to develop. The weeder had a very light draft, so third gear could be used. Ferguson claimed one of these machines could cover 100 acres (40 hectares) per day. Not surprisingly this efficient implement is much sought after today by organic growers, who by the very nature of their commitment do not use chemical sprays.

The implement that naturally follows the weeder is the four-, five- or six-row crop thinning machine. 4P-KE-20 was the designation for the four-row machine, which was developed with input from the National Institute of Agricultural Engineering at Wrest Park and was manufactured by Salopian. One should recall that prior to the development of this machine row crops such as sugar beet, mangolds, turnips, swedes and kale had to be thinned by hand-hoeing. This was before the advent of the precision seeding that we have today for these crops. The machine was three-point linkage mounted, and only needed the tractor driver to operate it. It was fitted with a pointer made of spring steel to the front axle and a steerage fin on the implement itself, as accuracy was the key to the successful use of this implement.

The plants were thinned by tines fixed on a revolving head which was wheel driven through simple bevel gears from the land drive wheels of the machine. Each head unit was fitted with an adjustable depth control wheel, one for each row. By altering the number of tines fitted to each head, it was possible to achieve gapping distances of 28in, 14in, 9.5in, 7in, or 4.625in (711mm, 356mm, 241mm, 178mm or 117mm). The whole unit could be lifted clear for transport but was linked together, and was controlled by a hand lever, fitted conveniently close to the driver, to enable him mechanically to set the depth of work simultaneously for all the heads. A weight tray was fitted to enable ballast to be added it necessary.

As selective weed sprays were coming on to the market, Ferguson commissioned Pest Control of Cambridge to manufacture a low-volume crop sprayer for use with the TE20 tractor. This was designated S-LE-20 and was three-point linkage mounted, with a latch-type linkage top link that took the weight off the hydraulic system. The 45-gallon (205 litres) tank supplied liquid to a PTO-driven pump. On the output side was a filter and pressure regulator,

The Ferguson low-volume sprayer S-LE-20 attached to a TE.E20 (the narrow TVO model).

The Ferguson four-row crop thinning machine 4P-KE-20.

The Ferguson medium pressure sprayer S-LE-21, a very rare machine today.

A TE.H20 with the early-type loader L-VE-20 being used to fill a manure spreader type A-IE-A20.

with its gauge generally set at 40psi, supplying material to the spray booms. These folded down to horizontal for field work, giving a covering width of 19ft 6in (5.95m) through thirteen nozzles which could accommodate three different sizes of inserts to give application rates of 5, 10 or 20 gallons per acre (56, 112 or 225 litres per hectare). The spray booms were height adjustable from 18in to 33in (457mm to 838mm) and were spring loaded, so if an obstruction was hit they would safely swing back out of harm's way. This machine was very popular with cereal growers and sold in large numbers.

A more sophisticated machine was also marketed, this being the medium-pressure sprayer, aimed more at potato growers and at orchard owners for tree spraying. A hand-held lance was available. The machine was designated S-LE-21 and featured a 92-gallon (418 litres) tank feeding to a twin-cylinder pump that could deliver 16 gallons (72.7 litres) at 180psi. It was PTO driven at 500rpm through a set of three belts. Again a pressure regulator and gauge were fitted, likewise an inline filter. Unlike the low-volume sprayer, this one had the facility to suck water into the tank from a pond or river through a strainer. Inside the tank, an agitator was fitted to ensure that powder chemicals mixed with water did not separate out. The folding boom gave a spray cover width of 21ft 6in (6.55m), and application rates could be varied between 20 and 85 gallons per acre (225 and 955 litres per hectare). These were expensive, rather specialist sprayers which did not sell in great numbers and are very rare today. When loaded with chemical spray the outfit was very heavy, and front wheel weights A-TE-91 had to be fitted, likewise the stabilizer bars kit A-TE-59.

A TE.D20 fitted with the high lift loader M-UE-20, commonly known as the banana loader, doing the same job. Note the rear concrete weight.

PLANT CULTIVATION: SPREADING MANURE AND FERTILIZERS

In the range of implements for fostering the growth and establishment of plants, there was equipment for loading and spreading farmyard manure as well as manufactured chemical fertilizers. One implement offered in the early range was the manure loader L-VE-20, which was mounted on a pair of special brackets attached to the front axle (as was the hay sweep, discussed below). Two hydraulic cylinders of 1.5in (38mm) bore by 15in (381mm) stroke took their pressure from the tractor's own built-in pump, and raised the loader arms and fork to a height of 66in (1.68m), which was quite sufficient for loading muck spreaders. The eight fork tines were of high-carbon steel, heat-treated to resist abrasion and bending. The fork was spring-loaded, so that after dumping its load it returned to the latched position. Its capacity was normally rated at 600lbs (272kg) with a tear-out force of 1000lbs (454kg). To achieve this in practice, it was essential to fit a concrete counterbalance weight to the rear of the TE20, attached by two substantial hooks cast into it. This fitted to the tractor's three-point linkage automatic pick-up hitch A-TE-20. The driver could now pick up the weight on to the rear of the tractor without effort, load the spreader with the front-mounted fork, drop off the concrete balance weight, and with the pick-up hitch connect to the spreader draw bar - all accomplished without leaving the seat of the tractor. This was advanced agricultural engineering for its time, and although it may sound rather puny by today's standards, it was a big leap forward from a man with a dung fork.

Turning next to the manure spreader, the Ferguson A-JE-A20 was produced by J Shankey & Sons of Hadley Castle Works, Wellington, Shropshire. The machine was of fairly conventional design but it did feature an all-steel body of about 70 bushels (2.5cu m) capacity that tapered towards the front by 2in (51mm). The taper helped to loosen the muck as the floor slats, which were ratchet driven from the 750x20 land wheels, moved slowly rearwards. The land wheels also drove the two beater-bar assemblies and the spreading rear auger, which was made half left-handed and half right-handed, to give a spreading width of about 7ft (2.13m). The operation of the spreader was controlled by a single lever within easy reach of the driver. The top notch was the neutral position for travelling. The second notch engaged the beaters and rear auger only, the conveyor remaining stationary. The third notch engaged the conveyor and gave distribution of four loads per acre (ten loads per hectare). The remaining four notches gave increments, each of four loads per acre, to a maximum of twenty. Third gear was recommended as the best choice when working.

As time went on, the early type manure loader was deemed to be rather weak and of inadequate lift capacity in terms of both weight and height, so Harry Ferguson engineers developed the high-lift loader M-UE-20 commonly known as the "banana loader", because of the profile of its lift arms, which were made from pressed fabricated steel. This loader was manufactured by Steel's Engineering Products Ltd of Crown Works, Sunderland. It had a maximum lift height of 11ft (3.35m) compared to the 5-6ft (1.52-1.83m) of the L-UE-20, and a maximum load of 1000lbs (454kg) as opposed to 600lbs (272kg) of the earlier model. Again the concrete balance weight and pick-up hitch were essential for successful operation. A nice feature was that a third ram was provided, to push a spring-loaded plate on the forks; this allowed control of the dumping of materials into a spreader or trailer. This cantilever-type loader was pivoted on a substantial frame positioned over the rear axle. The ram attachment was about a quarter of the way along its length, the lower ends of the rams attaching to a bracket mounted under the gearbox housing. An additional quadrant of smaller size had to be fitted to the left-hand side of the transmission housing; its function was to control a selector valve and it had three positions. The downward position diverted oil flow to the lift arm rams, the central position was neutral for transport, and upwards movement of the lever brought in the push-off ram circuit. The control of pressure-fed oil to the circuit was by the normal draft control lever. Ferguson engineers, who were anxious to protect the tractor's hydraulic system from shock loads imposed by loader operation, developed a patent valve bolted in place of the dipstick inspection plate on the right-hand side of the axle housing. This would blow off if pressure in excess of 2000psi developed within the system. In addition to recommending of the use of the concrete weight, it was suggested that the 400x19 tyres and wheels be changed to 600x16 due to the additional front axle loadings. No power steering kit was offered in those days! This was a good and popular loader.

A photograph taken in the Fletchamstead Highway engineering shop of the Massey-Harris-Ferguson mounted spinner broadcaster FE30 (721). What looks very much like an LTX is lurking in the background.

After the merger with Massey-Harris a three-point linkage fertilizer spinner broadcaster, FE-30, was made available to customers. This was very much based on Massey-Harris's MH721 trailed broadcaster, which was land wheel driven. The Ferguson version featured a hopper of 6.88cu ft (0.195cu m) with framework to connect to the tractor linkage, and built-in stands to assist parking. Drive was taken from the PTO through a rubber-jointed sliding shaft to a right-angle drive gearbox made of cast iron (and holding 1.5 pints/0.85 litres of oil). There were two vertical concentric drives: one drove the spinner plate at high speed, while the other drove the agitator at a relatively slow speed in the opposite direction. A regulating sliding tubular shutter controlled the rate of application. It was essential to use the stabilizer kit and front wheel weights with this implement. With wide variations in the nature of fertilizers, such as granular or powder types, it was rather hit and miss in practice, but experienced operators achieved good, even results. The author can remember using this machine for grass seeding by preliminary hand mixing of fertilizer and grass seed, a laborious process that would not find much favour today. Internally, the top of the hopper was braced with a tubular strut, and to this was welded a small triangle of flat steel in the midway position. This enabled paper and plastic sacks to be punctured and then torn open to discharge the contents into the hopper. It is believed that this was a patented feature, and it was certainly a nice alternative to dropping one's penknife into the fertilizer. A trailed version was also marketed.

The Ferguson buck rake being used on a cold winter's day. Note the drive for the Tractormeter adjacent to the dynamo.

MOWING AND HARVESTING

Turning our attention now to the range of crop harvesting implements that Ferguson marketed, the first to look at is the Ferguson agricultural mower 5A-EE-B2 with 5ft (1.52m) finger bar; a 6ft (1.83m) type was also available. This rear-mounted machine sold in large numbers and was deservedly popular; it was well-designed and, being PTO driven, drive was smooth and positive. Very early examples were imported from America; otherwise this mower was made for Ferguson by the Pressed Steel Company of Paisley near Glasgow. The centre bar could be raised and lowered by finger-tip control on the draft control lever. A wooden swathe board and stick were fitted as standard but, strangely, the parking stands were sold as an extra. If these were not fitted and used, mounting and demounting became a tractor driver's nightmare, and squashed fingers ensued! One helpful idea was that the stay bar for retaining the blade in the vertical transport position doubled as a puller for extracting the knife from the mower bed. While dealing with the mower, it is worth looking at an auxiliary piece of equipment designed to be used in conjunction with it. This, the game flusher PA-EE-20, was a rather unique device. It was mounted on the front of the tractor on brackets designed for the early manure loader, and the support bar carried nine adjustable chains terminating with cast-iron weights, rather like those used in sash windows. The idea was to scare game birds away before they were cut to pieces with the mower's knife. Very few were made, but this was nevertheless a nice idea to save game birds from a most unpleasant encounter.

The Ferguson side-delivery rake D-EE-20 was a beautiful design, very efficient in operation when compared to offerings from other makers of the day. Being rear mounted on the three-point linkage, transporting it was no problem apart from it being 9ft 11in (3.02m) wide. It was PTO driven, via a V-belt, so there was full power at all times to the rake and no risk from wheel slip, which often caused problems with other makes. Nevertheless, very few of these rakes were sold, and even fewer have survived. Normal operating speed was 4.5mph (7.2 km/h) in third gear. Where it was necessary to use a gear lower than third, as when dealing with a very heavy crop, a PTO speed reduction unit

The game flusher in the working position ahead of the mower.

FULLY EXTENDED IN WORKING POSITION

was available as an accessory. This was in effect a two-speed PTO unit, as both normal and reduced speeds were available from twin shafts projecting from the housing.

The grass having been cut, Ferguson offered a buck rake to collect and transport it to the silage clamp. The buck rake was not a Ferguson invention - that accolade goes to a pioneering farmer, Rex Patterson - but Ferguson engineers developed their own models, made of high quality materials. They were three-point linkage mounted, of course, and the fitment of the stabilizer kit was essential, as was the use of front wheel weights to maintain steering control on slopes. The buck rake was offered as a ten-tine model S-EE-20 7ft 2in (2.18m) wide, or with twelve tines (A-10-SEE) at 8ft 8in (2.64m) width. The weight of the twelve-tine model was 280lbs (127kg), and it had a rated carrying capacity of 750lbs (340kg). As well as providing the facility to raise the linkage and trip the tines to discharge the load, Ferguson design engineers incorporated a latch within the attachment linkage to take the load off the hydraulic system when travelling - a most worthwhile refinement since the shock loads transmitted to the system could be considerable. Apart from its primary design function, the buck rake quickly found many other uses around the farm: transporting hedge cuttings, straw bales or grain sacks, and even moving small wooden buildings such as hen runs.

A development of the buck rake by Ferguson engineers was the kale cut rake G-HE-20, an implement which as far as is known was not produced by any other organisation. It was 8ft (2.44m) wide, weighed 550lbs (250kg), and was basically a buck rake with triangular side panels, a reciprocating mower-type knife fitted to the ends of the tines, and PTO drive; again a stabilizer kit was needed, and front wheel weights were highly advisable. The special feature of the knife mechanism was that it was fitted with blunt-pointed fingers, and the knife sections were of the serrated type. The kale cut rake was attached in the normal way, but a Ferguson position control hitch was designed so that the tractor's lower links could be held in a number of positions, almost over the full length of their travel. For transport, a locking latch took the load off the hydraulic system. The method of operating was to lower the implement to the kale crop, set the height of cut, engage the PTO-driven knife and reverse gear, and drive at full throttle into the kale! By this expedient one could collect a full load of cut kale in a run of 10 to 12 yards (9 to 11m). Farm workers of fifty-odd years ago must have been very grateful when the gaffer lashed out and bought one of these luxury implements. Cutting kale 4ft (1.2m) high by hand on a cold, wet winter's day and loading it onto a trailer is not anybody's idea of fun!

An early implement that soon fell by the wayside and hence is very rare today was the hay sweep S-EE-21. Hay sweeps were common implements before the arrival of the pick-up baler on the hay field. They generally fitted to the front of a tractor or powerful old car, and were used to sweep hay windrows to a stationary baler strategically placed in the field. The hay was then hand forked into the baler. An alternative method was to sweep the hay to an elevator, into which it was hand-fed to be stacked. Haystacks with a crudely thatched roof of wheat straw were once a common sight in the English countryside. It is not surprising to find that the Ferguson hay rake was different from other makes in that the design was equipped with tines made of aluminium alloy for strength and lightness. The sweep fitted to brackets which were the same as were used for the weight frame and early manure loader, and which bolted to the front axle. It could be raised almost to the vertical for transport, achieved by a simple linkage connected to the rear lift arms of the tractor – yet another neat example of finger-tip control.

HARVESTING POTATOES AND BEETS

The Ferguson potato spinner D-HE-20 was manufactured by Steel's Engineering Products. This implement was desirable and popular because it represented a big leap forward from previous trailed wheel-driven machines that would jam up in wet ground conditions. An earlier version of the PTO-driven potato spinner was produced in Northern Ireland in the early 1940s, and would have fitted the Ford-Ferguson 9Ns that had been imported as part of the lend-lease arrangement. The D-HE-20 is three-point linkage mounted, and a rocker extension is fitted to the top to improve depth control. The stabilizer kit had to be installed. Incorporated into the PTO drive was a spring-loaded dog clutch, a safety measure to prevent damage to the machine. Drive was fed into a cast-aluminium gearbox through bevel gearing, with

Potato spinner D-HE-20 in action, possibly at Stoneleigh Park.

output to the main spinning wheel. This carries tines, is inclined at about 45 degrees to the vertical, and is responsible for flicking the potato tubers out of the soil. It rotates in a clockwise direction. A second disk carrying tines of a curved design rotates counter-clockwise and is also set at 45 degrees to the vertical, facing outwards by about the same amount. In operation, potatoes hit this rotating assembly and are relieved of any remaining adhering soil. They are confined by a curtain of hessian material hanging off a projecting arm. This results in neat rows of dug potatoes, ready for hand collecting into buckets - a good old-fashioned back-breaking job!

The Ferguson beet lifters made use of the toolbar frame, either the 1L-HE-20 single-row, or the 2L-HE-20 double-row. These implements were designed and produced with the intention of lifting sugar beet, but carrots and some other root crops such as parsnips could be successfully lifted. The principle of operation was that the 15.5in (394mm) diameter disc coulter running either side of the crop row would cut the soil, which in turn enabled the high carbon steel share to lift the crop and soil to a raised level, and thus enable a hand picker to collect the crop. The single-row model had an overall width of 34in (864mm) and a weight of 190lbs (86kg), while the two-row model had an overall width of 86in (2184mm) and weighed 360 lbs (163kg).

The beet topper L-HE-21 was developed to cut the cost of beet harvesting, with a low capital cost. Complete beet-harvesting machines were around in the mid 1950s, but due to their complexity they were expensive and beyond the reach of the smaller grower. The main frame of the Ferguson machine is an inverted U-section channel which at its front supports a transverse axle, carrying on the off-side a land drive wheel. The land wheel axle has a sprocket on the near-side which transmits drive to the feeler wheel by chain. The feeler wheel, mounted centrally at the rear, is comprised of four serrated rings. The cutting knife is mounted on a parallel linkage below the feeler wheel at 45 degrees to the direction of travel. As the feeler wheel rotates at a slightly higher speed than the forwards travel, it can ride the beet and hold it steady as the top is cut off at ground level. On the forward part of the frame are two adjustable foliage deflectors, mounted on guide shoes. The machine worked fairly well in good conditions, but it is understood that it never really made it into production. Only about five are believed to have been sold, so it is very rare today.

The cordwood saw A-LE-19 in action. This is the early type with angular saw guard. The trailer appears to be a very early example with drop-down sides and the channel steel chassis flanges facing outwards. On later production models they faced inwards.

OTHER FARMING JOBS

The early type of Ferguson logging saw was A-LE-19 and later became the A-LE-20. Both were basically similar and very popular, and were produced for Harry Ferguson by Robert Watson and Co Ltd of High Street, Boston, Lincolnshire. The concept of a tractor-mounted logging saw must be another Ferguson first. The blade, of 30in (762mm) diameter, ran at 1200rpm, being driven from the PTO via the Ferguson belt pulley attachment A-TE-66. It turned in roller bearings and was protected by a guard. A light cradle of steel and wood construction was spring counterbalanced and pivoted; the log to be cut was placed on this, and the operator then advanced the cradle into the blade to cut the log. Tensioning of the belt is achieved by a threaded adjuster between an A-frame on the saw and a receiving bracket on the belt pulley. As the saw is raised the belt tension comes off, and the blade slows down and eventually stops. An excellent safety feature, if only it stopped at once! They thought of almost everything, but as Health and Safety regulations advanced, a kit was produced that guarded the pulleys and the saw blade shaft.

The Ferguson winch W-UE-20. Note the fold-down parking stands.

An implement in the tidying-up category is the Ferguson linkage winch W-UE-20, manufactured by The Scottish Mechanical Light Industries Ltd, although some people believe they were produced by Hesford's of Orskirk. Perhaps both firms were involved. Like most Ferguson-designed implements, it was three-point linkage mounted, and required the fitment of a stabilizer kit. The winch is PTO-driven to a worm reduction gearbox. Drive to the cable drum via a cone friction clutch is controlled by a hand lever within easy reach of the driver. A similar lever controls the external-contracting brake on the winch drum. A tip-down sprag was fitted to

The Ferguson earth leveller and blade terracer with the adjustable top link that was supplied with these implements. In this shot the operator is not using a second levelling box on the left-hand side as per instruction book!

restrain the tractor when winching, and two fold-down parking stands were provided. This handy piece of equipment had a rated pull of 7000lbs (3178kg) and a rope speed of 50ft (15.2m) per minute. It was supplied as standard with 40ft (12.2m) of rope but could accommodate up to 100ft (30.5m). It was priced at £83 in 1953.

Also in the tidying-up category is the earth leveller and blade terracer B-FE-20. Again this implement was designed for a wide range of uses, such as creating shallow surface drains, levelling areas of soil, or digging silage pits. It was three-point linkage mounted and required the use of the stabilizer kit A-TE-20. Ferguson recommended wide track settings to the rear wheels, and the fitment of a levelling box on the left-hand side of the linkage, as a convenient expedient to gain more angle on the blade tilt. The terracer was supplied with a turnbuckle-type top link, to enable pitch adjustments to be conveniently made. Farmers found these came in handy with other implements, but their indiscriminate use was probably frowned upon by Ferguson.

The two compressors marketed by Ferguson are discussed in Chapter 9 on industrial models, likewise the Beresford irrigation pump.

The Ferguson earth mover 708 was probably introduced around 1954, just into the Massey-Harris-Ferguson era. At this time, mechanical earth-moving was the job of big, heavy and expensive machines. The concept of this implement was to make powered bulldozing available to the owner of a TE20 at a very affordable price. The front blade was concave and 5ft (1.5m) wide, and could be angled to either side; the pitch of the blade was also adjustable, with settings for 6 degrees or 12 degrees in either direction. Scarifer tines could be added as an

The Hydrovane compressor A-UE-20 complete with both large and small reciprocating hand-held hedgecutting blades.

The Ferguson hammer mill H-LE-A20 set up on a TE.F20.

accessory. The blade was mounted on a fabricated bracket attached to the engine front mounting bolts. The fitment of stabilizer brackets A-TE-59 was essential. The raising and lowering of the front blade was achieved by the tractor's lower lift arms, operating through a linkage system to the front blade. The tractor's

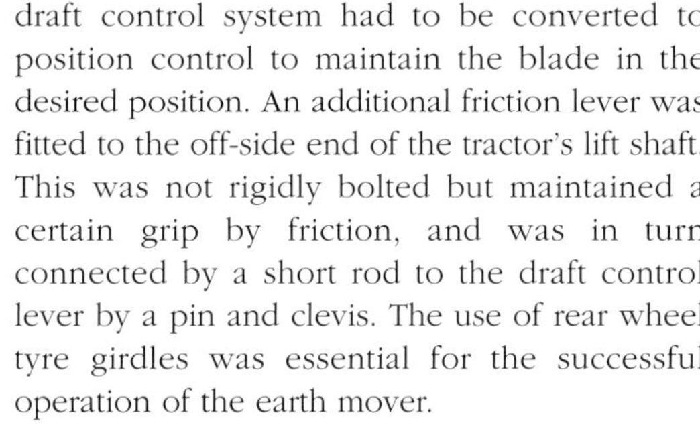

draft control system had to be converted to position control to maintain the blade in the desired position. An additional friction lever was fitted to the off-side end of the tractor's lift shaft. This was not rigidly bolted but maintained a certain grip by friction, and was in turn connected by a short rod to the draft control lever by a pin and clevis. The use of rear wheel tyre girdles was essential for the successful operation of the earth mover.

The earth scoop B-JE-A20, priced at £12.10s in 1951, was a handy and cheap tool for a farm to have available for digging drainage channels and light earth-moving. The bucket has a capacity of 0.2cu yard (0.15cu m), and is lowered into the ground by the tractor three-point linkage; when full it is lifted, hydraulically transported, and then mechanically tipped by hand lever placed carefully close to the driver.

Another popular piece of farm equipment was the mounted hammer mill H-LE-A20 made for Ferguson by The Scottish Mechanical Light Industries Ltd of Ayr. This was three-point linkage mounted for convenience, and driven by belt from the pulley attachment. It was suggested that a curved extension pipe should be fitted to the tail of the horizontal exhaust, to prevent charring of the drive belt. The top link had to be fitted with an adjusting rack to hold the yoke that could be set to take the weight off the tractor's

The Ferguson earth scoop B-JE-A20 fitted to a very early TE.A20, identified by its vertical oil filter and the riveted joint on the aluminium bonnet side panels.

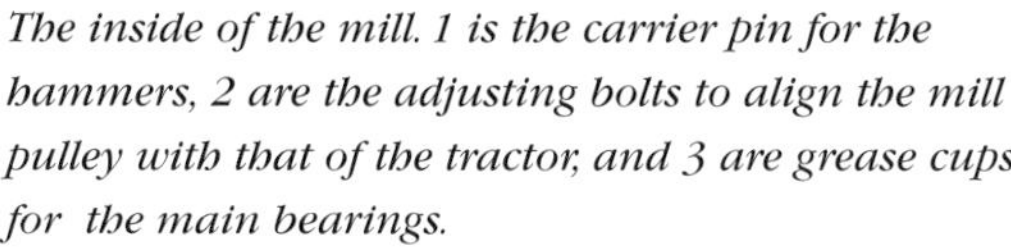

The inside of the mill. 1 is the carrier pin for the hammers, 2 are the adjusting bolts to align the mill pulley with that of the tractor, and 3 are grease cups for the main bearings.

hydraulic system during transport. Previously, hammer mills were fixed to the barn floor, and the tractor had to be carefully aligned to the mill to ensure that the flat belt did not run off the pulleys. These hammer mills worked on the principle of attrition. Basically, the hammers were swivel-mounted on the centre hub, and, running at the high speed of 3000rpm with the TE20 engine running flat-out, the hammers would fly out under centrifugal force and force the material being ground through a substantial sieve. The resulting meal was blown into a cyclone hopper to discharge the air. As well as grinding cereals and beans, other materials such as hay and straw could be dealt with. A metal and stone eliminator was fitted – a wise design feature. With economy of materials in mind each hammer had four cutting edges which could be used before renewal was necessary. Interestingly, Ferguson marketed two other models of static hammer mill, these being the only Ferguson implements that do not attach to the tractor. They were driven by electric motors, of either 3bhp (single-phase) or 5bhp (three-phase).

A hugely popular Ferguson attachment, and possibly another first, was the ubiquitous link box, which is still much sought after today. This simple device, designated T-JE-A20, attached to the lower links only, and had the great advantage that its floor could be lowered to ground level for loading heavy objects such as steel milk churns, which when full to 10 gallons (45 litres) weighed in excess of 133lbs (60kg). The link box could lift and carry five churns. Ferguson marketed a barrow attachment for the link box, enabling it to be pushed or pulled by hand (if

The electromatic hammer mill and cyclone (726) from the early MHF era.

The Ferguson link box F-JE-A20 fitted with the wheelbarrow conversion kit TE-JE-90.

The 3-ton tipping trailer F-JE-A30, retrospectively known as the Mark I.

Below: The rather cumbersome but effective coupling system of the Mark I trailer.

Below right: Lower attachment point of the coupling, which was in fact the draw bar.

you had the strength). It was mounted on a pair of 16x4 pneumatic tyres. A development of the link box was the transporter T-JE-21, which was three-point linkage mounted and needed the stabilizer kit. It was 68.5in (1.74m) wide, 35.25in (0.9m) deep and 27.25in (0.7m) high, and had detachable rear and side panels. It was available in both tipping and non-tipping versions, and was rated to carry 7cwt (356kg).

The 3-ton tipping trailer F-JE-40 was a handy piece of transport equipment and was another Ferguson first, featuring the concept of transferring some the load of the trailer to the rear wheels of the tractor, thus gaining additional traction. Early examples of this concept can be seen in the Ford-Ferguson era, but these 3-ton trailers were marketed in 1947. Although the principle of weight transference was undoubtedly effective, the method of connection of trailer to tractor was awkward and cumbersome to say the least - acceptable perhaps in a nice level concrete yard, but certainly not in a deeply

mudded yard. This type of 3-ton trailer has retrospectively become known as the Mark 1.

Harry Ferguson and his customers were not happy with this cumbersome coupling system, so Ferguson asked Theo Sherwen, who was a talented industrial designer and inventor of the time, to accept a commission to improve the system. The story goes that Harry Ferguson gave him a week to come up with a workable design that met the required parameters. This was achieved, and we have to thank Theo for what has now become the norm in tractor-trailer coupling even to this day, with only slight modification and development. Theo Sherwen's novel design basically used a hinged hook located under the centre of the rear axle which was raised and lowered by the tractor's lift arms; there was a built-in latching mechanism. This took the weight off the tractor's hydraulic system when the trailer was attached. All the driver had to do from his seat to attach a Ferguson trailer or muck spreader, fitted with a ring to the draw bar and a suitable prop stand, was to lower the hook and align it under the ring by carefully manoeuvring his tractor, then lift the draft control lever until the latch engaged, lower the linkage slightly, and drive off. This was such a big leap forward that a conversion kit F-JE-98 was offered to convert the Mark 1 type trailer to the improved model, which was designated F-JE-A30 (non-tipping) and type F-JE-A40 (with hydraulic tipping).

These trailers were very similar to the early models, with internal body size of 9ft 10.5in (3m) by 6ft 4in (1.93m), and lift-out front and sides 14.5in high (368mm), while the tailboard was hinged at floor level. By this time the floors and sides of trailers were made of keruing, a quality hardwood, and the sturdy chassis was fabricated from hot-rolled steel section of well-

A TE.T20 coupled to an industrial 3-ton tipping trailer of the MHF era.

The road springs and quarter mudguards fitted to these trailers. Earlier models had 12 wheel studs, later models five.

The brake lever of the 30cwt tipping trailer is easily accessible to the driver.

engineered proportions. The draw bar with ring hitch was fabricated from heavy pressed steel in two sections welded together. The axle and running gear were very well dimensioned, and 7.50x16 eight-ply tyres were fitted on rims with a twelve-stud fixing to the hub; later trailers had five studs. A parking brake was fitted with the control lever within easy reach of the driver. It operated on 12in (305mm) diameter brakes, and could be applied when descending steep hills. Provision was made for the fitting of the axle in two alternative positions, either on the rear of the trailer, giving maximum weight transference to the tractor, or 18in (457mm) further forward, for tipping into pits or to give greater manoeuvrability. All in all, these trailers were a very successful addition to the Ferguson System, and many thousands were sold.

By 1953 Ferguson were marketing a 30cwt (1525kg) tipping and non-tipping trailer, models L-JE-40 and L-JE-30 respectively. The chassis was fabricated from cold-pressed steel sections, and on the tipping version the lift cylinder was positioned horizontally in the chassis, actuating a tipping arm pivoted on the chassis. This arm was connected to a short length of multi-link chain connected to a stirrup that surrounded the lift cylinder. At the far end of the tipping arm were two rollers which pushed up on the underside of the trailer floor as the hydraulic cylinder was extended by the tractor's built-in pump. The trailer body was of sheet steel and able to hold 1.5cu yd (1.15cu m) of material. The tailboard hinged down and was detachable. As the body sat between the wheels (which were shod with 4.50x16 tyres) the floor was only 21in (533mm) above ground level. The empty trailer weighed 9cwt (458kg). These neat and compact trailers were a boon on small farms more geared to the horse and cart, but they also found wide acceptance with municipal authorities for park maintenance and similar jobs.

The detachable tailboard of the Ferguson 30cwt tipping trailer L-JE-30. The curved tops of the inclined side panels show up well.

The Ferguson post-hole digger type D-FE-20 was a development of an earlier implement made in America during the Ford-Ferguson era, and was probably another Ferguson first. The British version was made for Ferguson by Steel's Engineering Products Ltd. The implement was three-point linkage mounted to raise and lower it, while the drive to the boring auger was taken from the PTO through a universally-jointed driveshaft to a double-bevel gearbox whose casing was made of high-strength aluminium alloy. It was claimed that the machine could dig holes to a depth of 3ft (0.9m) in approximately 30 seconds, fourteen times faster than by hand! Initially 9in (229mm) and 12in (305mm) augers were available, but later a 6in (152mm) and 18in (457mm) sizes were added. The latter was ideal for tree-planting schemes. Stabilizers had to be fitted when using this implement to eliminate sideways movement. The instruction book recommended that if an auger became stuck in a stone or tree root, it was to be wound out in the reverse direction by using the Ferguson spanner on the rectangular section of the PTO – a well thought-out expedient.

Another Ferguson implement which has remained elusive is the 3in (76mm) self-priming irrigation pump 6PP-LE-20, made by Beresford. This was mounted in a cradle and attached to the three-point linkage, and was driven by the PTO pulley attachment A-TE-66 via a 5in (127mm) wide flat belt. It required the use of stabilizer kit A-TE-590. Performance was impressive: with the engine running at 1500rpm pump pulley speed would be 1400rpm, giving 1000 gallons (4546 litres) per minute with a 5ft (1.52m) suction and 5ft delivery head.

The cult harrow was a cultivation implement that was ahead of its time, but whether this was marketed by Ferguson is uncertain. It is illustrated in an industrial Ferguson brochure of the Massey-Harris-Ferguson period, showing it mixing scarified road metal following the application of cold bitumen emulsion by pressure tanker – but its design intention was as a power hammer. The machine is three-point linkage mounted and PTO driven via a conventional Hardy Spicer jointed shaft to a twin-belt drive system to give a step-up in speed. This was very similar to the drive used on the Ferguson mower 5A-EE-B20. Drive is then to a crank connected to a pitman which causes the front and rear tine bars to oscillate in opposite directions. The sideways oscillation causes a power harrowing effect which, coupled with the forward movement of the tractor, can achieve a fine seed bed rapidly. Each of the twenty-four tines is rubber-mounted to the carrier bars to absorb shock loads. This cult harrow was made by Horstman Ltd of Bath.

Post hole digger D-FE-20. There is a strange addition to the top of the hydraulic cover assembly.

Rear view of the cult harrow showing the guard concealing the twin belts which with suitably sized pulleys provides a reduction from PTO speed. The crank imparts a forward and backward movement to the pitman, which links to the rear tine bar. Three linking bars centrally pivoted on the main frame transmit an oscillating movement to the front tine bar.

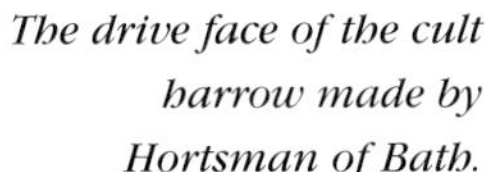

The drive face of the cult harrow made by Hortsman of Bath.

The rear-mounted Handy Loader, made by Cameron Gardner of Reading, fitted to a TE.A20.

To round off this chapter, I shall look at some implements, and a control system, which never reached the production stage but may well have been prototypes or precursors to implements that did eventually form part of the Ferguson line-up. I have seen photographs dated 1950 clearly showing what is obviously a prototype for what became the high-lift loader. The lift arms are fabricated from what looks like pressed channel steel. There was hydraulic tipping of the dung fork or mangold bucket. The front wheel centres were stronger, and Dunlop Land/Road tyres were fitted. The photographs show the evolution of the pivot point mounting bracket, to a design very close to the one used in the production version of the high-lift loader M-UA-20.

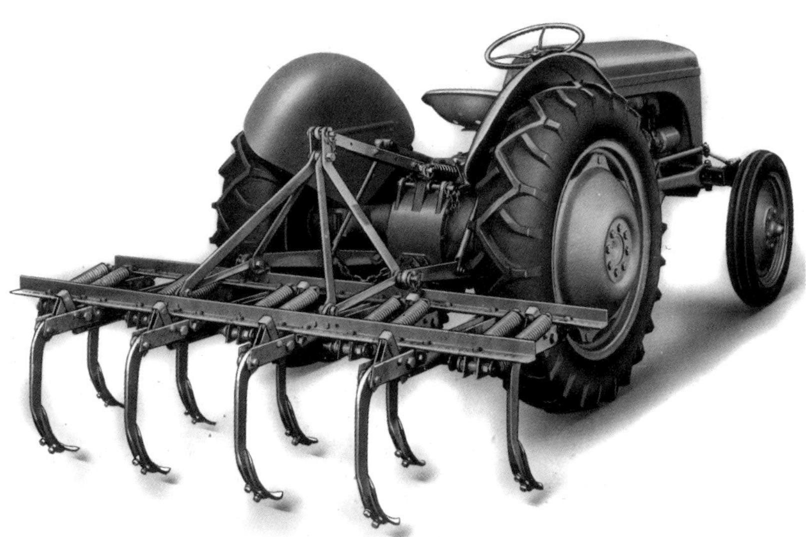

The Ferguson nine-tine spring-loaded tiller 9-BE-20.

Another loader which was developed but as far as is known, never reached production, is the Ferguson single-jack front end loader designated S-HE-20. The information on this loader is taken from Ferguson publication FP519/300/7/54, in the series *Information Vital to Your Business* issued to dealers in advance of marketing. From the above code, we deduce that 300 copies were printed in July 1954, so this development came after the high-lift loader M-UE-20 which was introduced to the farming community in around October 1952. Ferguson engineers made it quite clear that this loader did not have the high-lift capacity of M-UE-20, but was limited to a lift height of 8ft 2in (2.49m). Simplicity was the keynote of the design, with a single hydraulic ram positioned under the belly of the tractor, a pair of fabricated lifting arms, and attachment to the tractor at three major points. An isolator valve was positioned in the hydraulic circuit, to enable the lift arms to be locked off in any desired position. Other advantages of this design were the ease of attachment and detachment, the ability to lift 12.5cwt (636kg), and a low pivot point to the lift arms which gave better stability. On the downside, Alan Stanley recalls driving a TE20 fitted up with this loader and finding that very soon the tractor tended to bottom out, as the mud and muck got deeper in the stock yard!

Conceived as a means of direct reseeding, a seeding attachment for fitment to the 9-BE-20 spring-loaded tiller was developed, very much with the export market in mind. The pressed steel seed hopper had a capacity of 4.5cu ft (0.127cu m). Eleven adjustable apertures were located within the hopper through which seed fell by gravity via reinforced rubber tubes to special boots fixed to each tine. Provision was made to divide the hopper into eleven separate compartments, each with an independent regulating control lever. An ingenious design enabled the regulator levers to close each time the implement was lifted, and then revert to their original settings when the implement was lowered into the soil. Of course the width of drills could be varied by moving the tine spacing on the frame in increments of 1in (25mm) with a minimum setting of 7in (178mm). The "wavy" disc agitators were driven from a forward-mounted land wheel which helped to maintain constant depth – a rare use of a depth wheel on a Ferguson implement.

The rick lifter S-EE-22 was built upon the buck rake tubular frame, strengthened to deal with the greater loads incurred when transporting ricks of 9ft (2.74m) diameter. Six tubular steel tines are fixed to the frames, reinforced to resist bending while still having a degree of flexibility. The outstanding feature of the rick lifter design is its ability to lift from the ground loads in excess of the limitations of the tractor's hydraulic lift system. Bulky loads of 11cwt (559kg) can be dealt with by finger-tip control. This is achieved by using an auxiliary hydraulic arrangement, operating in conjunction with the tractor's lift system. The first stage is to lift the front end of the implement by the tractor lift links, the rake pivoting about the tine points on the ground. The height of lift is restricted by a telescopic carrying link arresting the movement of the lift links before the pump shut-off point is reached. Oil from the tractor pump is then directed through a stop valve connected to the control lever, into a small contracting ram used in place of the normal top link attachment. Movement of this ram's piston pivots the implement about the lower link attachment pins, and so raises the tines and the load. By lowering the control lever, the auxiliary hydraulic system becomes a closed circuit supporting the load with the latch of the mechanical telescopic link, thereby relieving the tractor's hydraulic system of strain and damage in transport. With all this overhanging load, front wheel weights were essential: A-TE91 for loads of up to 7cwt (356kg), and for the full capacity of 9cwt (458kg), the front-mounted weight tray and weights A-TE-131. Alternative tines were available to convert the rick lifter to a hay sweep.

The hydraulic engineering firm of E & G Norbury near Redditch in Worcestershire produced the "Mowless" bale loader of patented design number 76691. These were designed to fit a range of tractors including the Ferguson TE20 range, and were priced at £34.10s for the petrol and TVO models, while a bale loader for the TE.F20 diesel cost £35.5s. This was mounted directly on the tractor and used the movement of the lift arm on the near side through a mechanical linkage, the lower link having been removed. As an alternative, it was possible to buy the loader with its own built-in ram, when the complete package was priced at £42.17s.6d. Choosing this model meant that the tractor's linkage could be used, which was pretty necessary if one was using a Ferguson 3-ton trailer with extensions for carting bales. The Ferguson automatic pick up hitch was essential when using this trailer.

Finally, mention must be made of a prototype depth control system that was experimented with for the TE20 tractor. What appears to be a spring-loaded jockey wheel attached to the implement, but having an arm making contact with the tractor, gives reference to the relative movement that is transmitted via a Bowden cable to the tractor draft control level: but this is all open to individual interpretation!

Rick lifter S-EE-22. Note the assistor hydraulic ram in place of the top link.

Haysweep S-EE-21. The twelve tines appear to be longer than those of the buck rake and there is the pair of shorter upward-pointing tines.

Chapter Twelve

Options and Accessories

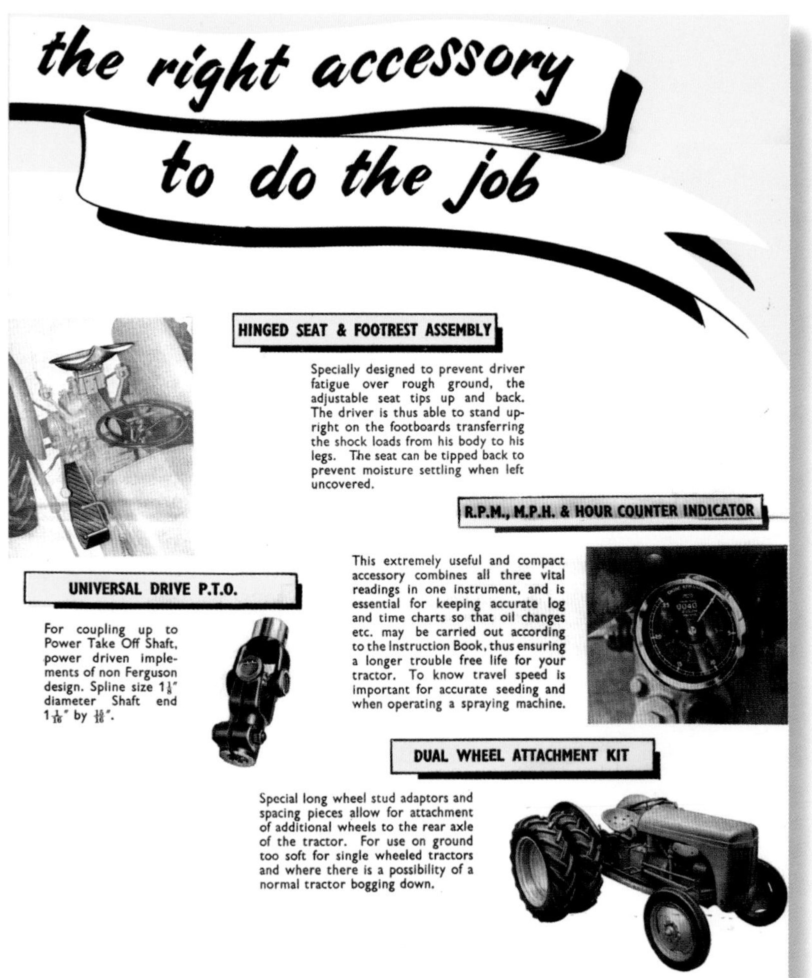

the right accessory to do the job

HINGED SEAT & FOOTREST ASSEMBLY

Specially designed to prevent driver fatigue over rough ground, the adjustable seat tips up and back. The driver is thus able to stand upright on the footboards transferring the shock loads from his body to his legs. The seat can be tipped back to prevent moisture settling when left uncovered.

R.P.M., M.P.H. & HOUR COUNTER INDICATOR

This extremely useful and compact accessory combines all three vital readings in one instrument, and is essential for keeping accurate log and time charts so that oil changes etc. may be carried out according to the Instruction Book, thus ensuring a longer trouble free life for your tractor. To know travel speed is important for accurate seeding and when operating a spraying machine.

UNIVERSAL DRIVE P.T.O.

For coupling up to Power Take Off Shaft, power driven implements of non Ferguson design. Spline size 1$\frac{1}{8}$" diameter Shaft end 1$\frac{1}{16}$" by $\frac{15}{16}$".

DUAL WHEEL ATTACHMENT KIT

Special long wheel stud adaptors and spacing pieces allow for attachment of additional wheels to the rear axle of the tractor. For use on ground too soft for single wheeled tractors and where there is a possibility of a normal tractor bogging down.

A page from a Ferguson accessories brochure.

In an attempt to meet customer needs and requirements to the full, and to maximise the profit as well as the kudos that would accrue to the organisation, Ferguson offered its customers a wide range of options and accessories that they could use to tailor their tractors and implements precisely for the duties to which they put them. This could only increase the sense of satisfaction felt by customers. Of course, this is what any business should strive to do. Harry Ferguson, being the perfectionist that he was, no doubt endorsed and fostered this aspect of sales promotion.

It should be remembered that the development of some of these products was customer-driven, because by the early 1950s the versatile TE20 was being used in more and more unconventional areas, away from the basic realm of agriculture. Likewise, outside manufacturers were not slow to climb on the bandwagon with their own versions of what they thought Ferguson owners would appreciate and buy.

In working through the options and accessories that were on offer I will confine myself to the period up to the demise of the TE20 series in 1956.

AIDS TO TRACTION

Ferguson tractors were promoted as having excellent traction when used with the Ferguson System implements and this was generally true, but often outfits were called upon to operate in terrain that was far from ideal, such as steep slopes, soft muddy ground, etc. To meet these special needs, a range of accessories was developed, mostly by Ferguson engineers in-house, but also by outside organisations. One of the most often used aids to traction was wheel girdles for the rear wheels, especially on the landside when ploughing. These girdles were

The Tamkin steel wheels used the TE20's wheel centres.

The Ferguson steel wheels AT-E-74, 40in diameter and with detachable lugs.

simple, light, and inexpensive at £9.10s in 1950. They were available in two widths, 10in and 11in (254mm and 279mm), under part numbers A-TE-89 and A-TE-89A respectively, to suit the tyre size fitted to the tractor. To fit a pair of tyre girdles, they were laid flat on the ground and the tractor driven up on to them. The driver then wrapped them around the rear wheels, pulled the ends together with a simple lever tool provided with the kit, and bolted together the end sections. These girdles were manufactured for Ferguson by Donaldson at Linwood near Paisley in Scotland. Shay of Basingstoke produced their own version of the girdles, to a patented design.

For extreme ground conditions, 10in (254mm) wide steel rear wheels A-TE-74,

Ferguson wheel girdles, made by Donaldson.

A TE.D20 fitted with tyre tracks A-TE-113.

The special spacer plate and extended studs developed to enable the fitment of dual wheels, used as an aid to flotation and stability. The kit was marketed under product code A-TE-78.

The spring tensioning device for the tyre tracks also incorporates a hydraulic damper.

The front idler tyre, which is of 500x15 size.

without centres but with bolt-on lugs, were available to fit in place of the normal rear wheels with pneumatic tyres, and were priced at £26 for a pair. Ferguson never offered steel front wheels. For special row-crop work, steel rear wheels of skeleton type were available under part number A-TE75. Another type of skeleton wheel was available from Tamkins of Chelmsford, who made the rather bold claim that they "trebled the pulling power of your Ferguson."

Allman produced narrow pneumatic rear wheel assemblies featuring 400x32 tyres. Opperman, Darville & Stanhay produced their own design of wheel strakes to fit on the rear wheels of the TE20. The advantage of wheel strakes was that they could stay bolted to the rear wheels and be retracted for road work after a day's work in the field. An interesting method of aiding traction, flotation and stability, was the dual-wheel fitting kit, part number A-TE-78, that enabled a second standard rear wheel to be bolted to the outside of the existing wheel. Another expedient for gaining flotation and traction was the development of a simple, light and very effective half-track conversion kit, known as tyre tracks, part number A-TE-113, which was beneficial in snow, peat bogs, soft sand, and for forestry work. A development of this idea into a full track was successfully used by Edmund Hillary on his trip to the South Pole in 1956 (see Chapter 14).

Yet another attempt to gain traction was the development by Selene of Turin in Italy of a four-wheel drive conversion kit, discussed in detail in Chapter 10. The ultimate conversion to aid traction must be the full track kit made by Bryden of Lincolnshire, called Track Part. In this case front and rear tyres were dispensed with and the steering was locked up. A pair of drive sprockets and five idler rollers supported the lower side of the track, and a front roller spring tensioner kept the steel track taut. It was claimed that one man could fit this conversion in one and a quarter hours and take it off in one hour, to return the tractor to normal wheeled configuration, but this seems rather optimistic!

The front-mounted weight tray with axle brackets, part number A-TE-131.

It was found necessary with some of the heavier rear-mounted implements, such as the three-furrow plough, link box, hammer mill, medium volume sprayer, and loaded buck rake, to fit weights to the front of the tractor: this became essential if the tractor was working on steep gradients. There were two methods of attaching additional weight. An early expedient was a tray that bolted to the front axle, where the user could add weights at his discretion. Later, in 1950, specially-made front wheel weights were produced, to bolt on to the inside of the wheel discs. Earlier solid front wheel centres did not have the facility to accept these weights, but could be adapted by drilling the wheel centre. Weights were produced to fit 400x19, 600x16 and 500x15 wheels and tyres, with those for the 600x16 size made in two halves. Wheel weights were also produced to fit inside the rear wheel rims, but these generally were confined to industrial applications. Of course, another cheap method to gain wheel weight was to water-ballast the tyres, making sure that the appropriate amount of calcium chloride was added in winter to prevent freezing. It would be a rather hard ride with ice in the tyres!

Yet another aid to traction was the Ferguson concrete block, which was designed to complement the manure loader and the high-lift loader. It was slung by two hooks on the cross-member of the automatic pick-up hitch. Usually these weights were cast by the local dealer, with the necessary hooks supplied by Harry Ferguson Ltd.

AIDS TO DRIVER COMFORT AND SAFETY

Most of today's tractor cabs have all the "mod cons" – air conditioning with heating and cooling, hi-fi systems, adjustable air sprung seats, and cool boxes, but in the 1940s and 1950s this sort of luxury was not the norm for the agricultural tractor driver. Harry Ferguson never offered even a cab to owners of TE20s, yet he himself was quite well acquainted with the style and luxury of his Rolls-Royce and Bentley cars! It was left to outside manufacturers like Weathershields and Scottish Aviation, or sometimes to the farmer himself, to construct some crude weather protection for the TE20 driver. The manufactured cabs were very basic by today's standards and did not incorporate any roll-over protection for the driver; in the case of a tractor overturning the driver was bound to be crushed, as the light cab would have collapsed around him. He even lost the chance of being thrown clear. If these early proprietary cabs were fitted with the luxury of a windscreen wiper, it was usually hand cranked.

It is strange to consider that Ferguson engineering could come up with a footbrake parking latch design which would release the brake if you happened to step on the brake pedal as you climbed off the tractor. Yet on the other hand safety was to the fore in many other areas, such as the overload protection to stop the tractor rearing up if an implement struck an obstruction, or the starter operated by the gear-lever. It was left to outside manufacturers to correct this gross deficiency in the parking brake arrangements. Bulldog, Meadonian and Western Engine Products of Delabole, Cornwall offered proper handbrake levers which linked to the tractor's brakes, and held them firmly on, when set in the park position. Eventually Harry Ferguson did offer a spring-loaded parking latch

The light-alloy cab made by Scottish Aviation Ltd.

A handbrake lever manufactured by Meadonian for the Ferguson TE20 range. The small lever on the side of the main lever had two positions: handbrake out of use and handbrake operative for parking.

that could be installed in place of the previous hazardous one. This was issued under part number A-TE-12B.

As we all know, seating for tractor drivers in the late 1940s was pretty basic, with a pressed-steel pan seat mounted on a flat spring-steel C-bracket. Additional padding was traditionally provided by stuffing a bit of hay in a hessian sack. This was refined by Ferguson engineers by offering a seat cushion, part number A-TE-103, made of Sorbo rubber and covered in Rexine. A further refinement was the offer of a tip-up seat pan, which was standard on industrial tractors: why this discrimination against agricultural users? Also optional on the agricultural TE20s were foot steps, which again were considered essential for the industrial driver. Likewise on offer was a rear view mirror A-TE-2123, found as standard equipment on industrial tractors to comply with the Road Traffic Act.

The early lighting kit for the TE20 was produced by Joseph Lucas of Birmingham, the major supplier of electrical equipment to the British motor industry, so it was no surprise that they were called upon to produce a basic lighting kit that just met the then-current Road Traffic Act requirements. This comprised a centrally-mounted bonnet headlamp (type S575) and a pair of side lamps (type LD109A), mounted on folding brackets bolted to the front bonnet side panels. Rear lighting was provided by a Lucas flood light (type SFT575) and tail lamp (type AT201L). The change-over between these two was controlled by a Lucas dip switch (type FS22/1), and there was provision for a two-pin trailer plug. Later Road Traffic Acts demanded that two double-dipping headlamps and twin tail lamps be fitted. For those users wanting to have a horn on their tractor, the Lucas type HF1235 was usually specified.

A grey canvas tractor cover, part number A-TE-A68, was available; it was neatly tailored to fit over the bonnet, steering wheel and seat, and came complete with tie-down eyelets. Interestingly it featured a sewn-up pocket in the area of the central headlamp – the stitching could be cut to open the pocket and enable it to fit over the lamp.

Outside manufacturers produced a locking device to take the load off the hydraulic lift arm when it reached full height. This was quite

The "Bulldog" handbrake. When the lever is moved forward the pawl on the footbrake pedal engages with the toothed sector, so if foot pressure is applied to the pedal it is restrained from returning by the pawl. To release the brakes, move the lever to the rear and tap the pedal. This device must have saved a lot of Fergusons from running away.

A genuine Ferguson tractor cover A-TE-A68. Note the Ferguson logo towards the front. A pocket was provided in the cover to accommodate the central headlamp if fitted; if this facility was needed the stitching in that part had to be cut.

useful when transporting heavy loads or implements on the road. The PTO could then be put out of gear to save wear, in the confidence that the linkage-mounted load would not drop, nor would shock loads be imposed on the hydraulic system. This device was a good idea, and Nuffield incorporated it in some of their tractors, including the BMC Mini.

A short, slightly curved piece of pipe was available as an accessory to extend the exhaust system so that gasses were not directed at the belt pulley, heating up the belt being driven. Also in the area of exhaust systems, Ferguson offered a vertical exhaust silencer and elbow that bolted directly to the manifold and was steadied by a short steel bar bolted to one of the clutch housing bolts. Very often this was used to replace the standard down-swept system, and was essential if operators were behind the tractor – for instance on the potato planter or steerage hoe. It was also often fitted in markets with hot dry climates, such as Australia, where the standard arrangement was a potential fire hazard.

A tractormeter A-TE-93 became available which recorded hours worked with the engine running at 1500rpm. It also indicated engine speed and road speed in top gear in mph (or km/hour for export markets where required, part number A-TE-95). A special version for Diesel engines had a letter F in the part number, thus A-TEF-93. This instrument was driven by a flexible shaft from a pulley with a rubber tyre fitted to the dynamo shaft. It was a handy guide when using the compressors, sawbench, or crop sprayers and seeders, and for monitoring regular servicing. In a similar vein, but less sophisticated, was the Ferguson hour-meter T-AE127, which was strapped to the dynamo housing and was gear driven by a special cog fitted to the dynamo

An hour counter made by ENM (English Numbering Machines). It is gear driven off the dynamo shaft.

The Smiths Tractormeter A-TE-93 correctly mounted. On the left, the handbrake lever of this TE.T20 is just visible.

The Allman speedometer fitted to a Ferguson TE.E20. It is calibrated in mph and furlongs. Drive is taken from the inside tyre wall but can be put out of engagement by simply turning it out.

shaft. This instrument recorded one hour when the engine ran at 1500rpm, so it was possible to keep a check on engine service hours.

A speedometer for the TE20 was produced by the Allman Sprayer Company. It was friction-driven by small wheels 2.5in (64mm) in diameter, contacting the inside wall of the front tyre; a scraper was provided to prevent the build-up of mud. The housing for the speedometer and odometer was made of cast aluminium and it was bolted to the steering arm on the nearside of the tractor. The drive pulley bracket was spring-loaded on an over-centre linkage, so it could be swung away from the front tyre when not needed. Drive was taken from this wheel to the head by a flexible drive cable. The dial was 4in (102mm) in diameter and calibrated up to 20mph, while the odometer read in furlongs and chains. This actual instrument was made by Smiths of London. When these units were produced in the 1950s, they were priced at £12, or about the same price as a Ferguson earth scoop, so it is natural to assume that not many were sold, as most farmers preferred to save the cost and make do with guesswork. No metric equivalent was available.

ATTACHMENTS RELATED TO POWER APPLICATION

Outside manufacturers were the first to offer Ferguson owners a TVO (Tractor Vaporising Oil) conversion. As one would expect, Harry Ferguson personally preferred petrol, but with rising fuel costs TVO became the preferred option. Lawrence Edwards, Fishleigh, the Loddon Engineering Company (LEC), and Vapourmatic all produced TVO conversion kits. When eventually Ferguson engineering did concede to offer its customers a TVO conversion kit in 1950, it was well-engineered, and attempted to compensate for the slight loss of power when running on this lower-octane fuel (see also Chapter 4).

The kit was generally fitted at a time when a top overhaul was required, as the cylinder block had to be machined out to accept the slightly bigger liners. The kit basically consisted of replacement liners and pistons, with an increase in the bore from 80mm to 85mm, a thicker cylinder head gasket to lower the compression ratio to 4.8:1, and a thermostat with a hotter opening setting of 75 degrees C. The aluminium heat shield designed by Alex Senkowski was attached to the manifold by extended bolts and a pressed-steel base bracket. A temperature gauge was included, to fit into the blanked-off hole on the left side of the dash. To complete the kit, there was a flat tank holding about 0.75 gallons (3.4 litres) of petrol, to be used for starting purposes only. A 1948 TE.A20 petrol engine developed 23.9bhp, and when converted to run on TVO with the Ferguson kit it still produced 23.9bhp. Not a bad conversion!

One of the most popular accessories sold in the 1940s and 1950s was the belt pulley attachment A-TE-66. This unit could be bolted in three different positions relative to the rear axle housing, and fitted over the PTO shaft from which it took its drive. Clockwise or counter-clockwise rotation of the belt were both possible. The flat cast-iron pulley was 6.5in (165mm) wide and 9in (229mm) in diameter, and with the engine running at maximum 2000rpm, a pulley speed of 1358rpm was achieved, and a belt speed of 3190ft (972m) per minute. The reason for the belt pulley's popular appeal at the time was the fact that rural electrification was in its infancy, so most farmers only had lighting plants. For the operation of barn machinery which demanded more horse-

The Ferguson belt pulley assembly

BELT PULLEY ASSEMBLY

PART 1193

This unit is supplied as an accessory to the tractor and may be fitted or removed with ease in a few minutes.

Rotation may be obtained in either direction by mounting to the right or left of the rear axle centre.

power, the tractor equipped with a belt pulley was the obvious choice.

For some strange reason, the TE20 tractors, like the earlier Ford-Ferguson 9N, were equipped with a PTO shaft of 1.125in (29mm) diameter, rather than the usual SAE standard size of 1.375in (35mm). To overcome this anomaly, a Hooke-type joint, A-TE-8950, was offered which fitted the TE20 PTO spline of 1.125in and had a rectangular output shaft of 1.0635in by 0.9375in (27mm by 24mm), quite a handy size, because the larger dimension was the same as the larger end of the Ferguson spanner. So a jammed PTO-driven implement could be wound backwards by hand to release a blockage, using the Ferguson spanner.

The American-made PTO shaft extension kit, which not only brings the PTO up to the SAE standard of 1⅜in 6-spline but also brings it to 14in from the centre draw-bar pin hole and thereby complies with another SAE standard.

The Ferguson organisation in Detroit marketed a different type of PTO adaptor. This neat accessory not only brought the PTO shaft up to 1.375in with six splines to the SAE standard, but by extending it rearwards from the axle housing, also bought the PTO shaft within 14in (356mm) of the centre draw bar hole, which again was an SAE standard. This standard was designed to provide the correct geometry for the PTO shaft, as articulation took place between tractor and trailed implement.

An interesting and expensive piece of power application equipment on offer was the epicyclic reduction gearbox A-TE-118. With this unit installed to the rear of the gearbox, the tractor was extended in length by 4in (102mm), so extension pieces had to be supplied to lengthen the brake rods and, interestingly, the extra legroom made the tractor more comfortable to drive. The benefits of installing the complicated epicyclic gearbox, which had its own built-in hydraulic pump to power the slave cylinder on the brake band assembly, was the doubling of the number of gear ratios available, and in low range a 3:1 reduction from standard,

The epicyclic gearbox casing with the planet wheels and carrier assembly removed but showing the brake band and PTO drive.

The Ferguson epicyclic reduction gearbox A-TE-118 provided the facility of live PTO when operating in low range. It increased the length of the tractor by 4 inches. Tractors equipped with this unit had a choice of 8 forward and 2 reverse gears.

with live PTO available in the lower range. To eliminate the possibility of excessive torque being applied to the rest of drive train, the hydraulic pressure applied to the brake band around the epicyclic housing was restricted, so that it would slip if subjected to an unsafe level of torque.

An outside manufacturer who offered a cheaper and less sophisticated version of this concept was Howard Rotorvator Co, but their design did not feature either live PTO or the built-in safety factor. Their design was based on a pair of sliding gears and a dog clutch, mounted on the output shaft of the gearbox, and all neatly accommodated within the existing casing. Tractors so fitted had the operating lever protruding from the inspection plate on the right-hand side, where the transmission dipstick was normally situated.

ACCESSORIES FOR CONVENIENCE

The Ferguson pick-up hitch A-TE-90 was developed to meet Harry Ferguson's requirement for a simplified method of connecting the 3-ton trailer to the tractor, while at the same time maintaining the one-third weight transfer to the rear wheels of the tractor. The system had to be capable of being operated by the driver while sitting on his seat. Prior to Theo Sherwen's design (see Chapter 11), the early Mark I 3-ton trailers had a most complicated two-point linkage method of attachment to the tractor. Part of this system was a plate mounted under the rear axle incorporating a special pin that mated to a part of the trailer which took the directional load from the trailer to the tractor. Ferguson

The automatic pick-up hitch A-TE-90, with the draw bar of the 3-ton industrial trailer coupled to the TE.T20 tractor.

The automatic pick-up hitch in the lowered position ready to back under the ring on the drawbar of a Ferguson trailer.

engineers used this pin to connect with the early type of swinging drawbar, which enabled non-Ferguson trailed equipment to be used. A later design of draw bar was offered: it was a high-carbon steel bar with eleven holes, attached to the ball ends of the lower links, and supported by adjustable stays. These were attached at their upper ends to the long pin hole on the back axle. With these stays in position it was imperative that the driver did not attempt to lift the hydraulic lift arms, and to obviate this risk a warning plate was fitted, and a locking bolt to the lever quadrant was attached on a long chain. But often the locking bolt was not put in place, with dire results in terms of a pair of severely bent stays, as can be vouched for from experience! It should be mentioned that a similar but shorter nine-hole drawbar was offered for vineyard tractors. This version featured slightly larger, countersunk holes on the extreme ends. This facilitated the fitment of

A pair of spanners from American production with TO prefix. It is up to the reader to find the difference between the two spanners! You may need a magnifying glass!

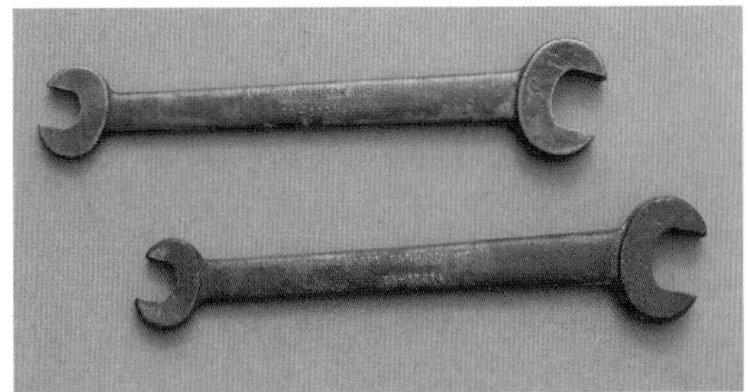

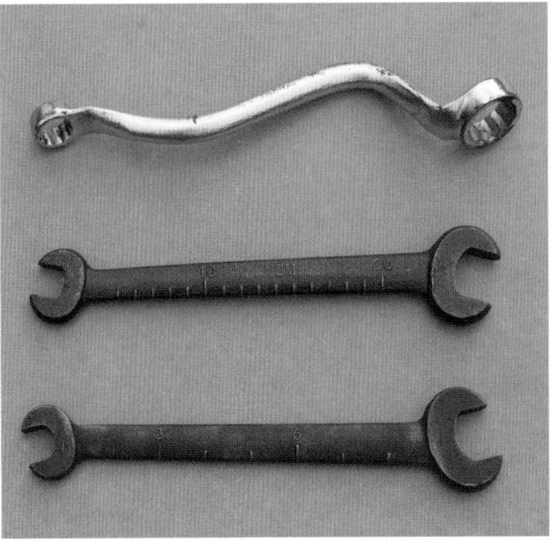

Three spanners from the British range. The ring spanner is made by Britool but marked Ferguson.

The safety chain and warning plate were part of the 11-hole draw bar kit. The purpose was to lock the hydraulic control lever in the lower position. If the linkage were lifted with this type of drawbar fitted both adjustable stays would be seriously deformed!

certain implements designed for vineyard work.

The famous Ferguson lifting jack, A-TE-A70, was a novel design, and many of these were sold, bearing in mind that very few farms had good workshop equipment and facilities at the time. The two-part design consisted of a tubular steel inverted U with sprags. This was positioned under the front axle mounting bracket, sprags digging into the ground. The tractor was then driven slightly forwards, causing the front end to rise, which elevated the front wheels clear of the ground. The rear section, also of light tubular steel design, attached to the lower lift arm balls and to cup-shaped brackets that were positioned under the inner rear ends of the lift arms. As the hydraulic linkage was raised, the tractor moved slightly forwards and upwards, bringing the rear wheels clear of the ground. Some designs took advantage of this fact by connecting the front and rear sections together with a light chain, thus lifting all four wheels simultaneously. It was essential to use this device on solid ground or concrete. To jack up a vineyard TE20 with its narrow track and lower ground clearance, a special version of this jack was produced under part number A-TE-K20.

Yet another simple piece of kit was the tyre inflation set A-TE-77, manufactured by Schrader. This was suitable only for spark ignition engines, as it was necessary to remove one spark plug and screw in the diaphragm air pump. This device used the suction force within the cylinder to drive the diaphragm pump, thus pumping clean air into the tyre. It was able to create ample air pressure to inflate both front and rear tyres. A pencil-type air pressure gauge completed the set. This must have been a huge step forward compared to the traditional hand or foot pump of the day. The instructions supplied made a point that the engine should be run at just a brisk tick-over. Having used this type of pump, I can vouch for its effectiveness.

A convenience item that one would have expected to be included in the original specification was the rear-mounted mower stand A-BE-B780, which stabilised the mower when detached from the tractor and was stowed clear of the ground when the machine was in use. Without the help of this simple stand, the mower was a pig to dismount, with a high risk of squashed fingers. Likewise, with the high-lift loader, if the optional stands were not available, fitting and dismounting was a tractor driver's nightmare. A top link rack with upwards-facing deep serrations was bolted to the standard top link. This piece of optional equipment was necessary when using implements that needed to be retained at a fixed height without the load being taken by the hydraulic system; examples of these were the hammer mill, the 65cu ft compressor and the rear-mounted mower. A yoke at the top end and a short length of chain attached at the lower front end of the implement were placed over the rack, and its relative position to the tractor determined the height that the implement was clear of the ground. Finally a turnbuckle-type top link (common today) was available; it was initially intended to be used on the earth leveller but it found uses with lots of other implements, where it provided quick and fine adjustment of the top link length.

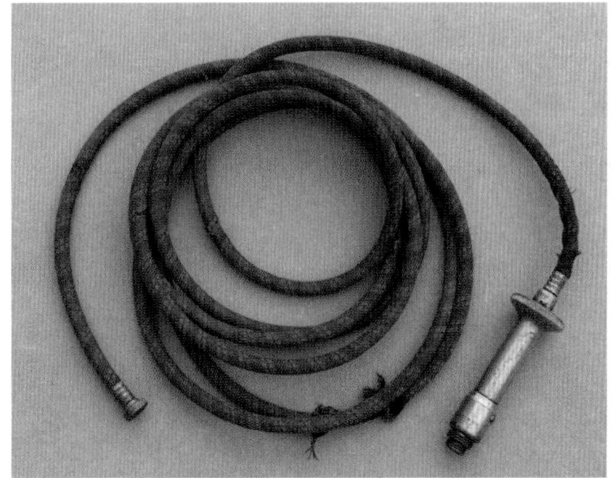

The tyre inflation device made for Ferguson by Schrader. The kit normally included a pencil-type tyre pressure gauge. It could only be used on spark ignition engines. Only clean air was pressurised into the tyre.

A New Zealand firm produced a simple device that enabled the operator to lock the steering wheel either straight ahead, or to the left or right on hard lock, while he walked behind the trailer or link box, throwing out animal fodder. It might not meet with the approval of today's Health and Safety regulations! Another design of steering wheel lock was probably produced locally in Scotland; with five holes for the pin to sit in, and three spokes on the steering wheel to choose from, this gave a wide range of steering locks the tractor could be set to.

To summarise this chapter, it is clear that the tractor was basic to keep its price down, but by buying additional pieces of equipment, it could be made to perform its role well on any particular farm or site. This equipment could be added easily, as and when required, quite an economic expedient in those far-off days when materials and money were in short supply, and wages were rising rapidly.

Chapter Thirteen

The LTX or Big Ferguson

To understand the development of the LTX (Large Tractor Experimental), which began in strict secrecy at Fletchamstead Highway back in 1948, one has to look further back to the mid-1940s, when a batch of five prototypes were built in America, based on scaling-up the Ford-Ferguson 9N tractor. One of these 4P-type machines was brought to Coventry in 1948, and probably used as a backdrop for the development engineers, who began with Harry Ferguson to formulate designs for a larger tractor based on the TE20.

A petrol-engined version of the LTX, one of four believed to have been built.

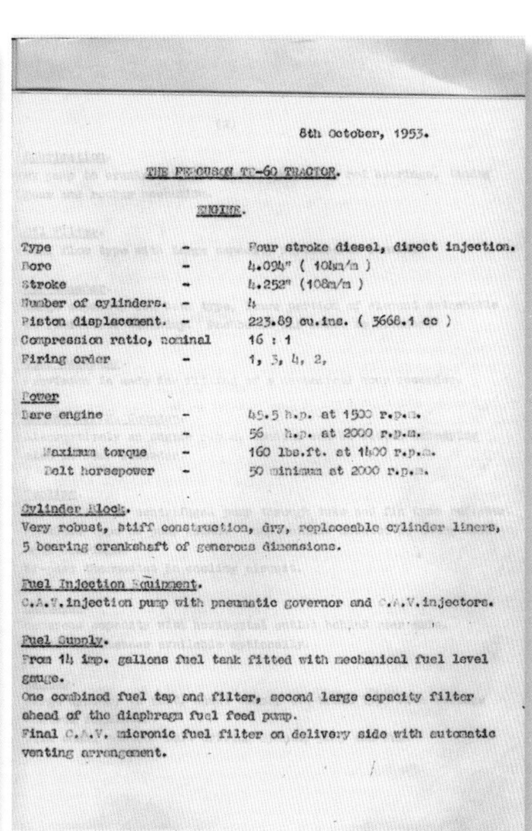

8th October, 1953.

THE FERGUSON TE-60 TRACTOR.

ENGINE.

Type	-	Four stroke diesel, direct injection.
Bore	-	4.094" (104m/m)
Stroke	-	4.252" (108m/m)
Number of cylinders.	-	4
Piston displacement.	-	223.89 cu.ins. (3668.1 cc)
Compression ratio, nominal		16 : 1
Firing order	-	1, 3, 4, 2,

Power

Bare engine	-	45.5 h.p. at 1500 r.p.m.
	-	56 h.p. at 2000 r.p.m.
Maximum torque	-	160 lbs.ft. at 1400 r.p.m.
Belt horsepower	-	50 minimum at 2000 r.p.m.

Cylinder Block.
Very robust, stiff construction, dry, replaceable cylinder liners, 5 bearing crankshaft of generous dimensions.

Fuel Injection Equipment.
C.A.V. injection pump with pneumatic governor and C.A.V. injectors.

Fuel Supply.
From 14 imp. gallons fuel tank fitted with mechanical fuel level gauge.
One combined fuel tap and filter, second large capacity filter ahead of the diaphragm fuel feed pump.
Final C.A.V. micronic fuel filter on delivery side with automatic venting arrangement.

Front cover and first page of the TE-60 data booklet.

Although the TE20 line of tractors was selling extremely well both in Britain and abroad, there was a growing demand from farmers with larger arable acreages for a more powerful tractor. Not only was more bhp needed at the power take-off for balers, trailed combines and forage harvesters, but with rising wage costs it became imperative that large-acreage farms should achieve as high an output per man as possible, necessitating the use of bigger implements. The sales staff who reported customer pressure for a larger Ferguson to head office probably provided the catalyst for the LTX's development. It is understood that Harry Ferguson was not too keen on the idea to start with, but understandably went along with it. He was of the view that the TE20 was just right for all sizes of farms, but then he was biased!

Larger farmers could of course turn to heavier-wheeled tractors, such as those produced by Ford, Nuffield, David Brown, International and others, or could opt for crawlers for heavy tillage work. Yet people liked the Ferguson TE20 because it worked well with its own specialist implements and was efficient on fuel. So what was obviously needed was a larger version, and this is what the LTX project sought to achieve.

The design team set up in 1948 was headed by John Chambers, who had worked alongside Harry Ferguson during the development of the Ferguson-Brown. Also in the team were Alex Senkowski, a Polish aircraft pilot who before the war had been involved in engine design, Bill Harrow, brought in from Daimler bus engines, and Alex Patterson, who like Ferguson was an Ulsterman and had worked with him on the Ferguson-Brown. He was in charge of the engineering shop where the prototypes were built up. As these tractors – six in total, four petrol and two Diesel (although a reference to a seventh and eighth has been found) – became available for field testing, it was up to Jack Bibby to organise the field test team, who generally worked two eight-hour shifts. The testers were Dick Dowdeswell, Nigel Liney (who by the way was a keen amateur photographer and whom we have to thank for some of his unofficial shots used in this chapter and elsewhere!), and Colin Stevenson. The fitter on the project was Nibby Newbold.

It is believed that prototype drawings were

under way by September 1948, and the first petrol-engined prototype was ready for field testing by April 1949 - not bad going when one remembers the material shortages of that time.

To give a broad insight into the LTX, I will first look at the design parameters and the brief the team set themselves, and then go on to look in more detail at the various elements that come together to make the tractor. Bearing in mind it is over fifty-five years since this project was in full swing, that this model never went into production, and that all six prototypes were scrapped, information in some areas is a bit vague.

This larger Ferguson was planned to be an upgrade of the TE20, not only in terms of engine bhp and performance, but also to improve on what was considered by most users to be a fine tractor complete with its own special implements. The LTX was designed to have a transmission capable of dealing with up to 100bhp, and a range of engine sizes using common components, such as individual blocks and heads for two-, three-, four- and six-cylinder configurations, suitable for petrol, TVO or Diesel fuels. This was a similar concept to the Ford 4D engine used in the new Fordson Major. It has not been possible to find much information on the petrol engine variants, but a two-cylinder engine was built and bench-tested, and was said to perform so well that consideration was given to installing it in the Massey-Harris Pony tractor.

More is known about the Diesel prototypes, but by the time they were produced the concept of using individual blocks and heads had been abandoned in favour of the more conventional monobloc arrangement. I was informed by Bill Buffery that as a twelve-year-old he was taken by his father, who was at the time farming in Shropshire near to the Stiperstones, to a ploughing demonstration of a Diesel LTX. Graham told me, "I was a bit of a clever dick as a twelve-year old and I can remember saying to the driver, 'I see it is fitted with a Perkins L4 engine.' The driver's reply was 'Well, Mr Clever Dick, it has got a L4 block, but a very special cylinder head!'" – no doubt designed by Bill Harrow. Although this is a true story, it is interesting to compare the information that has come to light on the Diesel LTX engine with the

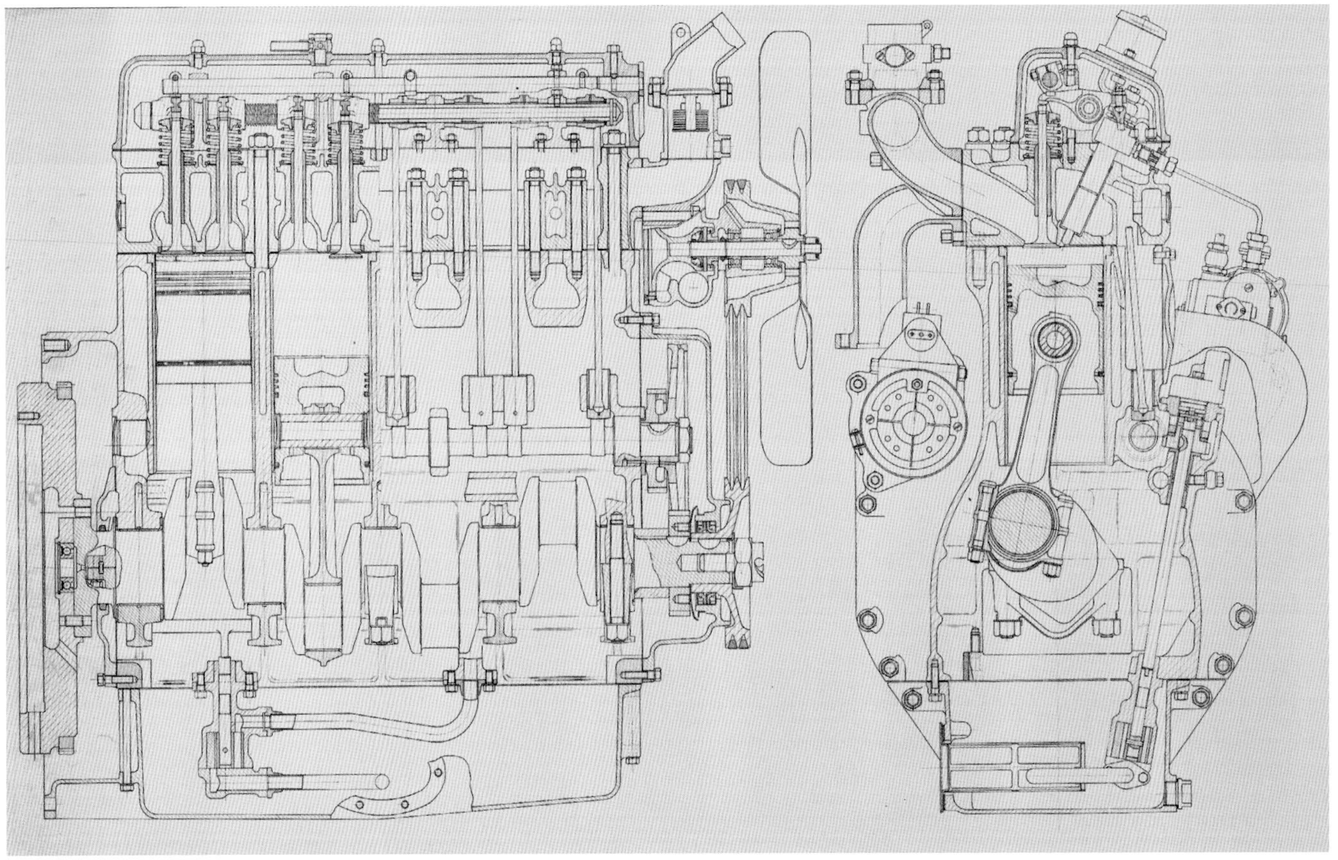

Undated engineering drawings of the LTX engine.

So one wonders how true that story is! A full size drawing of the LTX Diesel engine has been given to the Coldridge Collection by John Burge.

Fuel-injection equipment was by CAV, with a pneumatic governor. Nibby Newbold told the story of an LTX engine that was sent to CAV for injection testing. On its return to Fletchamstead Highway it was found to have been filled with varnish instead of oil! Yes, there were cock-ups even in those days! A Ferguson safety feature that was carried over from the TE20 was the use of the gearlever to operate the 12-volt pre-engaged starter motor, with a safety interlock to prevent inadvertent engagement. Power was provided by a pair of 6-volt batteries connected in series, and carried in recesses built into both rear mudguards. The dynamo to maintain charge was of the shunt-wound two-brush type; judging by photographs and the drawing it is of largish capacity and driven by twin A-section belts. Provision was made on the engine for the take-off of a drive for a tractormeter or hour-meter.

The hydraulic system and three-point linkage were similar to the TE20's, but more robust to cope with heavier loadings. Interchangeable balls of Category I (⅞in aperture) or Category II (1⅛in aperture) were available to fit the lower links. This dual arrangement meant that the tractor could be used with most existing TE20 implements, which had Category I attachments. Larger implements made specially for the LTX would be to Category II dimensions. The pump drive was taken from the constant-running PTO through a dog clutch having three positions:

	LTX	**Perkins L4**
BType	Direct injection	Indirect injection
Bore	4.094in (104 mm)	4.25in (107.95mm)
Stroke	4.252in (108 mm)	4.75in (120.65 mm)
Capacity	3668cc	4417cc
Liners	Wet liners	Wet liners
Power output at 1500 rpm	45.5	56

(i) Pump and PTO stationary.
(ii) Pump engaged.
(iii) Pump and PTO shaft engaged.
The three-cylinder pump ran at a maximum working pressure of 2500psi, and had an output of 2.4 gallons (10.9 litres) per minute at 1500rpm engine speed.

The LTX was fitted with the Ferguson System draft control, but this was refined in two respects, firstly by the fitting of a double-acting control spring which facilitated working with heavy-overhang but light-draft implements, and secondly by an independent overload release valve which opened if an obstruction was hit: this remained open until re-set by the operator moving the quadrant control lever to the "drop" position. A further development was the fitting of a sensitivity control, which permitted the variation of the ratio between movement of the control valve and draft spring deflection. This ratio was normally 8:1 as on the TE20, but with this improved facility a range from 4:1 to 16:1 was available.

For the first time in the Ferguson System, tractor position control was made available. At the flick of a small lever, the main control quad-

Testing the LTX's power with a specially made disc plough.

The five-furrow 10-inch plough specially developed for the LTX.

rant changed from draft control to position control, which in effect meant that the lower links moved in direct relationship with the control quadrant, so wherever the lever was set the lower links remained in that position, unaffected by any movement in the top link. The overload protection still operated when this function was selected. A take-off tapping for external hydraulic services was provided. Hydraulic lift lock for implement transport was tried on one or two prototypes.

The transmission of power from the engine flywheel was through a double clutch of 11in (279mm) effective diameter operated by two pedals, the main pedal operating only the transmission clutch, the second pedal operating both the transmission and PTO to provide true live PTO – another first! As before, Harry Ferguson insisted that no more than 35lbs (16kg) foot pressure be needed to depress the clutch pedal. Two PTOs were provided, the lower one running at the standard speed of 540rpm against an engine speed of 1500rpm, the upper PTO running at engine speed. The PTOs were detachable to give improved clearance for implements. A belt pulley could be fitted to the upper, engine speed PTO.

The gearbox featured five forward speeds and one reverse, and of course the start position on the gearlever gate. The gearbox layout was similar to the TE20's in that it featured helical cut gears running in constant mesh, and gear changing was achieved by selectors moving dog clutches. The final drive was by spiral bevel gear and had a ratio of 5.8:1, with a differential of four-pinion design, mounted on taper roller bearings, driving through final reduction gears to output drive shafts of semi-floating design, which were also mounted on taper roller bearings. The rear axle incorporated what is believed to be a friction clutch controlled differential lock. This was very smooth in action, and could be engaged by a hand lever, even if one wheel was spinning. I was told by John Handcock of Snowford Hall Farm in Warwickshire, who as a farmer tested some of the LTX prototypes for Harry Ferguson, that it was a brilliant tractor, and if you got wheel spin, you just pulled on this lever and you were going again. Telling this story, John mimicked being back in the seat and pulling the imaginary lever with his right hand.

The internal-expanding brakes, of twin-shoe design, 16in by 2.5in (406mm by 64mm), were of the fully self-energizing type, and were fitted to the high-speed output side of the differential. They operated together through a compensating linkage, or by independent pedals for sharp turning. The parking brake was fitted with a safety latch, a big improvement on the step-off and roll of the TE20!

The steering was basically a beefed-up TE20 system, with a double drop link steering box, and a 20in (508mm) steering wheel. The steering was a bit of a problem, because several drivers reported cases of kick-back. This was confirmed to me by Derrick Hiatt, who farms in Warwickshire and had the use of the last LTX until 1970. The other five had been broken up in June 1954. Derrick told me that one of his drivers was off work for a week following an encounter with the steering wheel of the LTX. Likewise, Dick Dowdeswell informed me he had a similar experience. He told one of the design engineers, who did not believe him but took an LTX out for a drive over rough ground and hurt his thumb. A modification quickly ensued!

To round off this chapter on the LTX, or TE60 as it would have been known in production, I would like to mention that back in 1999, with the help of the late Erik Fredriksen, I researched and commissioned the production of 1/18th scale models of these prototype tractors. As a result of my research, I was privileged to meet several of the men who were responsible for the LTX's design and development, as well as two farmers who had used them, John Handcock and Derrick Hiatt. Derrick, who retained "his" until 1970 when the clutch failed, 'phoned Banner Lane, just as he had done on several occasions before, to come and fix it. The only long-term problem he had with the tractor was a tendency to slip out of second gear, although this was easily remedied by jamming the gear-lever with... the Ferguson spanner of course! He also told me it was a bit of a sod to start on very cold mornings.

Sadly, after the Banner Lane engineers took the LTX from his farm in 1970, it never returned; it was cut up and scrapped. Derrick was devastated. When I first visited him in mid-1999 and told him of my plan to make some models of the LTX his words were, as we sat around his kitchen table one evening, "Well, whatever the cost I want one, it was a *fantastic* tractor." I can tell you I have dealt with lots of farmers over the years and never, ever have I heard them blow cost to the winds like that!

The demise of this project came at the time when Harry Ferguson was selling his business to Massey-Harris. He was by now enthusiastic about the LTX, and had even begun to encourage dealers to take orders for the Big Tractor, as is evidenced by the factory order ledger. He arranged for a demonstration field to be covered in muck, and in the presence of James Duncan, President of Massey-Harris, and other top staff, he instructed Jack Bibby to plough the field up and down the gradient, demonstrating the effectiveness of the combination of draft control and differential lock. Massey-Harris fielded their MH 744 against the LTX but there was no contest, Jack Bibby with the LTX just ran rings around it. Sadly, whether for reasons of ego or politics we do not know, at a crucial product policy meeting which took place in San Antonio, Texas between 6 and 11 March 1954, the North American sales staff were not impressed with the LTX on the grounds of the lack of a tri-cycle model for row crops, and felt that if a conversion were developed it might appear crude.

The styling prototype of the LTX, badged TE-60 on the bonnet sides, alongside a Fordson Major. This comparison gives an idea of the size of the new tractor.

Chapter Fourteen

With the TE20 to the South Pole

The assignment that brought world-wide attention to the TE20's prowess was the use of three slightly modified tractors driven by Edmund Hillary (later Sir Edmund Hillary) and his team on their historic trip across Antarctica to the South Pole in 1957-58. Preparations for Ferguson tractors to be used at the Scott Base Camp on the western side of the polar plateau initally took place at Northwoods on South Island, New Zealand. Keith Base was setting up a Ferguson training school in New Zealand in 1957, and it was considered prudent to train all of the team travelling to the South Pole on the internal workings of the TE20 and the efficient repair procedures to be adopted, should they have problems: a wise move.

A replica made by Bill Glennie of one of the projects tried out for the expedition, using skis at the front. It did not work too well and full tracks were adopted instead. The Trans-Antarctic tractors were petrol models and would not have had the heat shield shown in this photograph.

Concurrent with this training, various modifications were tried and tested in the snowy parts of South Island.

Keith recalls that one idea was to fit half tracks to the rear wheels (see Chapter 12) and to replace the front wheels with skis to enable the tractors to be steered. When this was tried out in the snow it was found to be totally unworkable. Keith recalled to me several years ago that he and his team, and Ed Hillary and some of his men, were gathered around in the tractor yard one day, scratching their heads over how to deal with this problem. Ed Hillary said, "Why not put the f...ing tracks over the front wheels as well and weld the steering in the straight-ahead position." Keith said to me, "Everyone looked amazed and a bit sheepish – why had they not thought of that!" Then some bright spark on Keith's team said, "Well, how are you going to steer, then?" Ed Hillary is reported as saying, "I am going straight to the South Pole so I don't want to be able to steer the f...ing thing" So this was the chosen track system. Here was a flash of inspiration by a man determined to reach his goal – a man not unlike Ferguson.

Let us look at the other modifications made to the TE.A20s to fit them for the arduous task ahead. Ed Hillary's idea was fine, but for it to work in practice oversize front wheels had to be fitted so that the rubber tracks would run true. To gain the required space for these meant extending the distance between the track idler wheel and the front wheel, which was achieved by installing the Ferguson epicyclic gearbox. This added 4.75in (121mm) to the wheelbase, and of course added another, lower range of gears. According to Ed Hillary's report on the five tractors used in connection with this expedition, the low-range gearboxes were hardly ever used. All five tractors were transported from Wellington in New Zealand to Scott Base on the *Endeavour*, three on deck and two in the hold. They were all given female names, no doubt to compensate for the lack of female company on this expedition! Those on deck were Liz, Aggie and Gert, those below were Daisy and Sue. Sue now resides in the Massey-Ferguson works museum in Coventry, and one of the others is in Christchurch, New Zealand. A third one of this type that did not go to the South Pole is in private ownership in New Zealand.

Other modifications to the three tractors taken to the South Pole included the fitting of home-made roll-over bars, which in turn allowed the fitting of a rudimentary cab to give the driver some protection from the wind and cold. They were painted red to make them easier to spot in the snow. Heavy-duty 110Ah batteries were fitted, with simple wooden top covers. The tyres were were of a special silicon rubber which was more suited to polar conditions than the standard compound, and this type of rubber was also used for insulating all electrical cables. There were problems with the brakes, bearing in mind that they were the only means of steering, unlike purpose-built crawler tractors which incorporate a steering clutch in the output shaft to each track drive sprocket. The main problem with the brakes was that snow got into them, reducing braking efficiency, and of course they froze up when they were not used. As a temporary "cure" for this problem, it was found that putting a small quantity of powdered resin in each brake greatly improved its effectiveness. Eventually, better sealing of the brakes was developed.

After about 300 hours' running, the tractors' engines were stripped to be given a valve grind,

One of the Fergusons on the Trans-Antarctic expedition. As the steering is locked, changes of direction are made by braking the appropriate rear wheel.

and some broken valve springs and some thrust bearings were replaced. The bores were found to be almost perfect, and oil consumption was nil. With temperatures often 40 to 50 below, the tractors had to be warmed up before attempting to start them. This was first achieved by the simple expedient of covering them with a tarpaulin and lighting a blow lamp under this cover. Using this method had its risks! Before long, sure enough, one caught fire, but luckily someone noticed the flames and the fire was put out with the use of many powder fire extinguishers, with little damage to the tractor. This method of pre-heating was then abandoned and alternative methods sought. One tried was the installation within the tractor's cooling system of a 1000-Watt immersion heater. This worked well, providing the tractor was parked near an electricity supply point but the generating capacity at Scott Base was very limited. At the base there were two Weasels, and as only one of these was being taken to the South Pole, the team decided to take the petrol-burning cab heater out of the other and modify it as a portable heater. Another novel form of heating which was used for the caboose sleeping quarters and the radio room (which was on skis), was to pass exhaust gas from a tractor into a radiator on the inside, where it gave up its heat before being exhausted to the outside. The idea worked perfectly so long as the radiator did not leak.

Another modification made was to move the batteries very close to the engines of the tractors, so that they benefited from the slightly raised temperature. It should be remembered that in a lead acid battery the production of electricity is dependent upon a chemical reaction within the plates of each cell. The speed of this reaction is proportional to the temperature of the battery.

The plateau of Antarctica rises to 10,000ft (3000m). Engines and humans lose 3 per cent of their efficiency per 1000ft (300m) of altitude due to thinning levels of oxygen. Thus at 10,000 ft the tractors' power output, normally 28bhp at sea level, was reduced by 30 per cent to approximately 16bhp. To compensate for this, the governors were adjusted to allow a

One of the expedition Fergusons is preserved in New Zealand.

maximum engine speed of 3000rpm. Hillary notes that when operating in low gear with engine running at this maximum, fuel consumption was down to 1 mile per gallon (over 280 litres per 100km). Despite this revving the engines gave no problems. The clutches were trouble-free, but there were a few minor problems with the hydraulic system. Most significant was when the crown wheel and pinion on one tractor broke up, causing metallic debris to circulate in the hydraulic system and scar the plungers in the pump. However, the system still worked, albeit with reduced effectiveness.

Mention might be made here of some of the implements and tractor equipment shipped to Scott Base. There was a Lincoln mounted and PTO-driven arc welder with 200-amp output. A Hydrovane 60cfpm compressor was another essential piece of equipment. A Ferguson post-hole digger was included, perhaps for boring holes in the ice to erect flag poles! A Ferguson forklift attachment was included, and fitted to a Ferguson with tyre tracks. Also a Ferguson winch was taken along: a wise precaution, bearing in mind the hostile topography. A Ferguson terracer blade was much used for clearing snow. An automatic pick-up hitch was part of the kit of each tractor, presumably used because it kept the point of attachment low, and reduced the risk of the tractor rearing up if a severe obstruction was encountered.

A rather unusual coolant was used in the engines when the neat Glycol antifreeze ran out. It was none other than kerosene! According to the expedition's engineer Jim Bates, this fluid worked well, and no problems ensued. The base engineers decided to strengthen the front axle by welding angle steel between the lower part of the swivel and the rear end of the radius arms. All the Fergusons and Weasels were fitted with short-range two-way radios to ease communication between drivers. It should be mentioned here that while Ed Hillary and his team were setting out from Scott Base and heading towards the South Pole with three Fergusons, Vivian "Bunny" Fuchs and his team had set off from Shackleton Base, where two modified Fergusons were used, with two Snow Cats named Rock'n'Roll and Able, two Weasels named Rumble and Wrack & Ruin, a Muskeg tractor called Hopalong, bearing the emblem of a kangaroo, and, bringing up the rear, another Snow Cat, County of Kent.

Hillary and his team with their three Fergusons finally reached the South Pole Station at 12.30pm on 4 January 1958, and were met by two commanders of the American base there, Dr Houk and Major Margesson. Ed Hillary wrote, "On the circle of drums and flag poles that mark the South Pole itself they were greeted by a battery of cameras and friendly faces!" Bunny Fuchs arrived at the South Pole at midday on 20 January, with his Snow Cats and a Weasel plus dog teams. Ed Hillary recalls how all the vehicles were parked together beside his three Fergusons. "I have to admit there was quite a contrast in the vehicles!" Ed Hillary and his team were the first people to drive to the South Pole, and they achieved this distinction with three Ferguson TE.A20s.

On his arrival at the South Pole, Hillary sent this appreciative telegram to Banner Lane, Coventry: "Despite quite unsuitable conditions of soft snow and high altitudes our Fergusons performed magnificently and it was their extreme reliability that made our trip to the South Pole possible. Thank you for your good wishes. Hillary."

Principal data on the Ferguson TE20 tractors used on the Trans-Antarctic Expedition:	
Compression ratio	6:1
Power	28bhp, reduced to 16bhp at altitude
Ground pressure of full track	1.3psi
Turning radius	20ft (6.1m)
Overall width	6ft (1.83m)
Overall length	10ft (3.05m)
Overall height less cab	4ft 4in (1.32m)
Dry weight with full tracks	3370 lbs (1530kg)
Coolant capacity	15 pints (8.5 litres)
Engine oil capacity	12pints (6.8 litres)
Petrol capacity	9 Gallons (41 litres)

Summary of major modifications in addition to full tyre tracks
Epicyclic reduction gearbox
All electrical leads covered in silicon rubber
Heavy-duty starter motor
110Ah batteries
Eventually, better sealing of brakes to keep out snow
Strengthened front axle
Crude cab
Fitting short range two-way radio to each tractor
Tractors painted red to make them easier to spot in the snow
Silicon rubber tyres fitted

Chapter Fifteen

TE20 Ownership Today

It is not surprising that, given the high standard of their engineering, many of the over half a million Ferguson TE20 tractors made more than fifty years ago have survived to this day and are still used as working tractors, albeit often in a part-time way. This is almost unique in the field of vintage vehicles – excepting working steam railways. While a lot of vintage cars, commercial vehicles, horticultural machinery and aircraft have been preserved and restored to full working order, generally these machines are kept for occasional use, for shows and displays, and, most importantly, for having fun. Large toys, one could say! Other makes of agricultural tractors from the TE20 era could well fall into this category.

While it is always dangerous to make generalisations, if you look around it is usually a TE20 of some sort that is found doing a job of work, from pulling a set of gang mowers or a heavy roller on a village sports field to working as a scraper tractor on a dairy farm. Likewise, they are found in market gardens, where their compact size and wide range of implements make them as well suited to the purpose as they were fifty-odd years ago. Some farmers today prefer them as a runabout vehicle to the ubiquitous ATV or quad bike, being cheaper to buy, cheaper to run, and easy to repair. These comments hold true in all the countries to which the TE20 was exported.

What is the reason for this almost unique phenomenon? The fact that the TE20 was an advanced design for its time, with refined steering, braking and hydraulics, and light weight, makes it a very handy little tractor. The Diesel version TE.F20 is deservedly the most popular model for everyday use, as it uses cheap Red Diesel fuel. But every TE20 is a maid of all work, with a very wide range of available attachments. These can be of new manufacture, such as grass toppers, log splitters, transport boxes and trailers, or they can be secondhand implements from the whole of the original Ferguson range.

To set these tractors up today to meet Health and Safety requirements is cheap and straightforward. Fitting a roll-over bar is essential, likewise fitting suitable guards to the sides of the bonnet to keep hands away from the cooling fan and belt. Foot boards need to be provided, and the rear mudguards extended to keep the driver's legs protected from the rear wheels. If any PTO attachments are used, the shaft must be guarded in the normal way. If belt pulley attachments are used, such as the Ferguson compressor, water pump or cutter bar mower, it is necessary to make guards for the belt drives, as they were never supplied as original equipment. One other requirement to bring the TE20 fully into line with current Health and Safety requirements is the clear marking of controls, and as there are few of these that is a simple process: marking the ignition switch on/off, the hydraulic control lever up/down, the throttle lever fast/slow, and perhaps highlighting the numerals cast on the gearbox top showing the gearlever positions.

The reasons for the continuing widespread use of TE20 tractors today are manifold. The tractors are reasonably priced, a nice tidy TE.F20 Diesel at today's prices being about £2000. Compare this to the cost of a new Japanese model of similar size and power. In addition, a complete range of re-manufactured parts is available at very realistic prices compared with the cost of spare parts for modern equivalents. Secondhand parts are also available from tractor breakers, again at realistic prices – a kind of recycling, which appeals to lots of people. As mentioned earlier, the TE20s were very well engineered and did not have "built-in obsolescence". They were of simple, straightforward construction. Almost all repairs and servicing can be done by a capable amateur mechanic using basic tools, without the need for a diagnostic computer!

The only areas where specialist servicing is required are the injection system on Diesel tractors and the replacement of rear axle shaft oil seals. However, at least one firm has resolved the latter issue by developing an alternative seal that does not require the bearing to be removed. Supporting the ease of servicing and repair is the availability of reprints of the original dealers' workshop manual, giving clear instructions and guidance, aided by excellent line drawings of the procedures involved in the full range of workshop practice. This is completely unlike the ethos of today's tractor manufacturers, who like to maintain an element of mystique over all areas of repair, except basic oil changing and servicing. It is these user-friendly qualities, plus the magic of Ferguson, the man and his machines, that have endeared these little grey Fergies to the hearts of thousands of people. It would not be an exaggeration to say that the classic grey Ferguson TE20 tractor has attracted, over the years, almost a cult following of dedicated users, collectors, restorers, dealers and enthusiasts, all in their different ways paying homage to a design icon of the twentieth century.

But it is not just the tractor that appeals to users and collectors, it is the Ferguson System, whose basic principles are the three-point linkage and draft control, the basic principles invented by Harry Ferguson, but which also encompasses the enormous range of implements for almost all agricultural needs as well as a wide range of industrial and municipal functions. Collectors just love searching out and bringing back to life implements and accessories from the range that was on offer back in the early 1950s. Some reckon these might number as many as 100.

The type of display material Ferguson dealerships would have placed in their showrooms and offices.

The fact that so many TE20s around today have been bought, repaired and restored, often by people with very limited mechanical knowledge, is a clear indication of how basic and straightforward the design and construction are. There are magazines devoted to tractor collecting and restoration, and several clubs that cater specifically for Ferguson owners. Some of these clubs offer a technical advice service and publish articles on repair procedures, so the Ferguson TE20 owner is very well supported.

With the Ferguson System, using implements mounted on the three-point linkage, the implements themselves are vastly simpler than their trailed equivalents. Take as an example a two-furrow Ferguson plough, weighing about 360lbs (163kg). It is simplicity itself, with slender beams and a light headstock of high-quality alloy steel, two mould boards and a couple of disc coulters, together with a light spring-loaded furrow wheel. No levers, unless the owner has added the furrow width adjuster AE-7900 to the cross shaft – which is a convenient accessory. By contrast, consider a standard two-furrow trailing plough like a Ransomes Motrack. It weighed about 870lbs (395kg), so there was

Both sides of an illuminated dealer's sign. Obviously cash was as important in the early 1950s as it is today!

510lbs (232kg) of unnecessary steel when compared to the Ferguson design. How was this extra weight accounted for? For a start, all the beams and the framework of the plough were mild steel, so the sections had to be heavier than on the Ferguson design. Another area of weight gain was the adjustable draw bar with a break-away mechanism as a safety precaution to prevent rearing up in the event of the plough striking an obstruction. Weight was also added by the two wheels positioned either side of the frame towards the front, together with the smaller trailing wheel at the rear. One of these front wheels was used to control the depth of the plough, while the other, in conjunction with a complicated ratchet mechanism, was used to lift the plough out of the work at the headland and for transport, and as the lifting wheel had studs on it to facilitate operation in sticky conditions, transport along a road was very slow and liable to damage the surface.

The operation of the Ferguson draft control system is illustrated by the accompanying photographs of a full-size cut-away model, one giving a general view, the other a more specific view of the pump and control linkages. These models were produced not only for the Ferguson training schools at Stoneleigh and abroad, but also for selected educational establishments which had a strong bias towards agricultural engineering. The model is powered by an electric motor with a reduction gearbox, concealed where the differential normally resides.

The constant-running lower shaft drives the four-cylinder piston pump and the PTO. The plungers are moved by eccentrics on this shaft. The inlet port for the pump is just below the oil level, and is controlled by a sliding valve and linkage. When the valve is opened by raising the draft control lever, oil enters the pump and is pressurised and fed up the vertical pipe to the main lift cylinder, where it forces the piston up in the cylinder until it reaches the limit of its travel. At this point the piston contracts the control linkage and shuts off the inlet port, while the outlet port remains closed. Oil is thus retained in the cylinder and the lift arms remain raised. When the control lever is lowered, the inlet port remains closed whilst the outlet valve opens, thus allowing oil to escape from the cylinder, and the lift arms descend. This is the simple bit!

The next part to look at is the function of the draft control, the Ferguson System. Notice that there is a large compression spring on the top link attachment rocker. The top link transmits a compression force towards the rear of the tractor when a draft implement is in work, such as a two-furrow plough. The spring is compressed in a direct relationship to the force being applied to it. It is this movement that is used to operate the control valve in the pump, the precise setting being pre-set by the position of the draft control lever in its quadrant on the right-hand side of the driver.

When a tillage implement is operated, it tends to dig in. The more it digs in, the more force is transmitted through the top link, causing the compression spring to deflect even more. A rod in the centre of the spring transmits this movement through the internal linkage to the inlet port valve, causing it to open, with the effect that oil is pressurised, forces the piston along the cylinder, and thus lifts the implement slightly out of the soil. As soon as an equilibrium is struck, the implement starts to sink deeper, and the process is repeated. Constant correction is made automatically, as the tractor and plough proceed across the field. This is draft control. The depth will depend on the soil structure, so to keep a reasonable constant depth, the control lever will need to be altered manually.

Another special feature of this Ferguson System is the built-in safety device. This comes into operation if excessive forces are transmitted through the top link and compression spring. This would cause the control valve to move to the drop position, thus effectively taking weight off the rear wheels and causing them to spin safely.

There are a few questions which are commonly asked about fuel.

Q. Will they run on unleaded petrol?
A. Yes.
Q. What do you substitute for TVO (tractor vaporising oil)?
A. Four parts of burning oil "28 second", and one part of petrol.

On the subject of oils, in petrol or TVO engines it is preferable to use a straight mineral oil of SAE 20 grade in winter and SAE 30 grade in summer, and for the Diesel engine, Diesel SAE 20 and Diesel SAE 30 respectively. For the transmission and steering box throughout the year, use a straight mineral oil SAE 50. It is most important that extreme pressure (EP) gear oils are not used in the transmission, as the additives they contain will erode the bronze used for the gear selectors and parts of the hydraulic pump.

May I round off this chapter by quoting part of a letter Alan Stanley wrote to me. Alan was a development engineer at Fletchamstead Highway and a life-long Ferguson enthusiast. "Non-professional owners may not fully appreciate the technical or commercial implications of the features and concepts embedded within that innocent-looking transmission housing of the TE20. The visual impact and the operational hands-on requirement of the Ferguson three-point linkage may be why many give this particular aspect of the Ferguson System so much attention. Surely Ferguson's draft-controlled weight transfer must be given priority? A concept so simple, yet so difficult to engineer and bring to commercial fruition. It continues to amaze me how Harry Ferguson did what he did, when he did it, and how."

Apart from still performing the everyday tasks of work that they were built for, in modern times Fergusons have sometimes been called on to transport a bride to church for her wedding ceremony, and transport the newly-wedded couple to the reception afterwards. A very different recent achievement, by Bobbie Pellow in 2006, was driving a TE.F20 towing a 3-ton trailer from Land's End to John O'Groats for charity.

Cutaway transmission housing, used to demonstrate the workings of the hydraulics. It is electrically powered.

The hydraulic pump and control linkage.

Chapter Sixteen

Ferguson Spin-offs

In this final chapter, I shall take a look at three developments which are beyond the strict remit of this book but nevertheless were in many ways brought about by the pioneering and entrepreneurial spirit of Harry Ferguson. The first of these is the Standard Motor Company's tentative foray into tractor design in 1958. The catalyst for this was Massey-Ferguson's purchase of the Diesel engine maker Perkins. It was natural that Massey-Ferguson would now use Perkins engines in its Diesel models rather than buy engines from Standard. Thus Standard found 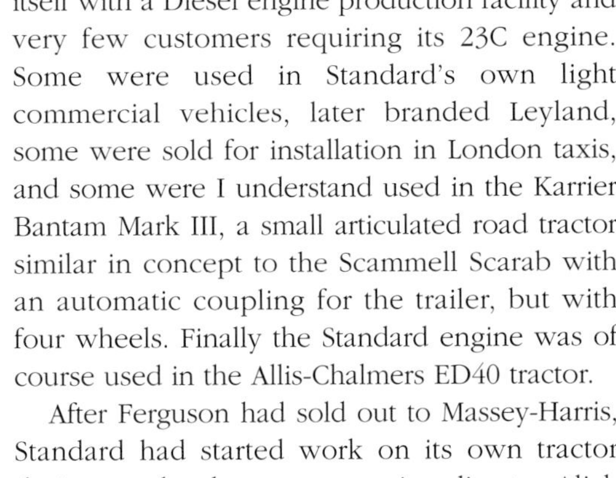 itself with a Diesel engine production facility and very few customers requiring its 23C engine. Some were used in Standard's own light commercial vehicles, later branded Leyland, some were sold for installation in London taxis, and some were I understand used in the Karrier Bantam Mark III, a small articulated road tractor similar in concept to the Scammell Scarab with an automatic coupling for the trailer, but with four wheels. Finally the Standard engine was of course used in the Allis-Chalmers ED40 tractor.

After Ferguson had sold out to Massey-Harris, Standard had started work on its own tractor designs under the new managing director Alick Dick, with a team headed up by John Chambers. Perhaps they perceived the very real possibility of Massey-Ferguson eventually buying Perkins as they did. A pair of tractors were designed and produced, and one of these has survived. It is now in the Coldridge Collection.

These tractors were built in great secrecy at Standard's Canley Works, as confirmed by a fitter on the project. The Standard tractor featured the 23C engine, fitted with a cylinder head with a heater plug in each combustion chamber - although I have never had to use them, as the engine starts instantly, even at 0 degrees C, just as a direct injection Diesel would. The shape of the combustion chambers must have been slightly modified from that of the earlier design. The transmission incorporates a dual clutch similar to that fitted to Ferguson FE35s, but not quite the same. The gearbox is a four-speed and

An offside view of an early Standard Motor Company prototype. Note the fuel tank to the rear of the engine.

reverse unit, with a high/low epicyclic reduction unit fitted to the output shaft of the gearbox; again very similar in concept to that used on the Ferguson FE35, and giving in effect eight forward ratios and two reverse speeds. Interestingly, the main gearbox and the epicyclic unit are operated by the same lever. This is achieved by having two sets of slots in the selector rods. In the neutral position of the gate containing the high/low selection there is a switch for the starter solenoid circuit, which can only be closed when the lever is in neutral.

The hydraulics offer both draft and position control, again operated with one lever, selection of mode being determined by which quadrant the lever moves in – a neat idea. There are tappings for external services selected by their own valve. The rear axle, like the gearbox, is somewhat over-engineered, and is similar in layout to the Ferguson FE35, but is 11in (279mm) wide between the axle trumpets, whereas the FE35 is only 9in (229mm). The brakes are dry disc, very similar to those fitted to an MF65, but not exactly the same. The PTO is two-speed, but is only live in the lower ratio. There is also the facility for ground speed PTO. The Stanpart number N00003 and the Bean logo are cast into the transmission housing. Stanpart was Standard-Triumph's name for marketing parts, while Bean Industries of Tipton which had long been a Standard subsidiary.

The steering system is interesting, and I speculate that it was designed to get around Ferguson patents in that it does not have double drop-arms, but it does feature twin steering rods, as found on the TE20. Standard's engineers achieved this solution by using a Ford single drop-arm box to articulate a lever that passes through a gap in the transmission housing, being centrally pivoted and connected to a short drag link. At the extreme ends of this horizontal lever the steering rods are connected on either side, essentially following the Ferguson layout, in fact using a TE20 front axle, but with repositioned radius arm fitting points.

There is provision for a linkage to operate a differential lock but none is fitted. Obviously they were planning ahead. The mudguards and foot boards were taken directly from a Fordson Dexta, whilst the bonnet, although it looks like a Ferguson, has slats in the grille that are pressed integrally, unlike the TE20 grille that is made up of separate pressings crimped into position. The seat is from an FE35 de luxe. The air filter is of the dry type. The dash-mounted instruments include a tractormeter, an oil pressure gauge and an ammeter. The battery and fuel tank are positioned to the rear of the engine, parallel to each other under the bonnet. The fuel tank was probably taken from a Standard Atlas van.

A second, totally different design followed, and although it is believed that Standard's intention was to build five of these later prototypes, it is thought that only three were produced. Two are known to have survived, and one is owned by Robert Crawford. The tinwork was now more stylish, and obviously by this stage some thought

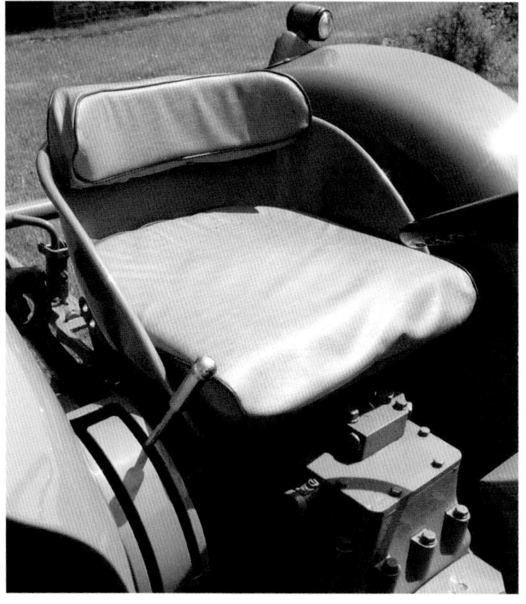

The hydraulic control lever showing the arrangement of the draft and position quadrant. The valve for the external hydraulic services can be seen below the seat.

A nearside view of the prototype's Standard 23C engine with a heater plug in each combustion chamber. Notice how the steering link passes through a hole in the transmission casing.

Another Standard prototype. This one is number three of the second batch.

was being given to how the tractor might be perceived by prospective purchasers. The specification of this second batch of prototypes still included the 23C Diesel engine, but this time fitted with an oil-bath type air filter. Apart from the fact that it had a dual clutch, the transmission was totally different from the previous project's. It had a forward and reverse shuttle 'box, with a four-speed main gearbox, and a high and low auxiliary gearbox. The brakes were inboard discs on the high-speed side of the differential, with spur gear reduction to the rear hubs. A two-speed PTO was also fitted, with an adjacent external services hydraulic coupling with its own control valve, and a built-in differential lock was fitted to these prototypes. However, the takeover of Standard-Triumph by the Leyland group in 1961 sounded the death knell for any future development of this tractor.

As was mentioned in Chapter 1, Ferguson set up a research company, Harry Ferguson Research Ltd, in April 1950, eventually based at Toll Bar End in Coventry and with the telegraphic address "Progress Coventry", to foster his pioneering work on four-wheel drive systems, limited-slip differentials, torque converter designs and anti-lock braking systems. These were developed very much with the idea in mind of offering motorists increased levels of active automotive safety. As a spin-off from the research company, another company was formed, trading as Tractor Research Ltd. One of their earlier commissions came in 1960 from BMC, who had identified a need for a small 15bhp tractor to complement their rather limited Nuffield tractor range. They had at one time considered the possible purchase of Brockhouse Engineering, who produced a lightweight tractor of about 10bhp powered by a Morris sidevalve engine. Nuffield actually tested a BMB President in secret but found it not to their liking. Eventually, in 1959, Nuffield started development work on their own small tractor, codenamed 2DL, but progress was slow, and in 1960 the development work was handed over to Tractor Research Ltd.

After some delicate negotiations, BMC were persuaded to drop the original design and start again from scratch, with the basic concept of producing a tractor with an under-body clearance similar to a TE20's. There would be two versions, a basic model with no PTO or hydraulics, and a de-luxe version with all the extras of the day, including PTO, hydraulic lift, differential lock and a full lighting set. This was just before Harry Ferguson died in October 1960. In the latter part of his life, he suffered bouts of depression, interspersed with periods of great energy and enthusiasm when his old spirit seemed to return. On these occasions he was often fired-up with his pet dreams of creating a tractor of around 15bhp incorporating many Ferguson patents. Perhaps it was this dream that became a reality, if posthumously, in the form of the BMC Mini Tractor. The design team at Tractor Research was headed by Alex Senkowski of LTX fame, Charles Black who was the agricultural advisor, and six engineers - Gordon Edwards, Dennis Langton, Frank Inns, Bruce Cosh, Ray Tyrer and Geoff Burton - plus a similar number of draughtsmen. The earliest known drawing is dated 19 May 1961.

At an early stage, 5.50x15 and 10x24 rear and front tyres were decided upon, as was the spur gear reduction drive at the outer ends of the rear axle, similar to the BMB President. Dry disc brakes were incorporated on the high-speed axle shafts. For the hydraulic linkage, the normal Ferguson draft control system was dropped in favour of the simpler and cheaper expedient of height-adjustable mounting points for the attachment of the forward ends of the lower links. The system proved to work well in reasonably consistent soil conditions pulling a two-furrow

A nearside view of Tractor Research 495 EUE - the first of a batch of four prototypes for BMC that were registered consecutively. Note the handmade bonnet and rear wings. These prototypes had on six forward and two reverse gears, whereas the production models introduced in 1965 had nine and three respectively.

Ferguson plough to which a depth wheel had been fitted (Harry Ferguson would have turned in his grave!) just in case maintaining an even depth became a problem, but in practice this was not needed. Frank Inns has confirmed that at an early stage one of the BMB Presidents was fitted with the Count Teramala torque converter, to which Harry Ferguson had bought the patent rights; one had previously been installed in one of the Ferguson prototype four-wheel drive cars. The converter performed reasonably well, but as one would expect fuel consumption was increased; not a feature that would appeal to farmers. Also a sudden reduction in torque requirement, such as when the plough was lifted at the headland, caused the tractor engine to speed up dramatically, which could catch a driver unawares, with possible dire consequences! The general conclusion was that this sophisticated type of transmission should be dropped in favour of a three-speed gearbox coupled to a high/low auxiliary 'box.

At around this time BMC had been developing an automotive Diesel engine of 948cc capacity under the direction of Alec Issigonis, with the intention of installing this in Morris 5cwt vans for the GPO, quite a pioneering concept. This indirect-injection engine was a Ricardo design, and was claimed to develop 15bhp. The early experimental engines, with engine numbers prefixed SPL (for "Special", a common BMC practice for prototype engines and cars), had glow plugs in each combustion chamber and one in the inlet manifold, together with a small push-button pump for spraying a small quantity of Diesel into the inlet manifold. It was this engine that BMC were adamant should be

An offside view of the diesel version of the BMC A-Series engine of 948cc. Note the belt guard fitted adjacent to the hydraulic pump pulley.

Another product of Tractor Research, the Calor Ranger. This is a later example made by Turner Engineering of Alcester known as the Turner Ranger Four.

used in the new tractor to be developed by Tractor Research. From mid-1961, work was under way to produce some working prototypes for evaluation. It is unclear how many were in fact built. The author has heard that it may have been eight. One is known to exist in the Midlands and one is in the Coldridge Collection. This was registered with Warwickshire County Council on 30 November 1962, with the registration mark EUE 495, for Tractor Research Ltd, colour blue, type TR MK1, chassis number TR 503/1. It has been established that a batch of four were registered consecutively on the same date, with marks from EUE 495 to EUE 498. An archive photo exists showing EUE 496. On this tractor a good number of Ferguson patents were incorporated, including the adjustable front axle, double drop arm steering box, stepped adjustable rear wheels and the Category I three-point linkage, but not the draft control.

Many differences are apparent when comparing the prototype design to the production version. The most noticeable differences are the hand-fabricated bonnet and rear mudguards, followed by the more crudely fabricated radius arms, particularly at the yoke end. The rear wheels have eight-stud fitting to the hubs, as opposed to the production versions which have six studs. Likewise, the wheel centre to rim attachment uses six bolts on the prototype, while four were considered sufficient for production tractors. The front wheels have six-bolt fixing, but again on production versions four were used, no doubt as a cost cutting measure. The gearbox arrangement is totally different, as the prototypes had six forward ratios and two reverse, with a three-speed and reverse gearbox coupled to a high/low range box, and with no facility for isolating the starter circuit. The production tractors had nine forward ratios and three reverse. The starter motor was controlled by the lever on the main gearbox, while the other lever controlled the high-medium-low and reverse 'box, with medium and reverse being conveniently arranged in line and having the same ratio, thus giving a forward and reverse shuttle, very convenient for loader work. Of other small details that are apparent, the hydraulic oil tank and its pipework are different. The final production model, designated the BMC

Mini Tractor, was launched in 1965, the publicity material of the time claiming that five years' development work had gone into its evolution. It should be added that the details given of the prototype are based on the example in the Coldridge Collection; the others may have been slightly different.

Another vehicle that Tractor Research Ltd was involved in developing was the Calor Ranger Four, this time for Calor Gas. Later the design rights and manufacturing were taken over by Turner Engineering of Alcester in Warwickshire, after about fifty of the original batch had been made. The later models were renamed the Turner Ranger Four, which eventually gained a Design Council Award. For those unfamiliar with this piece of British engineering let me set down the details. The project was to produce a versatile four-wheel drive vehicle which was economical in terms of both purchase cost and fuel cost, using Calor propane gas. This was realized for Calor by Tractor Research Ltd using a British Leyland 1100cc A-series power unit with integral four-speed synchromesh gearbox driving two BL diff units from a Triumph Herald, giving four-wheel drive, four-wheel steering, all-round independent suspension by Mini-type Moulton units, and no risk of transmission wind-up.

To complete this specification, PTO and Category I hydraulic lift (taken directly from the BMC Mini tractor) were offered as optional equipment for both front and rear of the vehicle. Further optional equipment was available to widen the range of applications it could be used for. This included roll-over protection with or without cab, twin seats, road lighting, a hydraulic power take-off, and a choice of gas or petrol as the fuel. The machine was aimed at factory and light aircraft operations as a tug tractor, with a basic specification but with a ballast weight, or at municipal users who might take advantage of the front and rear PTO and lift options. This gave it the ability to drive various types of grass cutters, including Turner's own flail type. It could be used for gritting or salt spreading, chemical weed control, etc. It is understood that about 250 of these vehicles were built in total.

The Harry Ferguson legacy in the area of four-wheel drive systems and active vehicle safety designs could fill another volume. The company title Harry Ferguson Holdings Ltd continues to this day. Harry Ferguson once said on the subject of vehicle safety design, "If it saves your life just once, that is enough." What an epitaph for a man whose ideas were often ahead of his time, but which are now mostly accepted and commonplace. An Isambard Kingdom Brunel of the twentieth century?

The mid-mounted BMC 1098cc engine. The hydraulic oil tank is taken directly from the BMC Mini Tractor.

Appendix 1: Identifying your TE20

Each model variation of the TE20 range was identified by a prefix to its tractor or chassis/frame number, all these prefixes starting with the general code TE20. The designation TE20, which stands for Tractor England 20hp, was used on its own for the first models fitted with the Continental Z-120 petrol engine. They were rated at 20.3bhp, which was 85 per cent of the maximum power of 23.9bhp. When the first derivative, a narrow version, was introduced in late 1948, this was prefixed TE.B20, and subsequent new models were similarly given an additional letter. Listed in the table below are these prefixes, together with the engine type and fuel they relate to. Using this information in conjunction with the production serial numbers given in the second table, you will be able to deduce the type of Ferguson a tractor was when it left Banner Lane, and the year in which it was produced. By a bit of calculation, it would be possible to put a rough date of production to the tractor, assuming daily output remained reasonably consistent.

The letter range continued through the alphabet although not all letters were used. There is one other special prefix that has come to light and that is TE.Y20, used on a quantity of 1996 Fergusons fitted with Perkins P3 Diesel engines for export to Yugoslavia and built between 15 November 1955 and 23 March 1956.

Engine type	Agricultural	Narrow	Vineyard	Industrial
Continental	TE.20	TE.B20		
Ditto, US built	TO.20			
Standard petrol	TE.A20	TE.C20	TE.K20	TE.P20
TVO	TE.D20	TE.E20	TE.L20	TE.R20
Lamp oil	TE.H20	TE.J20	TE.M20	TE.S20**
Standard Diesel	TE.F20	TE.G20*	TE.N20*	TE.T20
Perkins Diesel	TE.Y20			

*Only made in France **The rarest of all Fergusons, only one example was made!

A few Ferguson TE20s have survived without these prefixes and serial numbers on the commission plate. These were used for experimental purposes, being taken off the production line complete with prefix and serial number, and were allocated for use by the engineering department, who would remove the plate and hand it back to the last stage of the assembly line for fixing to an appropriate but un-numbered tractor. Engineering would then affix their own commission plate with the prefix EXP (for "Experimental") followed by a number. For instance, EXP16 survives in private ownership, and EXP11 is in the Coldridge Collection.

The following Ferguson TE20 production figures year by year have been taken from records kept at the end of the assembly line.

Year	Total For Year	Running Total	First tractor serial number in each year (approx.)
1946	314	314	1 (July 1946)
1947	20,580	20,894	316
1948	56,878	77,772	20,895
1949	38,689	116,461	77,773
1950	51,375	167,836	116,462
1951	73,500	241,336	167,837
1952	69,443	310,779	241,335
1953	57,219	367,998	310,780
1954	60,094	428,092	367,999
1955	60,486	488,578	428,093
1956	29,073	517,651	488,579

Production ended on 13 July 1956 with number 517,651, 148 tractors being made that day. Production of the FE35 started on 22 August. Records of models produced were kept from 1948 onwards, but those for 1951 are missing.

There is no definitive record of engine production numbers, but all engine numbers were prefixed either S for the petrol and TVO versions or SA on Diesel engines, while engine numbers were suffixed with the letter E for Engine, which was Standard's normal practice.

Getting the Most
out of the
FERGUSON SYSTEM
The
FERGUSON SYSTEM
A HANDBOOK ON OPERATION AND CARE

Appendix 2: Specifications

TE20 with Continental Z-120 petrol engine

Engine:
Four cylinders, wet liners
Bore and stroke 3.1875in by 3.75in (80.96mm by 95.25mm)
Cubic capacity 120cu in (1966cc)
Compression ratio 6:1,
Firing order 1-3-4-2,
Maximum power output 23.9 bhp at 2000rpm
Rated bhp 20.3.
Mechanical governor, variable speed 400-2000rpm
Lubrication by gear pump
Sump 10 pints (5.7 litres) capacity, replaceable cartridge filter in the sump

Electrical system:
6-volt, thirteen-plate battery 75Ah capacity,
Ignition by coil and distributor with automatic advance and retard
Dynamo Lucas C45X shunt wound two-brush with voltage control regulator
Starter motor Lucas M418G four-brush type with Bendix drive to flywheel, starter operated by gearlever.

Cooling:
By water with pump and radiator, fan assisted, thermostat in a hose in the cooling circuit. No temperature gauge fitted.

Fuel system:
Petrol tank 8 gallons (36 litres)
Carburettor Marvel-Schebler updraught type
Air cleaner of oil bath typ.

Transmission:
Clutch single dry plate 9in (229mm) diameter by Borg & Beck
Gearbox four speeds and reverse, constant mesh with helical-cut gears, all shafts mounted on taper roller bearings except reverse idler gear
Final drive by spiral bevel, ratio 6. 66:1, pinion differential mounted on tapered roller bearings, as are the wheel hubs.

Gear ratios and speeds	Overall gear ratios	Speeds in mph (km/h) at 2000rpm
First	78.5:1	3.375 (5.43)
Second (ploughing)	57:1	4.625 (7.44)
Third	41.3:1	6.375 (10.26)
Fourth	19.8:1	13.25 (21.32)
Reverse	68:1	3.875 (6.24)

Steering:
Both front wheels controlled independently by adjustable bevel gear pinions, oil-filled steering box,
steering wheel 18in (457mm) diameter.

Brakes:
14in by 2in (356mm by 51mm) internal expanding twin shoe brakes, operated together or independently.

Wheels:
Front 400x19,
rear 10x28, drop centre with detachable and adjustable wheel centres.

Hydraulic draft control:
Four-cylinder piston pump, engaged by PTO lever,
manual control of pump by draft control lever,
automatic overload protection through top link.
Pump should be disengaged when not in use.
PTO engaged by lever on left-hand side of transmission,
1.125in (29mm) diameter shaft turning at 1500rpm engine speed giving 545rpm PTO speed.
Draw bar: Standard equipment, adjustable with stays and eleven-hole bar.

Dimensions (for normal agricultural model):
Wheelbase 70in (1778mm),
Normal track front 48in (1219mm), rear 52in (1321mm),
when using 8in or 10in (203mm or 254mm) plough both front and rear tracks 48in
Track adjustment front up to 80in (2032mm), rear up to 76in (1930mm)
Overall length from front tyre to end of lower link 115in (2921mm)
Overall width 64in (1626mm)
Overall height 52in (1321mm)
Ground clearance under centre 13in (330mm), under axle 21in (533mm)
Turning circle diameter with use of brake 16ft (4.9m)
Weight approx. 2500lbs (1135kg).

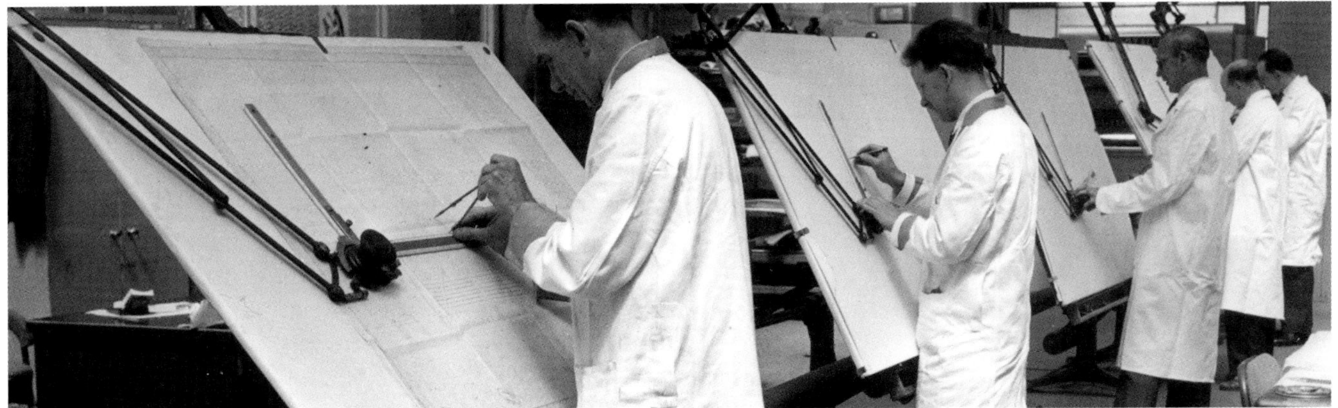

170

As the basic specifications of all the TE20 models are so similar, there is little point going through the specification model by model. Instead, the differences between various models are outlined below. Obviously with a production run spanning ten years, lot of subtle variations were made, so for this reason be very careful about mixing second-hand parts!

TE.A20 with the Standard petrol engine, where different from the Continental-engined model

Engine:
Bore and stroke 80mm by 92 mm, later 85mm by 92mm
Capacity 1850cc, later 2088cc,
Power output 23.9bhp, later 28.2bhp
Valve clearance (cold) inlet 0.010in (0.245mm), exhaust 0.012in (0.249mm)

Electrical system:
at tractor number 200001, a 12-volt electrical system was introduced with a Lucas GTW 7A/1 seven-plate battery of 38Ah capacity, a Lucas CP39P2 dynamo, shunt wound, two-pole output controlled by Lucas RB107 regulator, and a Lucas M45G starter motor.
Spark plugs Champion L10, gap 0.030in to 0.032in (0.762mm to 0.813mm).

Cooling system:
Capacity 15 pints (8.5 litres). No temperature gauge fitted.

Fuel system:
Carburettor Zenith updraught type 24T2 or 28G.
From tractor number 200001, the air intake was ducted from a perforated mesh grill in the dashboard to the oil bath air cleaner.

Standard TVO engine fitted to TE.D20, TE.E20, TE.L20 and TE.R20 model

Specifications basically similar to the later petrol engine (85mm bore, 2088cc) with the following changes:
Compression ratio 5.1:1
Power output 25.4bhp
Spark plugs Champion N7 with a gap setting of 0.030in to 0.035in (0.762mm to 0.889mm).
Fuel tank with two compartments, main tank 7 gallons (31.8 litres) TVO, petrol tank for starting 1 gallon (4.5 litres), with a two-way tap supplying the carburettor. A temperature gauge was fitted to facilitate correct change over from petrol to TVO.

Standard lamp oil engine fitted to TE.H20, TE.J20, TE.M20, and TE.S20 models

Similar to the TVO version but
Compression ratio 4.5:1
Power output 22.9bhp
Cooling system capacity 17 pints (9.6 litres), caused by the fitment of a different cylinder head incorporating the water pump and a water distribution tube. A temperature gauge was fitted.

Narrow tractor TE.B20, TE.C20, TE.E20, and TE.J20 models

Dimensions:
Front track adjustable from 44in (1118mm) to 60in (1524mm), in increments of 4in (102mm), rear track similarly adjustable from 42in (1067mm) to 66in (1676mm), turning circle with track on narrow setting with brake 18ft (5.5m), dry weight up to tractor number 32500, 2327 lbs (1056kg), after this number 2397 lbs (1088kg).

Perkins P3/TA Diesel engine, factory fitted to 1996 Ferguson tractors for export to Yugoslavia in 1955-56, carrying a commission plate with the TE.Y20 prefix

Engine:
Indirect injection Diesel with swirl chambers, three cylinders
Bore and stroke 88.9mm by 127mm (3.5in by 5in), capacity 2360cc, maximum speed 2000rpm
Power output 32bhp – a useful improvement on the output of the Standard 20C engine!

Vineyard tractor TE.K20, TE.L20, and TE.M20 models

Transmission:
Overall gear ratios are the same as the normal model, but speeds are lower because of the fitment of smaller front and rear wheels, 500x15 and 10x24 respectively.

Gear ratios and speeds	Overall gear ratios	Speeds in mph (km/h) at 2000rpm
First	78.5:1	3.000 (4.82)
Second	57:1	4.125 (6.64)
Third	41.3:1	5.750 (9.25)
Fourth	19.8:1	11.875 (19.11)
Reverse	68:1	3.625 (5.83)

Dimensions:
Wheelbase 75in (1905mm),
Front track adjustable from 37in to 58in (940mm to 1473mm) in increments of 4in (102mm)
Rear track similarly adjustable from 32in to 56in (813mm to 1422mm)
Overall length 119in (3023mm)
Minimum overall width 46in (1168mm)
Overall height 50in (1270mm)
Turning circle diameter with brake on narrowest track setting 18ft 6in (5.6m),
Weight approx. 2410 lbs (1094kg).

Standard Diesel engine 20C, fitted to TE.F20 and TE.T20 models made in England and TE.G20 and TE.N20 models made in France

Engine:
Indirect injection Diesel engine with combustion chambers to Freeman Sanders patent and wet replaceable cylinder liners
Bore and stroke 80.96 mm by 101.6mm
Capacity 2092cc,
Compression ratio 17:1, decompression by lever on three or four cylinders
Firing order 1-3-4-2
Power output 26bhp at 2000rpm
Valve clearance (cold) 0.012in (0.249mm) both inlet and exhaust.
Governor: variable speed, pneumatic type mounted on injection pump. Regulates up to 2200rpm. CAV type BEP/AMN80A102X with excess fuel override facility to aid cold starting.

Electrical system:
12-volt, two Lucas 6-volt batteries in series, type T/TX19/TE, 115Ah capacity, dynamo Lucas C39P-2 two-brush shunt wound, starter motor Lucas type M35G-1 with mechanical pre-engagement of pinion. On the right hand side of the gear box casing is a brass button that has to be depressed before the starter motor can be operated via the gearlever in the normal Ferguson fashion.

Cooling system:
Capacity 15 pints (8.5 litres), pressurised at 4psi.

Fuel system:
Injection pump CAV type in-line with override button, one of the following types: BPE4A60Q120S6200EL, BPE4A60Q320/356293EL, BPE4A60Q120S6292E, BPE4A60S120S6341EL, or BPE4A60S120S6402EI, with spill cut-off at 32 degrees BTDC. Fuel injectors CAV type BDN4S1.
Air cleaner, oil bath type with centrifugal-type pre-cleaner.
Cold start system by Ki-Gass and a heater plug on the induction manifold.
Fuel tank 7 gallons (32 litres), auxiliary tank 0.75 gallons (3.4 litres).

Hydraulic system:
Relief valve set at 2000psi, fitted in pump on early tractors and on left-hand side oil gallery on later tractors, so be careful if swapping second hand parts, it could be disastrous if you get the wrong parts fitted!

Appendix 3: Suppliers and dealers

Suppliers to Harry Ferguson Ltd

In 1951, Harry Ferguson held a Manufacturers' and Dealers' conference, and the following is a list of manufacturers and suppliers to Harry Ferguson who attended this gathering:

The Standard Motor Company Ltd, Coventry, Warwickshire
Steel's Engineering Products Ltd, Sunderland, Co. Durham
Rubery Owen & Co Ltd, Darlaston, South Staffordshire
Thos. Blackburn & Sons Ltd, Preston, Lancashire
Robert Watson & Co Ltd, Bolton, Lancashire
Sun Engineering (Crowle) Ltd, Scunthorpe, Lincolnshire
John Garrington & Sons Ltd, Bromsgrove, Worcestershire
Frank Wade Ltd, Stourbridge, Worcestershire
Midland Industries Ltd, Wolverhampton, Staffordshire
Joseph Sankey & Sons Ltd, Wellington, Shropshire
Dowty Equipment Ltd, Cheltenham, Gloucestershire
Pressed Steel Co Ltd, Paisley
John Lysaught's Bristol Works Ltd, Bristol
Wellwinch Engineering, Sittingbourne, Kent
William Donaldson (Engineers) Ltd, Paisley
Joseph Lucas Ltd, Birmingham
Hattersley & Ridge Ltd, Sheffield, Yorkshire
Midlands Repetition & Auto Manufacturing Co Ltd, Bedworth, Warwickshire
C & S Carburettors, Shirley, Birmingham
Scottish Mechanical Light Industries Ltd, Ayr
Coventry Hood & Sidescreen Co Ltd, Coventry
Tyzack Sons & Turner Ltd, Sheffield, Yorkshire
Weldall & Assembly Ltd, Stourbridge, Worcestershire
Helliwell's Ltd, The Airport, Walsall, Staffordshire

Implement suppliers to Harry Ferguson Ltd

The following list is taken from Bulletin No 185 domestic, 1952.

Thomas Blackburn manufactured the following implements: blade terracer, weeder, disc harrows and spike tooth harrows.
Rubery Owen & Co Ltd manufactured all the mould board ploughs, also the universal seed drill and subsoiler.
John Garrington manufactured the ridge tine cultivator together with the spring tine revisions.
Scottish Mechanical Light Industries manufactured the mounted and stationary hammer mills, and the linkage-mounted winch and steerage hoes.
Joseph Sankey & Sons Ltd manufactured open wheel sets, all trailers and conversion kit, together with the automatic pick up hitch assembly and the muck spreader. They also produced the disc plough, conversion set and transport box.
Midlands Industries Ltd manufactured the chitted seed potato attachment, both types of potato planter, and the wood saw.
Pressed Steel Co Ltd produced the mower.
Robert Watson manufactured the earth scoop.
Steels Engineering Ltd manufactured the post-hole digger and both types of loader, the potato spinner, the ridger, the tiller and the stabilizer assemblies.
William Donaldson manufactured the wheel girdles.
Wellwinch Engineer made the hay ladders for the 3-ton trailer.
The Standard Motor Company, Coventry, supplied not only the tractors themselves but the belt pulley attachment.
Midlands Repetition & Auto Light supplied the dual wheel attachment kit.
Sun Engineering Ltd fabricated the jack.

Ferguson dealers in the British Isles

For the purposes of dealerships, Britain was divided up into six areas or zones.

Zone A: The South West and South Wales

Abergavenny Motors Co (1919) Ltd, Monmouth Road, Abergavenny, Monmouthshire
Aberystwyth Tractors Ltd, Park Avenue, Aberystwyth, Cardiganshire
Auto Services Ltd, The Ivy Motor Garages, Bridge Street, Lampeter, Cardiganshire
Brecon Motors Ltd, 41 The Watton, Brecon
B S Bird & Co (Gloucester) Ltd, Wallbridge, Stroud, Gloucestershire
B S Bird (Tractors) Ltd, Cowbridge, Glamorgan
A H Christopher, Broadmayne, Dorchester, Dorset
College Motors Ltd, Triangle West, Queens Road, Bristol, Somerset
Farm Aids (Wilts.) Ltd, New Road, Marlborough, Wiltshire
Farmex Ltd, Lowman Green, Tiverton, Devon
J Gliddon & Sons, Williton, Somerset
Morris Isaac Ltd, Service Garage, Llandovery, Carmarthenshire
G Llewellyn & Sons, Royal Prize Churn Works, Haverfordwest, Pembrokeshire
J T Lowe Ltd, Longham, Wimborne, Dorset
E Mitchell & Sons, Mounts' Bay Stores, Penzance, Cornwall
Moxhams (Newport) Ltd, Clarence Place, Rodney Road, Newport, Monmouthshire
W Mumford Ltd, Agricultural Depot, Skew Bridge, Plympton, Devon
Par Engineering & Motor Works Ltd, Par, Cornwall
Salisbury Tractor Co Ltd, Waterloo Road, Southampton Road, Salisbury, Wiltshire
Tractors (Bath) Ltd, Bathford, Somerset
Tractors (Swindon) Ltd, Groundswell Road, Swindon, Wiltshire
West Regional Autos Ltd, Newport Road, Barnstaple, Devon
West Regional Autos (Launceston) Ltd, 25 Broad Street, Launceston, Cornwall
Western Garage (Newton Abbot) Ltd, 40 Wolborough Street, Newton Abbot, Devon
Western Motors (Carmarthen) Ltd, Riverside, Carmarthen
Percy Winsor Ltd, Vicarage Street, Yeovil, Somerset

Zone B: The South East and East Anglia

Anna Valley (Tractors) Ltd, Upper Clatford, near Andover, Hampshire
Barclay Motors Ltd, Devonshire House, King's Road Corner, Bury St. Edmunds, Suffolk
The Chiltern Tractor Co Ltd, Woodley Aerodrome, Reading, Berkshire
L F Dove (Tractors) Ltd, Nicholls Farm, Redbourn, St. Albans, Hertfordshire
Eastern Roadways (Engineers) Ltd, Newmarket Road, Cambridge
Eastern Tractors Ltd, Springfield, Chelmsford, Essex
Farm Mechanisation Co, Egerton's Corner, Gt. Colman Street, Ipswich, Suffolk
M O Harper (Tractors) Ltd, 19 Commercial Road, Guildford, Surrey
G R Hartwell Ltd, 205 Charminster Road, Bournemouth, Hampshire
Holloway, Hinson & Co Ltd, Oving Road, Chichester, Sussex
Lenfield Engineering Ltd, Lenfield Works, Ashford Road, Maidstone, Kent
Lenfield Engineering (Ashford) Ltd, North Street, Ashford. Kent
Lenfield Engineering (Canterbury) Ltd, Broad Street, Canterbury, Kent
Moore of Brighton (1924) Ltd, Russell Square, Brighton, Sussex
Norfolk Tractors Ltd, 66 King Street, Norwich, Norfolk
Penwarden & Frost, Farningham Service Station, Farningham, Kent
The Reigate Garage Ltd, 23-36 & 51a Bell Street, Reigate, Surrey
Shaw & Kilburn Ltd, Bedford Street, Ampthill, Bedfordshire
Shaw & Kilburn Ltd, 546-550 Dunstable Road, Luton, Bedfordshire
Smith & Whitehead Ltd, Pan Engineering Works, Newport, Isle of Wight
F A Standen & Sons Ltd, King's Dyke Works, Whittlesey, Cambridgeshire
F A Standen & Sons Ltd, "Stanpoint" Works, St. Ives, Huntingdonshire
F A Standen & Sons Ltd, Hereward Works, Lynn Road, Ely, Cambridgeshire
Stortford Agritractors Ltd, 26 Hadham Road, Bishop's Stortford, Hertfordshire
Sussex Tractors Ltd, 33 High Street, Uckfield, Sussex
Wadham Bros. Ltd, Swan Lane, Winchester, Hampshire
H E Williams & Co Ltd, 152 High Street, Colchester, Essex
Walter A Wood & Co Ltd, Mill Bay Lane, Worthing Road, Horsham, Sussex

Zone C: The Midlands, mid-Wales, part of Lincolnshire

Avon Valley Tractors Ltd, Greenhill Garage, Evesham, Worcestershire
Baines Bros. Ltd, North Street & Church Street, Gainsborough, Lincolnshire
Boston Tractors Ltd, Kirton, Boston, Lincolnshire
H A Browett & Co Ltd, 64-66 Granby Street, Leicester
Burgess Motors Ltd, Wolverhampton Road, Stafford
Central Motor Co 1919 (Kettering) Ltd, Dalkeith Place, Kettering, Northamptonshire
Derby Engineering (Tractors) Ltd, Alfreton Road, Derby
G R Hartwell Ltd, Horse Fair, Chipping Norton, Oxfordshire
Kesteven Tractors Ltd, Cattle Market, Bourne, Lincolnshire
F Mitchell (Nottingham) Ltd, Derby Road, Lenton, Nottingham
S H Newsome & Co Ltd, Corporation Street, Coventry, Warwickshire
Pheysey Ltd, Bridge Street, Stourport-on-Severn, Worcestershire
Rogers & Jackson Ltd, Whittington Road, Oswestry, Shropshire
Shuker & Sons (Shrewsbury) Ltd, Old Church Place, Newtown, Montgomery
Shuker & Sons (Shrewsbury) Ltd, Battlefield, Shrewsbury, Shropshire
Stratford Tractors Ltd, Henley Street, Stratford-Upon-Avon, Warwickshire
Tractamotor Services Ltd, Thorpe End, Melton Mowbray, Leicestershire
Tractors (Hereford) Ltd, Holmer Road, Hereford
West's (Lincoln) Ltd, 116 High Street, Lincoln
James Windsor & Son, Nottingham Road, Mansfield, Nottinghamshire

Zone D: The North of England, North Wales, part of Lincolnshire

Agricultural Equipment & Contracting Co, Armley Park, Stanningley Road, Leeds, Yorkshire
Anchor Motor Co Ltd, The Newgate, Chester, Cheshire
Central Garage (Halifax) Ltd, 89 King Cross Street, Halifax, Yorkshire
W Clayton & Sons Ltd, Gilberdyke, Brough, East Yorkshire
Corlett, Sons & Cowley Ltd, 19 North Quay, Douglas, Isle of Man
County Motors (Carlisle) Ltd, 14a Butchergate, Carlisle, Cumberland
Edwards Motors (Doncaster) Ltd, Station Garage, Doncaster, Yorkshire
Glovers of Ripon & Harrogate Ltd, Borrage Bridge, Ripon, Yorkshire
Greenacres (Engineers) Ltd, Legbourne Road Station, Louth, Lincolnshire
Hoggarths Limited, Sandes Avenue, Kendal, Westmorland
Hoggarths (Tractors) Ltd, Moor Hall Works, Brook Street, Preston, Lancashire
Hollingdrake Automobile Co Ltd, Town Hall Square, Stockport, Cheshire
Hollingdrake Automobile Co Ltd, Llanrwst, Denbighshire
H Hughes & Sons Ltd, Agricultural Dpt, Glan Hwfa Road, Llangefni, Anglesey
Jones Bros., Bala, Merionethshire
Myers & Burnell Ltd, Ferguson Tractors, Swinegate, York
North Wales Agricultural Engineers Ltd, St. Asaph, Flintshire
North Wales Agricultural Engineers Ltd, Pwllheli, Caernarvonshire
J D Ord & Co Ltd, 177 Victoria Road, Darlington, Durham
Saville & Ezard Ltd, Falconer's Road, Scarborough, Yorkshire
Steel & Robinson Ltd, Paley Street, Sunderland, Durham
Sun Engineering (Crowle) Ltd, Crowle, Scunthorpe, Lincolnshire
George Thompson (Hull & East Riding) Ltd, 83-85 Anlaby Road, Hull, East Yorks.
Samuel Wilson & Son Ltd, 125-137 West Street, Sheffield, Yorkshire

Zone E: Scotland

John Davidson & Sons (Engineers) Ltd, 51-53 High Street, Turriff
Farm Mechanisation Co Ltd, Commercial Road, Ladybank, Fife
Hamilton Bros. Ltd, Ralston Garage, 255 Glasgow Road, Paisley
Geo. Henderson Ltd, 18 Forth Street, Edinburgh
Geo. Henderson Ltd, Kelso
Geo. Henderson Ltd, Bellevilla Road, Stranraer
L O Tractors Ltd, Coupar Angus, Perthshire
Mackay Bros., Central Garage, Dingwall
Morayshire Motors Ltd, Forres, Morayshire
Reekie Engineering Co Ltd, Lochlands Works, Arbroath
Daniel Ross, Newhouse Engineering Works, Lanark
John Scarth, Ayre Road, Kirkwall
Stirling Tractors Ltd, Menstrie, near Stirling
James Tweedie Ltd, Holmston Road, Ayr
Tweedies Motors Ltd, Rosefield Mills, Dumfries

Zone G: Northern Ireland, Eire and the Channel Islands

Harry Ferguson (Motors) Ltd, Donegall Square, Belfast
Ferguson Limited, Lower Baggot Street, Dublin
St. Helier Garages Ltd, First Tower, Jersey

Bibliography

Ferguson, A Living Biography, by Norman Wymer, Phoenix House, 1961

Harry Ferguson, Inventor and Pioneer, by Colin Frazer, John Murray, 1972

Harry Ferguson, A Tribute, by Duncan Russell

As Happy as Kings, by Constantia Arnold, Wilton, 1965

Harry Ferguson, by Bill Martin, Ulster Folk and Transport Museum, 1993

Harry Ferguson Memorial Lecture, by GBR Feilden, Queens University, Belfast, 1970

Harry Ferguson, A Brief History of his Life and Tractors, by George Field, John Barber and John Walker, a Massey-Ferguson publication, 1993

The Ferguson Story, by Alan Condie, Alan Condie, 1985

Ferguson, The Story Continues, by Max Smith, an AGCO publication, 1998

Ferguson Implements and Accessories, by John Farnsworth, Farming Press, 1996

The Ferguson Tractor Story, by Stuart Gibbard, Old Pond Publishing, 2000

Fergusons: the Hunday Experience, by John Moffitt and John Farnsworth, Japonica Press, 2000

Great Tractor Builders: Ferguson, by Alan Condie, Ian Allan, 2001

Ford and Fordson Tractors, by Michael Williams, Farming Press, 1985

Ferguson i Sverige, by Sture Tufresson, Värmlands Bygden, 1996

Tracteurs Ferguson, by Jean Cherourrier and Jean Noulin, ETAI, 1999

The Legendary LTX Tractor, by Erik Fredriksen, published by the author, 2000

Harry Ferguson and I, by Michael Winter, 1995

A Global Corporation, by EP Neufield, University of Toronto Press, 1969

Massey at the Brink, by Peter Cook, Collins, 1081

The David Brown Tractor Story Vol. 1, by Stuart Gibbard, Old Pond Publishing, 2003

Sir Edmund Hillary, an Autobiography, Corgi, 1999

The New Ferguson Album, by Colin Booth and Alan Condie, Alan Condie, 1986

Ford Tractor Implements, by Chester Peterson Jr and Rod Beemer, MBI Publishing Co., 1998

Ferguson Publications Index 1922-1964, by Andrew Boorman, published by the author, 2005

Know Your Tractor, a Shell Guide, Shell Petroleum, 1955

The Nuffield Album, by Michael DJ Irwin, Alan Condie, 2003